BRITISH ROYALTY
COMMEMORAT

19TH & 20TH CENTURY ROYAL EVENTS
IN BRITAIN ILLUSTRATED BY COMMEMORATIVES

REVISED AND EXPANDED
2ND EDITION

With Value Guide

DOUGLAS H. FLYNN
AND
ALAN H. BOLTON

Schiffer Publishing Ltd®

4880 Lower Valley Road, Atglen, PA 19310 USA

Revised value guide: 1999
Copyright © 1994 & 1999 by Douglas H. Flynn and Alan H. Bolton
Library of Congress Catalog Card Number: 99-62568

ISBN: 0-7643-0864-5
Printed in China
1 2 3 4

Published by Schiffer Publishing Ltd.
4880 Lower Valley Road
Atglen, PA 19310
Phone: (610) 593-1777; Fax: (610) 593-2002
Email: Schifferbk@aol.com
Please visit our web site catalog at **www.schifferbooks.com**

In Europe, Schiffer books are distributed by Bushwood Books
6 Marksbury Avenue Kew Gardens
Surrey TW9 4JF England
Phone: 44 (0)181 392-8585; Fax: 44 (0)181 392-9876
Email: Bushwd@aol.com

This book may be purchased from the publisher.
Include $3.95 for shipping. Please try your bookstore first.
We are interested in hearing from authors with book ideas on related subjects.
You may write for a free printed catalog.

Contents

A selection of crowns and coronets by Caverswall.

Acknowledgments

We owe a debt of gratitude to those below for their contributions to the first edition of this book.

Our thanks go to the following in the United Kingdom for their help: Dennis Colton, Peter Gray, John May, Susan and Peter Prior, David Warburton; Colin Terris of Caithness Glass; Steven N. Jackson of the Commemorative Collectors Society; Kevin Pearson of Kevin Francis; Tania Foster-Brown of Mappin & Webb Ltd.; David Williams-Thomas of Royal Brierley; Joan Jones and Julie McKeown of Royal Doulton; M. E. Frost, Dyson Perrins Museum (Royal Worcester); Bibby Cole of Rye Pottery; Robert Copeland of Spode Ltd.; Christine Golledge of Stuart Crystal; and Lynn Miller of Wedgwood.

We also thank Christina Watkinson of Crowns and Sceptres in the United Kingdom for supplying photographs from her collection.

Carol Stobaugh of Alexandria, Virginia, and Betty Browne of Lancaster, Pennsylvania, also permitted us to photograph commemoratives from their collections, and we sincerely thank them.

We are indebted to Alan's sisters, Barbara Holt and Margaret Jenkins, for tirelessly reading through our drafts and making some much needed corrections, as well as some excellent suggestions.

Stephen M. Davey, Manager of CPI Photo Finish of Lancaster, Pennsylvania, gave our jobs his personal attention. When our negatives were less than great, he made sure we had the best pictures that could be made from them. His special effort and contribution to the book are greatly appreciated.

We cannot say enough about the help given us by Anne and Lisle Minns of the United Kingdom. Anne has one of the finest collections of commemoratives we have ever seen, and she graciously gave us access to her entire collection. Her husband, Lisle, did the photography, and they both worked hard to supply us with the photographs and relevant information. A heartfelt "thank you" goes to Anne and Lisle.

Peter Schiffer, our publisher, gave us the widest leeway in planning and writing the book, and we are especially grateful for this freedom. Douglas Congdon-Martin, our editor at Schiffer Publishing, is an all-around nice guy, and one couldn't have a more helpful friend as editor. Peter and Douglas were always there when we needed help. By sharing their knowledge and experience, and making thoughtful suggestions, they made our job easier.

The help provided by those who contributed to the first edition has carried over into this revision, and we again thank them. In addition, we want to thank our revision editor, Ian Robertson, and photographer Bruce Waters. Cindy Brown gave special attention to developing and printing the new color photographs for this book. Again, Peter gave us wide latitude in developing this revised edition.

G6-341: A hooked rug made for the 1939 Canada Visit of King George VI and Queen Elizabeth.

Introduction

British royalty commemoratives — items made to commemorate coronations and other royal events — date from the 17th century. In addition to coronations, events for which commemoratives have been issued include royal weddings and wedding anniversaries, royal births and birthdays, jubilees celebrating anniversaries of a monarch's accession or coronation such as 25th, 50th, etc., and royal visits. In memoriam pieces, regretting royal deaths, are also made.

Commemoratives come in a wide variety of physical forms, from the conservative to the bizarre. Some of the more popular forms are pottery or china mugs, plates, cups and saucers, beakers, covered boxes, tankards, plaques, tea sets, loving cups, figurines and small dishes. Glass tumblers, crystal goblets and paperweights are also made. Frequently found are souvenir spoons, tins, pins, pendants, and medallions — all made of metal. Paper items such as postcards, calendars, jigsaw puzzles, playing cards, booklets and paper dolls are also common. Handkerchiefs, table cloths, tea towels, flags and various kinds of needlework comprise the more commonly found fabrics. Less frequently seen are soaps, socks, teddy bears, neckties, pocket knives, letter openers, stereo viewers, key rings and even bikinis.

Starting a collection of British Royalty Commemoratives is easy, and it's fun. You can begin with the less expensive pieces. Later, as your expertise grows, better and sometimes rarer pieces can be added to your collection, or they can replace some of the pieces acquired earlier. See Chapter 1, *Hints About Collecting*, for further suggestions on starting a collection.

Few pieces for events prior to Queen Victoria's reign are found today at popular prices. Very early commemoratives, such as those for King William III and Queen Mary, King Charles II or King George I, are now found mostly in museums or private collections. Their prices reflect their rarity.

The coronations of King George IV in 1821 and King William IV in 1831 were well commemorated; pieces for these events can still be found at fairly affordable prices. Items for Queen Victoria's coronation in 1838 are sometimes more difficult to find and are more expensive than those for the above monarchs. Many commemoratives were made for her golden and diamond jubilees in 1887 and 1897, celebrating her 50th and 60th anniversaries on the throne. They are frequently found today at reasonable prices.

The pages that follow contain a brief history of the reign of each monarch from King George III to Queen Elizabeth II, as well as information about the two princes next in line for the British throne. Some little-known facts and the truth about a few misconceptions are also covered.

Three new chapters have been added to this revision: Autographs, Enamel Boxes and Figurines. There is also a Manufacturers chapter showing examples of commemoratives made by a number of different potteries.

The second part of the book is a Value Guide with black and white photographs and descriptions of over 2,300 commemoratives with their suggested values.

Suggested values are also included for many of the commemoratives pictured in the front section of the book. All values shown in the book are based on the authors' experience and knowledge and should not be used in pricing commemoratives for sale. Values vary greatly from one part of the country (or world) to the other and are affected by condition and rarity. Neither the authors nor the publisher accept any responsibility for problems arising from the use of these suggested values.

A selection of royal bride figurines.

Royal House of Windsor 1917—1977 Diamond Jubilee Three-Handled Loving Cup. Limited edition of 250, produced by Spode for Thomas Goode & Co., London. $975.—$1025.

Transvaal Three-Handled Loving Cup 1900 (Subscriber's Copy). Made for Thomas Goode & Co. by Copeland. $1975.—$2075.

Chapter 1

Hints About Collecting

Starting A Collection

There is a wide range in quality, rarity and cost among commemoratives. Start with those you can afford. Pottery is usually cheaper than bone china, and tins are inexpensive items for the beginner. If there is a monarch or royal personage you especially admire, start your collection with commemoratives for that person. As time and finances permit, you can upgrade your collection with better pieces. Always buy what you like and think you will enjoy. Naturally, you hope the commemoratives you buy will appreciate in value over time, but don't buy for investment alone — again, buy what appeals to you.

Many collectors prefer commemoratives with portraits of the principals. However, it is not uncommon to find pieces bearing the royal arms or other decorations. A few, such as the birth pieces for Princesses Elizabeth and Margaret (shown in Chapter 4) do not at first appear to be commemoratives to the inexperienced eye.

As your collecting experience and knowledge grow, you will learn that some manufacturers' designs and shapes are common to many of the commemoratives they have made. Chapter 13 shows commemoratives made by various manufacturers. These will help you recognize the distinguishing features of different makers' products.

From the beginning, it is a good idea to keep an inventory of your collection. Obtain receipts for your purchases whenever possible. Your inventory should include a brief description of each item, the name of the manufacturer, the date and place of purchase and the price paid. Especially useful for insurance are photographs taken periodically of your collection. These can be still pictures or video tape.

Sources of Commemoratives

A few years ago, Doug Flynn wrote an article, "Fantastic Finds", for *Sceptre*, in which he described some of his good commemorative buys in somewhat unexpected places. For example, he bought a King Edward VII coronation plate, found in a stack of dinner plates at a yard sale, for 25¢. Even though a trip to England offers a great opportunity to buy commemoratives, and you'll see more at antique fairs there than anywhere else, you don't always have to go far from home for good finds.

Many times, dealers who do not specialize in commemoratives will underprice them — a boon for the sharp-eyed collector. Likewise, this same lack of knowledge of the commemorative market can lead to overpricing, and you have to pass when you see such a piece.

Some sources for commemoratives are:

  China and Glass Sections of Department Stores
  Museum Shops
  Auctions
  Antique shops, malls and shows
  Flea markets
  Advertisements in antiques publications
  Garage or yard sales
  Specialist dealers
  Other collectors

Condition

The condition of a commemorative affects its value — and its price. Pieces which have been used are more apt to show wear and damage than those which have been displayed and handled carefully. Look for small chips, hairlines, scratches, and pieces of missing transfers on china and pottery commemoratives. In the case of tins, the worst enemies are usually rust and dents. While some older tins can still be found in good condition, expect to see some scratches and dents.

On items with gold trim, look for touch-ups in the gold. The new gold will usually not match the original, but the difference might not be apparent without close inspection. A touched-up area may also cover slight damage such as a tiny chip which has been ground down. When shopping for commemoratives, always take along a magnifying glass.

Very old ceramic commemoratives, such as those for Queen Victoria's coronation and earlier, frequently have been restored. If the restoration has been done well by a professional, it usually will not affect the desirability of the piece. However, a perfect item is obviously more valuable than one which has been restored. But a good, almost invisible restoration might allow you to own a piece you could not otherwise afford.

Keep in mind that pottery tends to craze (show fine surface cracks) over time. Therefore, you should be somewhat forgiving of older pottery pieces if they show crazing. Staining is also more prevalent among older pieces than newer ones.

Reproduction mugs. Note that all are "waisted."

Limited Editions

Limited editions were begun around the turn of the century and are quite common today. They range from small editions, each individually numbered, to very large ones. Sometimes, the edition is limited to the number made during the year of the event. When a commemorative has a notation such as "A Limited Edition" and nothing further, it means very little. The more desirable limited editions are those which state the exact number in the edition and are individually numbered.

Official Designs

Official Designs were first introduced by the British Pottery Manufacturers Federation for King George V's Silver Jubilee in 1935. They were continued through the coronation of Queen Elizabeth II. Contrary to what some collectors have thought, the designs were not approved by the royal family. These commemoratives bear the "Official Design" logo of the British Pottery Manufacturers Federation.

Care of Commemoratives

China, pottery and glass pieces should be washed in mild detergent and water. Be careful of the gilding. Many times, on older pieces especially, it is not under the glaze and therefore not protected. Do not use abrasives in cleaning your commemoratives. Lighter fluid can be used to remove residue from labels, price stickers, etc.

Tins can be cleaned with a damp sponge and mild detergent. Lighter fluid can be used to remove glue or residue from labels. If it is to be used on the decorated portion of the tin, test a small area first. Never use fingernail polish remover or other acetone based cleaners. They will remove the finish from the tin. A light coat of a good wax will also help prevent rust. Do not use lacquers or shellac which will harden and discolor.

Reproduction mugs.

Reproductions

Fortunately, there has been little reproduction of commemoratives. A group of mugs, ranging from Queen Victoria's coronation to Queen Elizabeth II's, were produced a few years ago. Some of the mugs have a notation stating that they are reproductions, but many have no mark at all. The mugs are "waisted," that is, more narrow at the center than at the top and bottom. Thimbles with the same transfers were also made. There is also a reproduction teapot stand with a commemoration for Queen Victoria's 1887 Jubilee.

Seven examples of reproduction thimbles.

Monarchs of the House of Windsor

Shown below are Royal Doulton loving cups made for the four Monarchs of the House of Windsor.

Left, G5-301: King George V and Queen Mary 1935 Jubilee. Limited edition of 1000. $1250.—$1350.
Right, E8-227: King Edward VIII 1937 Coronation. Limited edition of 2000. $1050.—$1200.

Left, G6-379: King George VI and Queen Elizabeth 1937 Coronation. Limited edition of 2000. $1050.—
$1200. Right, E2-679: Queen Elizabeth II 1953 Coronation, Limited edition of 1000. $1000.—$1150.

E2-610: Three Queen Elizabeth II 1953 Coronation Dishes by Minton. $385.—$425. Set.

E2-611: Queen Elizabeth II 1953 Coronation Needlepoint. $185.—$215.

Chapter 2
Queen Elizabeth II
1952—

Upon her accession, Queen Elizabeth II had just begun a tour of East Africa and Australia on behalf of her ailing father, King George VI. In the early morning hours of February 6, 1952, the King died peacefully in his sleep at Sandringham. Prince Philip broke the news to his wife, the new Queen, at Treetops in Kenya where they had stopped en route to Australia. They flew back to London at once and were met by Prime Minister Winston Churchill and other government officials.

Princess Elizabeth Alexandra Mary, the first daughter of the Duke and Duchess of York, was born April 21, 1926, in the London home of her maternal grandparents. Her family and close friends have called her Lilibet since she was a little girl.

During her first ten years, Princess Elizabeth lived a relatively quiet life with her parents and her sister, Margaret Rose. The young Princesses were separated from

On the May morning of their father's 1937 coronation, Princess Elizabeth and her sister, Princess Margaret, under the watchful eye of the Princess Royal, rode in their own coach to Westminster Abbey.

Coronation commemoratives for King George VI sometimes include portraits of Princesses Elizabeth and Margaret together or separately. Royal photographer Marcus Adams took many pictures of King George VI's family. One of the most popular of these appears on china and tin commemoratives, as well as on paperweights, postcards, calendars and many other items. See Chapter 4 for examples.

While visiting South Africa, Princess Elizabeth celebrated her 21st birthday. Upon her return to England, her engagement to Prince Philip of Greece and Denmark was announced June 9, 1947. They were married at Westminster Abbey on November 20th. Throughout the streets of London, thousands of well-wishers celebrated the first post-war royal ceremonial event. Very few commemoratives were produced for this occasion.

E2-612: Queen Elizabeth II 1953 Coronation Set of Six Goldtone Anointing Spoons. Woven Macclesfield silk coronation scene. $215.—$240.

their parents only when the Duke and Duchess of York traveled in Britain or different Commonwealth countries representing King George V.

In 1936, the abdication of her uncle, King Edward VIII, changed the future of the young Princess Elizabeth forever. He had succeeded to the throne in January, only to abdicate in December to marry the American divorcee, Wallis Warfield Simpson. Princess Elizabeth's father, Prince Albert, Duke of York, succeeded his brother to become King George VI. These quick changes in Britain's kings made Princess Elizabeth heir presumptive to the throne at age ten.

E2-407: Queen Elizabeth II 60th Birthday Plate, Caverswall. Limited edition of 600. $285.—$300.

E2-560: Princess Elizabeth and Prince Philip Wedding Silk Bookmark, 1947. $85.—$95. *Courtesy of Anne Minns.*

On her Coronation Day, June 2, 1953, Queen Elizabeth II was crowned in accordance with her proclamation as "Elizabeth the Second, by the grace of God of the United Kingdom of Great Britain and Northern Ireland and of Her other Realms and Territories Queen, Head of the Commonwealth, Defender of the Faith." The three-hour ceremony was attended by many heads of state and world leaders. In addition to the thousands who thronged the streets to capture a glimpse of their new Queen, millions of people viewed Queen Elizabeth II's coronation on television.

Shortly after her coronation, the Queen, as head of the Church of England, faced a crisis which focused upon Princess Margaret's love affair with Group-Captain Peter Townsend. The Princess's marriage to a divorced man would be against the laws of the church. Therefore, she chose duty to her church and country before love.

In 1957, Queen Elizabeth II made her first state visit to the United States.

Prince Charles was born November 14, 1948, and became second in line of succession to the throne. On August 15, 1950, Princess Anne was born.

Following in her parents' footsteps, Princess Elizabeth and her husband, the Duke of Edinburgh, traveled together on many official visits. These journeys included many different Commonwealth countries. One of the most popular trips, their 1951 Canada Visit, was well commemorated.

E2-412: Queen Elizabeth II 1957 USA Visit Plate. $27.—$31.

E2-561: Princess Elizabeth and Prince Philip 1951 Canada Visit Cup and Saucer, Paragon. $85.—$95.

In 1958, when Prince Charles was nine years old, Queen Elizabeth II created him England's 21st Prince of Wales. His formal investiture did not take place until July 1, 1969, at Caernarvon Castle in Wales.

For the opening of the St. Lawrence Seaway in 1959, Queen Elizabeth II visited Canada and joined American President Dwight D. Eisenhower for the ceremony opening the new waterway. Many commemorative pieces were done for this event.

E2-613: Queen Elizabeth II and Prince Philip 1959 St. Lawrence Seaway Opening Plate, Tuscan. $85.—$95.

E2-328: Queen Elizabeth II 60th Birthday Mug, Wedgwood. Limited edition of 500. $235.—$250.

Left, E2-614: Queen Elizabeth II 40th Anniversary of Coronation Dish. Limited edition of 2500. Royal Crown Derby. $65.—$75. Right, PC-425: Prince William 1982 Birth Dish. Royal Crown Derby. $90.—$100.

In 1960, Princess Margaret married Anthony Armstrong-Jones, who was given the title, Earl of Snowdon, by the Queen. This was the first major royal event of Queen Elizabeth II's reign. Television cameras were set up inside Westminster Abbey to chronicle the royal wedding.

E2-615: Queen Elizabeth II/Prince Philip 1997 Golden Wedding Anniversary Mug, Royal Doulton. $35.—$40.

The Queen's second son, Prince Andrew was born February 19, 1960. On March 19, 1964, the Queen and Prince Philip celebrated the birth of their third son, Prince Edward.

During her long reign, Queen Elizabeth II has succeeded in breaking down some of the barriers between the monarchy and her people.

On a trip to New Zealand in 1970, the Queen made her first walkabout. She exited her car to walk and talk with the people who had come to see her. Prince Philip accompanied her as they greeted many elated and surprised families who had never dreamed they would be so close to the sovereign and her husband. Walkabouts have now become traditional practices by many royals.

The 1970's proved to be a prolific decade for the production of British royalty commemoratives. In November, 1972, Queen Elizabeth II and Prince Philip celebrated their silver wedding anniversary.

E2-249: Queen Elizabeth II and Prince Philip 1972 Silver Wedding Anniversary Loving Cup, Paragon. $152.—$168.

E2-030: Queen Elizabeth II and Prince Philip 1972 Silver Wedding Anniversary Bowl, Limited Edition of 500, Royal Worcester. $440.—$490.

PA-026: Princess Anne and Captain Mark Phillips 1973 Wedding Plate, Crown Staffordshire. $71.—$78.

On November 14, 1973, Princess Anne married Captain Mark Phillips.

Despite Queen Elizabeth II's plea for less fanfare during her 1977 Silver Jubilee Year, hundreds of celebrations took place throughout England. Ox roasts, bonfires, parades, street fairs, church services and other festivities marked twenty-five loyal years of service to her country.

The 1980's heralded two more royal weddings and several royal births. The Prince of Wales married Lady Diana Spencer on July 29, 1981. Unlike previous royal matrimonial unions, St. Paul's Cathedral was chosen for this well-attended and commemorated event.

Prince William of Wales was born to the Prince and Princess of Wales in 1982, and his brother, Prince Henry, in 1984. Queen Elizabeth II celebrated two new grandsons and two more heirs to the throne.

Early in 1986, Prince Andrew's engagement to Miss Sarah Ferguson was announced. The morning of their wedding day, July 23, 1986, Queen Elizabeth II announced the conferment of the title of Duke of York on Prince Andrew.

Princess Beatrice, the Duke and Duchess of York's first daughter, was born August 8, 1988. Their second daughter, Princess Eugenia, was born March 23, 1990.

Queen Elizabeth's 60th birthday was celebrated in 1986.

In 1987, Queen Elizabeth II and Prince Philip celebrated their 40th wedding anniversary.

The following year, the Queen conferred the title of Princess Royal on her daughter, Princess Anne.

E2-405: Queen Elizabeth II 60th Birthday Plate, 1986, Coalport. $82.—$88.

The early 1990's have not been kind to Queen Elizabeth II. Although 1992 marked the 40th anniversary of the Queen's succession to the throne, the celebration

E2-012: Queen Elizabeth II and Prince Philip 40th Wedding Anniversary Beaker, 1987, Caverswall. $88.—$100.

PA-031: Princess Anne Created Princess Royal Plate, 1987, Coalport. $70.—$75.

PA-032: Princess Anne and Captain Mark Phillips Divorce Mug, 1992, Mayfair. $75.—$83.

lost its fanfare when Buckingham Palace announced the separation of the Duke and Duchess of York in March.

In April, the Princess Royal was granted a divorce from Captain Mark Phillips.

A raging fire at historic Windsor Castle in November added to what The Queen called an "Annus Horribilus."

On the brighter side, the Princess Royal married Commander Tim Laurence on December 12th in a small church near Balmoral Castle, the Queen's Scottish home.

Still another somber event happened a week before Christmas: the separation of the Prince and Princess of Wales.

E2-563: Queen Elizabeth II Windsor Fire Mug, 1992, Coronet. $40.—$45.

E2-564: Queen Elizabeth II "Annus Horribilus Mug," 1992, J. & S. Chown. $50.—$55. *Courtesy of Anne Minns.*

In 1992, the Queen allowed television cameras to get reasonably close to her and her family — on private and public occasions. The BBC television production, *Elizabeth R: A Year In The Life of The Queen,* first shown in England, had an audience of more than half the popu-

Left, PA-033: Princess Anne and Commander Tim Laurence 1992 Wedding Mug, Aynsley. $65.—$72. Right, PA-034 Princess Anne and Commander Tim Laurence 1992 Wedding Beaker, Caverswall. $100.—110. *Courtesy of Anne Minns.*

G6-275A: Princess Elizabeth with Teddy Bear Figurine, 1935, Tuscan. $1000.—$1100.

lation of the country tuned in to watch their Queen. The two-hour documentary was also well received when presented on public television in the United States.

In October 1994, Queen Elizabeth II and Prince Philip visited Russia, the first visit to that country by a reigning British sovereign.

In May 1996, the Duke and Duchess of York were divorced. In August 1996, the Prince and Princess of Wales were divorced. This unfortunate event was to be overshadowed by the tragic death of the Princess of Wales in an automobile accident in Paris in August 1997.

In November 1997, the Queen and Prince Philip celebrated their 50th Wedding Anniversary.

The duties, celebrations and challenges will continue for the Queen and her family. And commemoratives, which chronicle these historic and personal events pertaining to the royals, will continue to be produced.

E2-565: Princess Elizabeth Figurine, Wade. *Courtesy of Anne Minns.*

Princess Elizabeth, Our Empire's Little Princess Group, 1928 — 1931, Paragon. *Courtesy of Anne Minns.*

E2-566: Princess Elizabeth of York Mug, Royal Doulton. *Courtesy of Anne Minns.*

E2-567: Pair of Queen Elizabeth II and Prince Philip 1952 Accession Plates, Grosvenor. *Courtesy of Anne Minns.*

E2-228: Queen Elizabeth II 1953 Coronation Jug, Burleighware. $235.—$260. *Courtesy of Anne Minns.*

E2-568: Queen Elizabeth II 1953 Coronation Loving Cup, Crown Staffordshire. $450.—$500. *Courtesy of Anne Minns.*

E2-233: Queen Elizabeth II 1953 Coronation Jug, Burleighware. $760.—$790. *Courtesy of Anne Minns.*

E2-569: Prince Charles and Princess Anne 1953 China Doll Heads. *Courtesy of Anne Minns.*

E2-570: Prince Charles and Princess Anne 1953 Figurines. *Courtesy of Anne Minns.*

E2-616: Queen Elizabeth II 1959 St. Lawrence Seaway Opening Plate, Paragon. $190.—$215.

E2-619: Queen Elizabeth II 1953 Coronation Bowl, Maling. $140.—$150.

E2-617: Queen Elizabeth II 1977 Silver Jubilee Needlepoint. $79.—$89.

E2-620: Queen Elizabeth II 1992 40th Anniversary of Accession Bowl, Wedgwood. $560.—$610.

E2-618: Queen Elizabeth II 1953 Coronation Tapestry, Usters of Bradford. $155.—$160.

E2-621: Queen Elizabeth II 1953 Coronation Cigarette Box and Ashtray, Gray's Pottery. $190.—$210.

E2-573: Queen Elizabeth II 1953 Loving Cup, Royal Crown Derby, Limited Edition of 250. *Courtesy of Anne Minns.*

E2-574: Queen Elizabeth II 1953 Coronation Mug, New Chelsea. $85.—$95.

E2-575: Queen Elizabeth II 1953 Coronation Mug, Royal Stafford. $110.—$120. *Courtesy of Christina Watkinson, Crowns and Sceptres.*

E2-576: Queen Elizabeth II 1953 Coronation Loving Cup, Hammersley. $350.—$385. *Courtesy of Christina Watkinson, Crowns and Sceptres.*

E2-461: Queen Elizabeth II 1953 Coronation Tin. $28.—$33.

E2-577: Queen Elizabeth II 1953 Coronation Plate, Chong Kee, Hong Kong. $78.—$89.

E2-578: Queen Elizabeth II and Prince Philip 1953 Coronation Framed Miniature Plaques, Wedgwood. $215.—$230.

E2-097: Queen Elizabeth II 1953 Coronation Cup and Saucer, Foley. $58.—$66.

E2-579: Queen Elizabeth II 1953 Coronation Mug, Royal Doulton. $45.—$50.

E2-675: Queen Elizabeth II 1953 Coronation Dish. $19.—$23.

E2-368: Queen Elizabeth II and Prince Philip 1953 Coronation Tin Plates, Metal Box Co. $38.—$44 Pair.

E2-351: Queen Elizabeth II 1953 Coronation Plaque, Tuscan. $40.—$45.

E2-622: Queen Elizabeth II 1993 40th Anniversary of Coronation Plate, Royal Doulton. $155.—$170.

E2-624: Queen Elizabeth II 1953 Coronation Plate, Gray's Pottery. $110.—$125.

E2-676: Queen Elizabeth II 1977 Visit to Derbyshire Plate, Royal Crown Derby. Limited edition of 500. $270.—$290.

E2-625: Queen Elizabeth II 1986 60th Birthday Plate, Royal Worcester. $55.—$65.

E2-623: Queen Elizabeth II 1977 Silver Jubilee Plate, Wedgwood. Limited edition of 1000. $185.—$205.

E2-626: Queen Elizabeth II 1977 Silver Jubilee Plate, Coalport. $370.—$400.

E2-627: Queen Elizabeth II 1977 Silver Jubilee Compact, Wedgwood. $90.—$100.

E2-630: Queen Elizabeth II and Prince Charles Tin. Birth, Marriage and Coronation Dates. *Bester's*. $70.—$80.

E2-628: Queen Elizabeth II 1957 Visit to France Covered Jar, L. Bernardaud & Co., Limoges, France. $350.—$385.

E2-631: Queen Elizabeth II 1953 Coronation Musical Teapot. $320.—$335.

E2-629: Queen Elizabeth II Silk Scarf, Liberty's of London. $120.—$135.

Left, E2-037: Queen Elizabeth II 1953 Coronation Covered Box, Wedgwood & Co. $85.—$95. Right, E2-041: Queen Elizabeth II 1953 Coronation Orb Shaped Covered Box, Wedgwood & Co. $90.—$100.

E2-632: Queen Elizabeth II 1953
Coronation Stand Alone Bronze Plaque.
$55.—$63.

E2-635: Queen Elizabeth II/Prince Philip
1997 Golden Wedding Anniversary
Plate, Royal Doulton. Limited edition of
2000. $155.—$175.

E2-634: Queen Elizabeth II 1977 Silver
Jubilee Urn. Coalport. Limited edition of
250. $415.—$440.

E2-633: Queen Elizabeth II 1977 Jubilee Water Colors. Reeves.
$57.—$65.

E2-636: Queen Elizabeth II 1992 40th Anniversary of Accession
Gold State Coach, Matchbox. $75.—$85.

Left, E2-637: Queen Elizabeth II 1953 Coronation Plaque Made for USA, Wedgwood. LE 150. $320—$345. Center, E2-358: 1977 Silver Jubilee Miniature Plaques, Silver Royal Arms, Wedgwood. $170.—$185. Right, E2-638: 1977 Silver Jubilee Plaque, Wedgwood. LE 2000. $145.—$160.

E2-443: Queen Elizabeth II 1953 Coronation Tea Set, Wedgwood Queensware. $265.—$295.

E2-639: Queen Elizabeth II 1993 40th Anniversary of Coronation Plate, Caverswall. Limited edition of 500. $215.—$235.

E2-641: Queen Elizabeth II 1977 Silver Jubilee Plate, Longton Hall Porcelain Co. Limited edition of 100. $375.—$410.

E2-640: Queen Elizabeth II 1953 Coronation Loving Cup, Tuscan. $420.—$465.

E2-642: Queen Elizabeth II/Prince Philip 1972 Silver Wedding Anniversary Loving Cup, Spode. Limited edition of 500. $585.—$625.

PA-034: Princess Anne, Captain Mark Phillips 1973
Wedding Mug. J&J May. $70.—$80.

E2-644: Queen Elizabeth II 1977 Silver Jubilee Beaker, Mulberry
Hall. Limited edition of 2500. $95.—$119.

E2-643: Queen Elizabeth II 1953 Coronation Paperweight,
Baccarat. $520.—$550.

E2-645: Queen Elizabeth II 1953 Coronation Paperweight, St.
Louis. $415.—$450.

MA-009: Princess Margaret, Anthony Armstrong-Jones 1960
Wedding Kneeler. $530.—$575.

MA-007: Princess Margaret, Anthony Armstrong-Jones 1960
Wedding Cup and Saucer, Paragon. $275.—$325.

DY-062: Prince Andrew and Sarah Ferguson 1986 Wedding Flask, Minton. $169.—$179. *Courtesy of Anne Minns.*

DY-041: Prince Andrew and Sarah Ferguson 1986 Wedding Plate, Royal Doulton. $129.—$139.

DY-063: Prince Andrew and Sarah Ferguson 1986 Wedding Mug, Britannia, Limited Edition of 150. $130.—$145.

DY-046: Prince Andrew and Sarah Ferguson 1986 Wedding Plate, Caverswall. $61.—$66.

DY-064: Princess Beatrice 1988 Birth Mug, Caverswall. $65.—$72.

DY-065: Princess Beatrice 1988 Birth Plate, Caverswall, Limited Edition of 250. $90.—$100.

Princess Margaret 1958 Canada Visit Pieces, Aynsley.
Courtesy of Anne Minns.

MA-006A: Princess Margaret Framed
Plaque, Wedgwood. $195.—$210.

MA-005: Princess Margaret's 50th Birthday Loving Cup,
1980. Queen Elizabeth, the Queen Mother's 80th
Birthday on Reverse, Caverswall. $119.—$129.

MA-008: Princess Margaret and Anthony Armstrong-Jones
Divorce Mug, 1978. $140.—$155. *Courtesy of Christina
Watkinson, Crowns and Sceptres.*

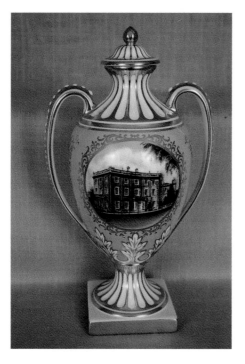 

PC-426: 1981 Wedding Vase, Spode.
Limited edition of 500. $595.—$635.

Reverse of PC-426, 1981 Wedding Vase.

PC-427: 1981 Wedding Chalice, Spode.
Limited edition of 500. $595.—$635.

Reverse of PC-427, 1981 Wedding Chalice.

Chapter 3
The Future Kings

Prince Charles Philip Arthur George was born on November 14, 1948, the first child of Princess Elizabeth and the Duke of Edinburgh.

Upon his mother's accession to the throne as Queen Elizabeth II in 1952, he was named Duke of Cornwall. The Queen made him Prince of Wales in 1958.

In 1969, Prince Charles was formally invested as Prince of Wales at Caernarvon Castle in Wales, only the second formal investiture of a Prince of Wales in modern times. A number of commemoratives for his investiture are shown on this and the following page.

Their first son, second in line to the throne, Prince William Arthur Philip Louis of Wales, was born on June 21, 1982. His brother, Prince Henry Charles Albert David, known as Prince Harry in the family, was born on September 15, 1984.

On December 9, 1992, Buckingham Palace announced that the Prince and Princess of Wales had agreed to a separation which was followed by their divorce in 1996. Tragically, the Princess of Wales died in an automobile accident in Paris in 1997.

PC-079: "Charles - Prince of Wales - July 1958" is on this Dish Commemorating His Creation as Prince of Wales. $125.—$140.

PC-408: Three Views of Prince and Princess of Wales 1992 Separation Mug. $65.—$68.

Prince Charles attended Hill House School in London, Cheam Preparatory School and Gordonstoun. He was not an outstanding student, but he did well during the two semesters he spent as an exchange student at the Geelong School in Australia. Later, he received a degree from Cambridge. Following Cambridge, he spent time in the Royal Air Force and later in the Navy.

The Prince became engaged to Lady Diana Spencer in February, 1981. Only a few commemoratives were made for the betrothal. A beaker, loving cup and mug are shown in the Value Guide. The marriage took place at St. Paul's Cathedral in London on July 21, 1981. Many commemoratives were made for this royal wedding.

PC-409: Prince Charles 1969 Investiture Dragon, Royal Crown Derby. $1600.—$1800. *Courtesy of Anne Minns.*

PC-035: Prince Charles 1969 Investiture Mug, Wedgwood. $80.—$85.

PC-016: Prince Charles 1969 Investiture Goblets, Royal Crown Derby for Harrods. Limited Edition of 25. $785.—$820. Pair.

Prince Charles 1969 Investiture Mugs, Lord Nelson Pottery. Left, PC-029; Center, PC-410; Right, PC-030. $40.—$45. Each.

Prince Charles 1969 Investiture Pieces. Left, PC-411: 5" Plate, Rye Pottery. $30.—$35.; Center, PC-412: Teapot shaped Pomander. $49.—$54.; Right, PC-036: Mug, Made in Wales. $47.—$51.

PC-078: Prince Charles 1969 Investiture Vase, Spode. $535.—$555.

PC-017: Prince Charles 1969 Investiture Goblet, Coalport. $138.—$153.

PC-428: 1981 Wedding Miniature Mug, Highland, Scotland. $85.—$95.

PC-188: 1981 Wedding Loving Cup, Royal Crown Derby. Limited edition of 1500. $280.—$295.

PC-430: 1981 Wedding Sterling Silver Chalice, London Hallmark. $425.—$465.

PC-429: 1981 Wedding Plate, Royal Worcester. Limited edition of 1000. $155.—$175.

PC-431: 1981 Wedding Plate, Royal Crown Derby. Limited edition of 750. $235.—$255.

31

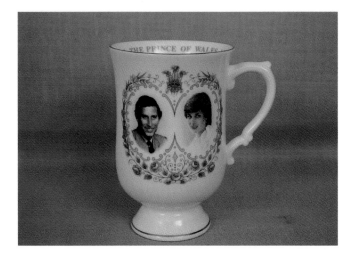

PC-201: 1981 Wedding Mug, Crown
Staffordshire. $42.—$46.

PC-181: 1981 Wedding Loving Cup,
Paragon. $94.—$99.

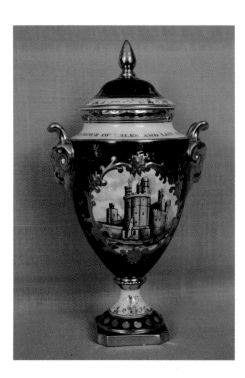

PC-432: 1981 Wedding Covered Vase,
Coalport. Limited edition of 100.
$795.—$855.

PC-432: 1981 Wedding Cuff Links. $185.—$205.

Left, PC-433: 1981 Wedding Ginger Jar, Mason's. $55.—$65.
Right, PC-189: 1981 Wedding Loving Cup, Mason's. $155.—
$165.

PC-434: 1996 Prince and Princess of Wales Divorce Mug. $65.—$75.

Reverse of PC-434, 1996 Divorce Mug.

PC-435: 1996 Prince and Princess of Wales Divorce Mug, Lady Grace. Limited edition of 896. $75.—$89.

Reverse of PC-435, 1996 Divorce Mug.

PC-279: 1981 Wedding Plate, Royal Worcester. Limited edition of 3000. $225.—$240.

PC-436: 1981 Wedding Plate, Hammersley. $210.—$225.

PC-437: 1982 Prince William Christening Goblet, Spode. Limited edition of 5000. $215.—$235.

PC-440: 1982 Prince William Birth Plate, Wedgwood. $55.—$69.

PC-438: 1984 Prince Henry Birth Plate, Royal Doulton. $110.—$125.

PC-441: 1996 Diana, Princess of Wales, Plate, Goss. Limited edition of 2500. $135.—$150.

PC-439: Princess of Wales 30th Birthday Mug, Aynsley. $110.—$125.

PC-442: 1982 Prince William Birth Plate, Royal Worcester. Limited edition of 1000. $190.—$220.

PC-443: 1997 Princess of Wales In Memoriam Russian Egg. $85.—$95.

PC-446: 1997 Princess of Wales In Memoriam Tree Ornament. $30.—$35.

PC-444: 1997 Princess of Wales In Memoriam Tea Plate. $49.—$59.

PC-447: 1997 Princess of Wales In Memoriam Paperweight. $59.—$69.

PC-445: 1997 Princess of Wales In Memoriam Kensington Vase, Aynsley. Limited edition of 1000. $250.—$275.

PC-465: 1997 Princess of Wales In Memoriam Doll, Society for Preservation of History, Inc. $175.—$189.

G6-342: 1939 King George VI and Queen Elizabeth USA Visit Tea Set, Wedgwood. Limited edition of 3000. $695.—$755.

Left, G6-343 and Right, G6-344: 1937 King George VI and Queen Elizabeth Coronation Plaques, Coalport. $800.—$950. each.

Chapter 4

King George VI

1936 — 1952

With the birth of a second son at Sandringham on December 14, 1895, the Duke and Duchess of York at last were able to satisfy one of Queen Victoria's wishes by naming the young prince Albert Frederick Arthur George, despite the fact that his birth came on the 34th anniversary of the Prince Consort's death. Young Prince Albert, like his grandfather, would be known in the family as Bertie. Little could anyone have imagined at the time that Bertie would one day become King George VI.

Prince Albert shared a tutor with his elder brother, Prince Edward, and later followed him to Osborne and Dartmouth. However, they were not classmates at the latter two institutions. He was a shy youngster and grew up in the shadow of Prince Edward who was being prepared for his future role as King. Prince Albert developed a stammer early in life which plagued him for many years, especially when he was under stress.

In 1913, the young prince completed his training on board the cruiser *Cumberland*, which went to the West Indies and Canada. Later that same year, he became a midshipman on *HMS Collingwood* and was still on duty aboard that ship when World War I broke out in 1914. Despite a tendency to sea sickness and gastric disorder, Prince Albert wanted to stay aboard *HMS Collingwood* for action in the war and was in one naval battle with the Germans. Afterwards, the gastric trouble flared up again, eventually being diagnosed as an ulcer. As a result, the Prince underwent surgery in 1917, effectively ending his naval career.

In 1919, he took flying lessons and qualified as a pilot. However, because of his ill health, he was not permitted to fly solo. Then followed a year at Cambridge with his younger brother, Prince Henry. In 1920, King George V created him Duke of York, Earl of Inverness and Baron Killarney.

In 1920, Prince Albert again met Lady Elizabeth Bowes-Lyon, whom he had first met in 1905 at a children's party. He fell in love with her in 1922, and early in 1923 they were engaged to be married. Their wedding took place on April 26, 1923, at Westminster Abbey. Few commemoratives were made for the occasion.

G6-204: Duke and Duchess of York 1923 Wedding Tin. $130.—$140.

G6-322: Duke of York Wedding Mug. (A similar mug was made showing the Duchess of York). $275.—$300.
Courtesy of Anne Minns.

Their first daughter, Princess Elizabeth, was born in 1926. Little was done to commemorate her birth.

For Princess Margaret's birth, Paragon made another series with budgies perched on marguerites for Margaret, pink roses for Rose, and heather for Scotland where she was born.

G6-345: King George VI and Queen Elizabeth 1937 Coronation Loving Cup, Minton. $1195.—$1295.

Reverse of G6-345 Coronation Loving Cup.

The Duchess of York was instrumental in helping her husband overcome his stutter. Eventually, with the help of a speech therapist and the encouragement of a warm family, he was able to speak in public. However, the stammer did recur from time to time.

Although the Duke of York represented the Crown on many formal occasions, he was not given access to the inner workings of the monarchy. This was understandable, since his older brother, Prince Edward, was the heir apparent, and there was little likelihood that Prince Albert would ever need such knowledge. He did make a few official visits to the Dominions on behalf of the King.

The Duke and Duchess of York were unprepared for the abdication of King Edward VIII. They were not kept well informed by the King of his intentions. Indeed, the King himself may not have known what he intended to do. Although the Duke was told by King Edward VIII in November of his intention to marry Mrs. Simpson, it was not until December 7 that Prince Albert learned of his brother's firm intention to abdicate.

Prince Albert decided to be known as King George VI, and his coronation date was set for May 12, 1937, the same date which had been planned for the coronation of his brother. Many coronation commemoratives which had been designed for King Edward VIII's coronation were simply modified to show the new King and Queen with a slight change in wording. There were, of course, additional commemoratives made exclusively for the coronation of King George VI and Queen Eliza-

G6-346: King George VI 1937 Coronation and 1939 USA/Canada Visit Cup and Saucer, Paragon. $295.—$325.

beth. Many coronation commemoratives also showed Princesses Elizabeth and Margaret.

In 1939, with war clouds looming over Europe, the King and Queen paid a visit to Canada and the United States — the first visit to the USA of a reigning British monarch. This visit did much to cement Anglo-American relations for the upcoming struggle.

G6-016: King George VI and Queen Elizabeth 1939 USA Visit Beaker, Minton. $525.—$595. *Courtesy of Anne Minns.*

G6-045: World War II "There'll Always Be An England" Cup and Saucer, Roslyn. $110.—$125. *Courtesy of Anne Minns.*

G6-324: King George VI and Queen Elizabeth 1939 USA Visit Loving Cup, Royal Crown Derby. $575.—$675. *Courtesy of Anne Minns.*

World War II "The King and Queen are Still in London" Cups and Saucers by Paragon. King George VI and Queen Elizabeth. *Courtesy of Anne Minns.*

In August, 1939, Germany invaded Poland — World War II had begun. In 1940, Germany began its aerial bombardment of Britain. The King and Queen remained in London and suffered the air raids along with their people. Buckingham Palace was itself bombed twice. Their example was an inspiration to the British people and helped keep their spirits high through this terrible ordeal. Paragon produced a number of items in their Patriotic Series, some depicting war ships and planes. The most famous of these —and most difficult to find today — show the King and Queen and are captioned, "The King and Queen are Still in London." Roslyn China also made a cup and saucer with their portraits and the caption, "There'll Always Be An England." These are more easily found.

In December, 1941, the United States joined the Allied cause following the Japanese bombing of Pearl Harbor. It was not until June, 1944, that the Allied armies were able to invade France and begin the assault that would end the war. It was a jubilant Royal Family who stood on the balcony of Buckingham Palace with Prime Minister Churchill on VE Day in May, 1945.

In 1947, Princess Elizabeth was married to Prince Philip. Very little was done to commemorate their wedding, since it came so soon after the end of World War II. In 1948, their first son, Prince Charles was born, insuring the line of succession to the throne.

In 1948, the King developed circulatory problems, and in 1949, he had to cancel a tour of Australia and New Zealand. In 1951, he developed lung cancer and underwent surgery to remove one lung.

On January 31, 1952, the King went to the airport to see Princess Elizabeth and Prince Philip off on the beginning of a tour of East Africa, Australia and New Zealand. Princess Elizabeth was making the tour on the King's behalf because he was too ill to make it himself. He returned to Sandringham the next day. On February 5, he spent the day shooting. That night he died peacefully in his sleep.

Following the death of King George VI and the accession to the throne of Queen Elizabeth II, Queen Elizabeth became Queen Elizabeth, The Queen Mother. She continued to take an active part in royal affairs and to make many official public appearances.

G6-348: King George VI and Queen Elizabeth 1937 Coronation Jug. $175.—$195.

G6-347: 1937 Coronation Teapot with Marcus Adams Royal Family Portrait, Royal Albert. $395.—$425.

Reverse of G6-348 Coronation Jug.

G6-349: 1939 King George VI and Queen Elizabeth Canada/USA Visit Plate, Paragon. $395.—$435.

G6-352: 1937 King George VI/Queen Elizabeth Coronation Bowl, Poole Pottery. $185.—$205.

G6-350: 1939 King George VI/Queen Elizabeth Canada and USA Visit Charger, Paragon. $595.—$655.

G6-353: 1947 King George VI/Queen Elizabeth Africa Visit Plate, Gray's Pottery for Heal's of London. $225.—$255.

G6-351: 1937 King George VI/Queen Elizabeth Coronation Cigarette Musical Box, Crown Devon. $995.—$1095.

G6-018: 1937 King George VI and Queen Elizabeth Coronation Plate, Copeland Spode. $225.—$250.

Group of Princess Elizabeth and Princess Margaret Pieces by Paragon. *Courtesy of Anne Minns.*

Two Mugs by Crown Ducal. Left, G6-332: Princess Elizabeth. Right, G6-333: Princess Margaret. $250.—$275. Each. *Courtesy of Anne Minns.*

G6-293: Princesses Elizabeth and Margaret Tin. Marcus Adams portrait. $56.—$62.

Top, G6-334: Marcus Adams Portrait Tin $49.—$55. Bottom, Left, G6-182: King George VI and Queen Elizabeth Coronation Tin. $36.—$41. Right, G6-202: Marcus Adams Portrait Tin. $39.—$44. *Courtesy of Christina Watkinson, Crowns & Sceptres.*

G6-284: Princesses Elizabeth and Margaret Mug. Marcus Adams portrait. $265.—$290.

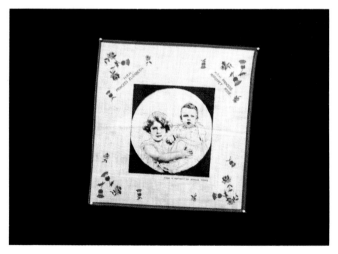

G6-282: Princesses Elizabeth and Margaret Handkerchief. Marcus Adams portrait. $55.—$60. *Courtesy of Anne Minns.*

G6-356: Queen Elizabeth, The Queen Mother, 95th Birthday Plate, Aynsley. Limited edition of 95. $595.—$635.

G6-354: Princess Margaret 1930 Birth Teapot, Paragon. $395.—$445.

G6-357: Queen Elizabeth, The Queen Mother, Portrait Plate, from a painting by Molly Bishop, Royal Worcester. $100.—$115.

G6-355: Queen Elizabeth, The Queen Mother, 90th Birthday Plate, Royal Doulton. Limited edition of 1000. $135.—$150.

G6-358: Queen Elizabeth, The Queen Mother, 90th Birthday Plate, Goss. $55.—$65.

Left, E8-124: King Edward VIII Accession Plate, Ruwaha, Belgium. $180.—$200. Right, E8-200: Accession Bowl by same manufacturer. $265.—$290.

E8-227 King Edward VIII 1937 Coronation Loving Cup, Royal Doulton. Limited edition of 2000. $1050.—$1200.

Chapter 5
King Edward VIII
1936

Edward, Prince of Wales, was at his father's bedside when King George V's life slipped away just before midnight on January 20, 1936. It is said that Queen Mary kissed her son's hand and said, "God save the King."

Prince Edward Albert Christian George Andrew Patrick David was born on June 23, 1894, at the home of his maternal grandparents, the Tecks, in Richmond Park. Throughout his life, he was known to his family and close friends as David.

Queen Victoria is reported to have wanted the new Prince named Albert. But Prince George told the Queen he and Princess May wished to name their first son in memory of Prince George's brother, "Eddy." Queen Victoria replied that whatever name they chose would be satisfactory. However, she pointed out that Eddy's real name was Albert Victor.

E8-179: Prince Edward Investiture Plate. $395.—$425.

E8-178: Prince Edward Birth Loving Cup, Aller Vale. $1050.—$1200.

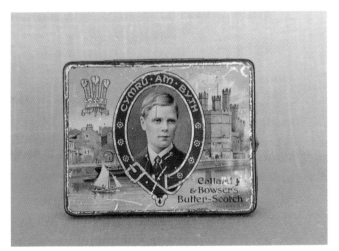

E8-180: Prince Edward Investiture Tin. $120.—$145.

In 1907, young Prince Edward was sent to the Royal Naval College at Osborne on the Isle of Wight, and then to Dartmouth in May, 1909. He was at Dartmouth when his grandfather, King Edward VII, died on May 6, 1910. Prince Edward then inherited the title of Duke of Cornwall.

On Prince Edward's sixteenth birthday in 1910, King George V gave the young prince the title of Prince of Wales. On July 13, 1911, he was invested as Prince of Wales at Caernarvon Castle in Wales — the first formal investiture of a Prince of Wales in more than 300 years. A relatively small number of commemoratives was made for this occasion.

Prince Edward went to Oxford in the fall of 1912. It was there that he met Walter Monckton who would later play an important role in his life, first during the abdication crisis and later as the Duke of Windsor's liaison in London.

With the outbreak of World War I in 1914, Prince Edward was given a commission in the Grenadier Guards. Although King George V permitted the Prince to go to France, the King always made sure his son was not in danger. In 1916, the Prince was awarded the Military Cross which he felt he did not deserve, especially when he compared his role to that of the men in the trenches.

In 1919, Prince Edward sailed for the new world — Canada and the United States. Very little was done to commemorate this trip. A mug for the Canada portion of his visit is shown below. It had been issued for his investiture, and a commemoration for the 1919 Canada trip was added.

Left, E8-181: Prince Edward 1919 USA Visit Medal. $195.—$220. Right, E8-182: Prince Edward 1911 Investiture and 1919 Canada Visit Mug. $250.—$275.

E8-183: Prince Edward 1920 Canada Visit Plate, Grimwades. $330.—$365.

In 1920, accompanied by his cousin Louis Mountbatten, Prince Edward went to New Zealand and Australia. Enroute they stopped in San Diego where they attended a mayoral ball. Also present were a young U.S. naval officer, Earl Winfield Spencer, and his wife, Wallis Warfield Spencer.

Tours of India, the Far East and South Africa followed. It was not until 1925 that the Prince completed the Imperial tours. During this period, he also made trips to Canada and the United States. Below is a tin with the Prince of Wales' portrait on the lid and scenes from India, Cape Town, Ottawa and Sydney around the sides. The tin was no doubt made for the tour, but it has no commemoration.

E8-175: Prince Edward Tin. c. 1920's. $97.—$107.

There were other Prince of Wales souvenirs made during this period, but many of them showed only his portrait and title and did not carry a commemoration. Commemoratives were also made for local events or visits, such as the tin made for the 1924 British Empire Exhibition at Wembley.

E8-184: Prince Edward 1924 Wembley Exhibition Tin. $95.—$115.

In 1929, King George V gave Prince Edward permission to use Fort Belvedere as a country residence. The Prince renovated the Fort, adding bedrooms, baths and a swimming pool. He enjoyed working in the gardens, clearing out underbrush and planting flowers and shrubs.

It was early in 1931 that the Prince of Wales first met Wallis Warfield Simpson. They were introduced by Thelma Furness, the Prince of Wales' favorite of the moment.

Bessie Wallis Warfield was born in Blue Ridge Summit, Pennsylvania, on June 19, 1896, two years after the Prince was born. Her father died of tuberculosis when she was only five months old. Her mother lived on the charity of relatives and the small amount she took in from boarders.

Anxious to get married, Wallis jumped at the first opportunity and married "Win" Spencer, a young naval officer. Because he was moody and a violent alcoholic, she left him and lived alone in Washington for several years. Afterward, they reconciled and she rejoined him in the Far East. Later she left him again and spent a year in China. In 1925, she returned to the United States and sued for divorce.

Wallis married Ernest Simpson in 1928. He was in the shipping business and was the son of an English father and an American mother. They settled down in rented quarters in London.

Following their first meeting in January, 1931, the Prince of Wales and Mrs. Simpson met again in May. In January, 1932, the Prince of Wales dined with the Simpsons at their London home for the first time. At the end of that month, the Simpsons were invited for a weekend at Fort Belvedere.

By early 1933, Mrs. Simpson had spent several more weekends at the Fort. Although Thelma Furness continued to be the Prince's favorite, Mrs. Simpson began to think she might take Thelma's place.

In early 1934, Thelma Furness made a trip to the United States. Before sailing, she asked Wallis to take good care of the Prince of Wales while she was away. It was reported that Thelma Furness had an affair with the Aga Kahn during that trip. On her first visit to the Fort after her return, the Prince of Wales was cool to her. At the dinner table that night, she came to realize that Wallis had indeed taken good care of the Prince while she was away. The next day Thelma Furness left the Fort and the Prince's life.

Wallis soon became the unofficial hostess at the Fort. She dismissed some of the servants who had been hired by Thelma Furness. An old friend of the Prince, Freda Dudley Ward, telephoned the Prince and was told by the operator she had orders not to put Freda's calls through. Mrs. Simpson was in charge. It was at the Fort that she introduced the American specialty, the club sandwich, to their British guests.

Before long, Mrs. Simpson was spending time at the Fort without Mr. Simpson. Until late 1934, King George V and Queen Mary had tacitly ignored Mrs. Simpson's existence. In November, the Prince of Wales managed, against his father's wishes, to have Wallis attend a party at Buckingham Palace. There she was introduced to Queen Mary, but the outraged King turned away.

The Prince and Mrs. Simpson enjoyed a holiday in Biarritz and then went on a cruise in 1934; in 1935, they went on a skiing outing to Kitzbuhel — all without Mr. Simpson. By now, the Prince of Wales was completely dominated by Wallis. He was deeply in love with her.

Following his succession to the throne in January, 1936, King Edward VIII in a radio broadcast to the nation said "I am better known to you as the Prince of Wales. I am still that same man." The last sentence of that statement appears on the reverse of the loving cup shown below which Royal Doulton made to commemorate his reign in 1936.

E8-075: King Edward VIII Loving Cup made by Royal Doulton to commemorate the year of his reign in 1936. $1100.—$1350.

Reverse of Loving Cup shown above.

King Edward VIII's coronation date was set for May 12, 1937. Thousands upon thousands of commemoratives were made and sold in anticipation of the coronation. Contrary to what many people believe, these coronation souvenirs are not rare today.

E8-203: King Edward VIII 1937 Coronation Cup and Saucer, Colclough. $200.—$225.

E8-202: King Edward VIII 1937 Coronation Plate, Wedgwood & Co. $95.—$110.

The story of the abdication crisis in 1936 would take many pages, indeed chapters, to tell. Suffice it to say that during the ten months and 21 days of the reign of King Edward VIII, there were many discussions and arguments about Mrs. Simpson's future role. Ideas ranging from a morganatic marriage (in which any children born of the union would not be successors to the throne) to Mrs. Simpson's becoming Queen were discussed on both sides of the Atlantic. At first, the discussions took place only outside the country because the British press agreed not to publish the stories. In the end, a constitutional crisis was averted only by the King's decision to abdicate. Following his abdication, he was styled Duke of Windsor. A number of commemoratives were issued for the abdication. However, very few were made especially for the occasion. Most were coronation souvenirs on which an abdication message had been overprinted.

On the evening of December 11, 1936, from Windsor Castle, King Edward VIII made a farewell radio broadcast to the nation. At two o'clock the following morning, he sailed for France enroute to Austria where he would reside temporarily while waiting for Mrs. Simpson's divorce to become final. She remained in France where she had been living with friends for the past few months.

In early May, 1937, Mrs. Simpson's divorce became final. On June 3, she became the Duchess of Windsor at a wedding ceremony in Tourraine, France. Much to the Duke's disappointment, no members of the royal family attended the wedding.

E8-188: King Edward VIII 1936 Abdication Cup and Saucer, Tuscan. $200.—$225.

E8-205: King Edward VIII 1937 Coronation Teapot, Royal Stafford. $225.—$250.

E8-188: Duke and Duchess of Windsor Wedding First Day Cover. $200.—$230.

E8-120: Duke of Windsor In Memoriam Plaque, Wedgwood. $115.—$130.

E8-189: Duke of Windsor In Memoriam Plate, Mercian. $115.—$130.

The Duke asked King George VI to announce publicly that Wallis would be styled Her Royal Highness. The King declined to do so and denied many similar requests through the years. The Duchess was never able to obtain the title of H.R.H. which she so coveted.

The Duke wanted to do some meaningful work, but the only job he was ever given by King George VI was that of Governor of the Bahamas during the World War II period. He had hoped that eventually he and the Duchess would be able to return to England to live, but this too was not to be. His beloved Fort Belvedere fell into disrepair and was eventually sold in 1955.

The Duke and Duchess spent most of their years in France, mainly because of favorable tax laws. They made frequent trips to the United States, and each of them published a book. He wrote *A King's Story* in 1951, and she wrote *The Heart Has Its Reasons* in 1956. The Duke also wrote a small book at the time of Queen Elizabeth II's coronation, *The Crown and the People — 1902— 1953*.

In August, 1970, at the Duke's request, Queen Elizabeth II gave permission for the Duke and Duchess to be buried at Frogmore on the grounds of Windsor Castle.

In May, 1972, the Queen visited the seriously ill Duke of Windsor in Paris. He died nine days later on May 28, 1972.

Following the Duke's death, the Duchess of Windsor continued to live in France. After several years of declining health, she died on April 24, 1986, and was buried next to the Duke of Windsor at Frogmore.

Duke and Duchess of Windsor In Memoriam Pieces by Dorincourt. Left, E8-190: Plate. $165.—$195. Right, E8-112: Mug. $85.—$95.

49

E8-206: British Empire Exhibition Miniature Vase. Left: Prince of Wales, President, 1924; Right: Duke of York, President, 1925. Grafton. $195.—$225.

E8-209: 1931 Prince of Wales Visit to British Exposition, Buenos Aires, Dish. Crown Devon. $225.—$245.

E8-207: King Edward VIII 1937 Coronation Dish, Tuscan. $65.—$75.

E8-210: King Edward VIII 1937 Coronation Tin. $75.—$89.

E8-208: King Edward VIII 1937 Coronation Press Molded Glass Bust. $110.—$125.

E8-211: 1937 King Edward VIII Coronation Plaques, M. J. Wood. $195.—$220. each.

Two 1937 King Edward VIII Coronation Mugs, Thos. Goode, London. Left, E8-211: Unlimited edition. $85.—$95. Right, E8-212: A limited edition of 12 made for Herbert Goode with fancier decoration. $110.—$125.

E8-215: King Edward VIII 1937 Coronation "E" Handle Mug, Royal Doulton. $130.—$155.

E8-213: King Edward VIII 1937 Coronation Covered Box, Wedgwood. $95.—$120.

E8-216: King Edward VIII 1937 Coronation Plaque, Poole Pottery. $595.—$655.

E8-214: King Edward VIII 1937 Coronation Plate, Charlotte Rhead design, Crown Ducal. $135.—$160.

E8-217: King Edward VIII 1996 60th Anniversary of Abdication Tray, Wedgwood. Also made in white on pale blue jasperware. $89.—$95.

51

G5-323: King George V Toby Jug by Carruthers Gould. Made as part of a series of World War I political and military leaders. $2000.—$2250.

Chapter 6
King George V
1910 — 1936

The future King George V was born on June 3, 1865, at Marlborough House in London, the second son of the Prince and Princess of Wales (later King Edward VII and Queen Alexandra). He was christened George Frederick Ernest Albert in St. George's Chapel, Windsor, on July 7, 1865.

Prince George and his older brother, Price Albert Victor, known in the family as Eddy, were inseparable throughout their youth. In 1877, it was decided that Prince George should begin his naval career by joining the training ship *Britannia* as a cadet. Prince Eddy joined him, as he did again in 1879 on the *Bacchante*, where they spent the next three years. The princes were separated for the first time in 1883 when Prince George joined the crew of the *HMS Canada*. He progressed in his naval career and was given his first command in 1889.

In 1891, while on leave at Sandringham, Prince George became ill with typhoid fever and was confined to bed for six weeks. During this period, Prince Eddy contracted influenza and died within a week. Suddenly, Prince George was thrust into the position of future King of England.

Prior to his illness, Prince Eddy had become engaged to Princess Victoria Mary of Teck, the wedding having been set for the following February. It has been said that Queen Victoria, who gave Prince George the title of Duke of York in 1892, encouraged a match between him and Princess Mary, known widely as Princess May. In any event, he proposed to Princess May in the spring of 1893 and was accepted. They were married on July 6, 1893, in the Chapel Royal at St. James Palace.

G5-264: Prince George and Princess May 1893 Wedding Tin. $250.—$275.

York Cottage at Sandringham became their home for the next 33 years. There they raised their children:

Prince Edward, born June 23, 1894, later King Edward VIII; then Duke of Windsor;

Prince Albert, born in 1895, later King George VI;

Princess Mary, born in 1897, later married to Viscount Lascelles;

Prince Henry, born in 1900, later Duke of Gloucester;

Prince George, born in 1902, later Duke of Kent, killed in an air crash in 1942; and Prince John, born in 1905, deceased at age 14.

When Prince George's father succeeded to the throne as King Edward VII upon Queen Victoria's death in 1901, he did not immediately bestow the title Prince of Wales upon his son. But the young prince did inherit the Duchy of Cornwall with its title, Duke of Cornwall.

In March 1901, Prince George and Princess May left on a tour of Australia, New Zealand and Canada. In Australia, he opened the first parliament of the newly formed Commonwealth of Australia. Eight days after their return in November, King Edward VII created his son Prince of Wales on the King's 60th birthday.

On April 17, 1910, King Edward VII returned from a trip to Biarritz. He continued a heavy schedule despite the fact he was not feeling well. On May 6, he died just before midnight.

Prince George and Princess May 1893 Wedding Items: Left, G5-297: Cup and Saucer. $245.—$270. Right, G5-298: Mug $185.—$200. *Courtesy of Anne Minns.*

King George V was almost 45 years old upon his accession. Princess May became known as Queen Mary. Their coronation, which was well commemorated, took place on June 22, 1911.

In the winter of 1911-12, King George and Queen Mary went to India for a second Coronation ceremony, a Durbar, held at Delhi on December 12. It was a spectacular affair, and the King and Queen were impressed by its splendor.

The new king inherited a number of problems which carried over from his father's reign: Irish Home Rule, the Parliament Act limiting the powers of the House of Lords, women's suffrage, labor strikes and other problems. These were at the forefront until World War I broke out in 1914, taking precedence over them.

In the fall of 1914, Princess Mary, the only daughter of King George V and Queen Mary, conceived the idea of sending a Christmas gift to all service personnel away from home. She helped form an appeal committee which raised funds for the project. The gift was a brass box which contained cigarettes, a pipe and tobacco, a lighter, and a card from Princess Mary. The lid of the box was embossed with Princess Mary's profile. The gift was later modified to contain candy for the Indian troops whose religion forbade their smoking and for nurses and other nonsmokers.

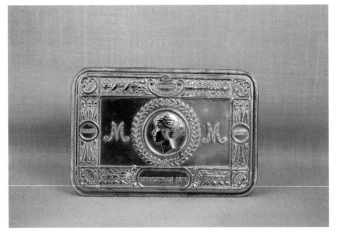

G5-285: Princess Mary 1914 Christmas Tin, Brass. $60.—$70.

The King made five trips to France during the war to visit troops in the trenches. On one of these trips, his horse fell and rolled over on the King, fracturing his pelvis — an injury which caused him a lifetime of pain.

In 1917, because of criticism of the royal family's German background, it was decided that their name should be changed from the House of Saxe-Coburg and Gotha. After considering many suggestions, the King chose the House of Windsor as the new royal family name.

Following the war, Ireland again became a major domestic problem. The final solution was dominion status for Southern Ireland, and the Irish Free State was born in January, 1922.

There were other farreaching changes following the war to which the King had difficulty adapting. Many of the European royal houses headed by relatives of the King had fallen. His first cousin, Tsar Nicholas II, and his family were murdered in Russia.

In February, 1923, Princess Mary was married to Viscount Lascelles, heir to the fifth Earl of Harewood.

Early in 1924, the first Labor government came into power, causing great concern at the time. The King got on well with the group in power, but the government lasted only until fall when Stanley Baldwin again became Prime Minister.

The King's health began to fail during the 1920's, and he suffered a number of personal losses. His mother, Queen Alexandra, with whom he had always been close, died in 1925. His sister, the Princess Royal, died in 1931.

1935 saw the King's Silver Jubilee. He was deeply moved by the outpouring of love for him and Queen Mary during the Jubilee celebrations.

As the year 1935 drew to a close, the King again became ill. He barely managed to make his Christmas broadcast and was not seen again in public. On January 20, 1936, with his family at his bedside, he died just before midnight.

G5-324: 1938 Mug. On the base: "A Christmas Gift from H.M. Queen Mary, December 1938", Paragon. $395.—$435.

G5-300: King George V In Memoriam Handkerchief. $60.—$66. *Courtesy of Anne Minns.*

G5-073: King George V and Queen Mary 1934 Manchester Library Opening Handkerchief. $42.—$47. *Courtesy of Anne Minns.*

MR-007: Princess Mary Mug. $265.—$280. *Courtesy of Anne Minns.*

MR-006: Princess Mary and Viscount Lascelles 1922 Wedding Tins. Left, 9¼" high: $75.—$82. Right, 8" high: $70.—$77.

Left, MR-008: Princess Mary Mug. $260.—$285. Right, MR-009: Princess Mary and Viscount Lascelles 1922 Wedding Mug. $315.—$345. *Courtesy of Anne Minns.*

MR-009-A: Princess Mary and Viscount Lascelles 1922 Wedding Bell, Crown Staffordshire. $290.—$315. *Courtesy of Anne Minns.*

G5-325: King George V/Queen Mary 1911 Coronation Loving Cup, Copeland for Thos. Goode, London, Subscriber's Copy. $2595.—$2800.

Reverse of G5-325 Loving Cup.

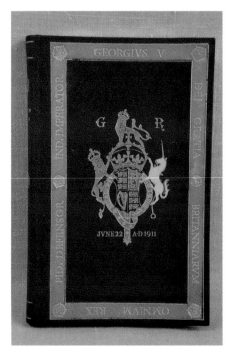

G5-326: King George V/Queen Mary Musical Tankard. $590.—$650.

G5-327: King George V/Queen Mary 1911 Coronation Book of Common Prayer Signed by Queen Mary. Leather binding. $390.—$430.

G5-328: King George V/Queen Mary 1911 Coronation Miniature Vases, Royal Doulton. $245.—$275.

G5-330: 1914 Allies Plate Featuring King George V, Czar Nicholas II and other Allied Leaders. $155.—$180.

G5-329: "George and May" 1893 Wedding Cup and Saucer. $280.—$310.

Left, G5-331: Duke and Duchess of York and Cornwall 1901 Canada Visit Jug. $145.—$160. Right, G5-332: Matching Dish. $89.—$105.

Left, G5-018: King George V/Queen Mary 1911 Coronation Beaker, Bishop & Stonier. $85.—$95. Right, G5-101: Matching Mug. $92.—$105.

G5-359: King George V/Queen Mary 1935 Jubilee Embroidery. $110.—$125.

G5-308: King George V and Queen Mary Coronation Flour Shaker. $115.—$125.

G5-309: King George V and Queen Mary Coronation Mug. $75.—$85.

G5-102: King George V and Queen Mary Coronation Mug. Harrod's Exclusive Design. $85.—$95.

G5-097: King George V and Queen Mary Coronation Mug, Royal Doulton. $99.—$109.

G5-121: King George V and Queen Mary Coronation Mug, Moorcroft. $495.—$585.

G5-062: King George V and Queen Mary Coronation Dish, W. H. Goss. $69.—$76.

G5-333: "George and May" 1893 Wedding Bowl, Wileman (Foley). $155.—$175.

G5-336: 1936 "Three Kings in One Year" Set of Medals. $185.—$210.

G5-334: "H.R.H. Prince of Wales" Mug c. 1911, Royal Doulton stoneware. $325.—$360.

G5-337: King George V/Queen Mary 1911 Coronation Cup, Saucer and Tea Plate, Williamson's. $95.—$110.

G5-335: "Edward Prince of Wales - Our Future King" Plate. $90.—$100.

G5-164: King George V/Queen Mary 1911 Coronation Plate, Royal Doulton. $120.—$135.

E7-221: King Edward VII/
Queen Alexandra 1902
Coronation Covered Vase,
Copeland. $2795.—$3075.

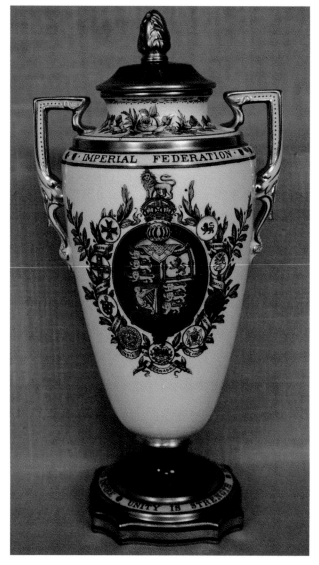

Reverse of E7-221: 1902 Coronation Vase.

Chapter 7

King Edward VII

1901 — 1910

Queen Victoria's oldest son, Albert Edward, was among the many children and grandchildren gathered around his mother's deathbed at Osborne House on the Isle of Wight. In the early evening of January 22, 1901, he succeeded his long-reigning mother to the British throne.

E7-200: King Edward VII 1901 Accession/Queen Victoria In Memoriam Plate. $250.—$285. *Courtesy of Anne Minns.*

Born on November 9, 1841, in Buckingham Palace, Albert Edward was created Prince of Wales by Queen Victoria on December 8th. The heir to the throne was known to his family as Bertie.

E7-201: Albert Edward, Prince of Wales 1841 Birth Plate. $530.—$565. *Courtesy of Anne Minns.*

When he was eighteen, Prince Edward made a state visit to Canada and the United States. His journey included a visit to George Washington's grave at Mount Vernon, Virginia.

In 1861, the future King of England was permitted to take a break from his university studies to spend a couple of months with the Grenadier Guards at the Curragh Camp near Dublin. After the Prince of Wales returned to Cambridge, the Prince Consort heard of his son's liaison with actress Nellie Clifden at Curragh. Already ill with typhoid, Prince Albert traveled to Cambridge on November 25 to discuss this disturbing incident with his son. Three weeks later the Prince Consort died, and Queen Victoria blamed her oldest son for her husband's death.

Still the widowed Queen felt it was urgent for the Prince of Wales to marry the right woman as quickly as possible. "The Grandmother of Europe" thought Denmark's Princess Alexandra would be a suitable bride for Prince Bertie.

The wedding took place at St. George's Chapel, located at Windsor Castle. On March 10, 1863, the Prince of Wales and Princess Alexandra became husband and wife.

E7-202: Prince and Princess of Wales 1863 Wedding Mug. $450.—$500. *Courtesy of Anne Minns.*

Following the newlyweds' Osborne honeymoon, the couple moved into Marlborough House. Their new home provided the perfect place for entertaining. Guests included not only the traditional London aristocracy, but also members of the upper middle class.

In 1864, Albert Victor was born—the first of Edward and Alexandra's six children. The next year their second son, George, later King George V, was born. Their daughters included Louise, born in 1867; Victoria, a year after; and Maud in 1869. Alexander, their last child, born in 1871, lived only a few hours. The Prince of Wales had a genuine affection for his wife and was devoted to his children.

Following the Mordaunt scandal in 1871, in which the Prince of Wales was accused as a corespondent in a divorce petition, Prince Edward focused on royal duties for which he had been trained all his life. Queen Victoria still held all authority of the Crown and was not willing to share any responsibility with her son. Later, he would take on such public duties as opening bridges, docks and buildings.

E7-203: King Edward VII Opening of Royal Edward Dock, Avonmouth, July 9, 1908, Coalport for S. J. Kepple & Son. $395.—$450. *Courtesy of Anne Minns.*

The Prince of Wales made many state visits to Europe which were interspersed with frequent trips to his favorite personal getaways: Paris, Marienbad and the French Riviera. He spent four months in India during 1875-6.

At Marlborough House, The Prince and Princess of Wales took on social functions which Queen Victoria either did not care about or refused to preside over.

Kind and generous to almost everyone he met, Prince Edward was loyal to his servants, as they were to him. Princess Alexandra shared her husband's sensitivity to people of all classes. When strangers wrote to her as Princess of Wales and later as Queen, she would often send five-pound notes in envelopes to those she felt were in need. Often these recipients were complete strangers.

The death of the Duke of Clarence in 1892 brought the Prince and Princess of Wales closer. They mourned the loss of their oldest son, Prince Albert Victor.

In 1893, the Duke of York married Princess May of Teck, who had been engaged to the Duke of Clarence before he died.

With his horse, Persimmon, winning the Derby in 1896, The Prince of Wales found increasing popularity among the British. He was also admired as a sportsman for his hunting and yachting, especially with his annual appearances at Cowes aboard the yacht Britannia.

When Queen Victoria's physical health declined, the Prince of Wales assumed greater constitutional responsibilities.

After his accession to the throne, King Edward VII pursued his royal duties, but not with the political acumen which Queen Victoria had possessed during her reign. As King Edward VII's coronation drew closer, he developed appendicitis. The ceremony at Westminster Abbey was postponed until August 9th.

E7-060: King Edward VII and Queen Alexandra 1902 Coronation Bisque Figures. $310.—$335. *Courtesy of Anne Minns.*

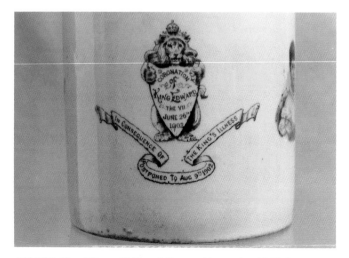

E7-108: King Edward VII and Queen Alexandra 1902 Coronation Mug with postponement notice, Royal Doulton. $135.—$149. *Courtesy of Anne Minns.*

Most coronation commemoratives bear the June 26th date. Only a few have the correct date. Some were overprinted with postponement notices.

Although King Edward VII's reign was short, and he cared little about domestic matters, he had an enthusiastic interest in foreign affairs. King Edward VII was highly praised on both sides of the English Channel for easing the tension between England and France.

Despite his reluctance, domestic matters demanded his attention following the general election in 1906 in which the liberals won a landslide victory. The King and the new government did not get along well. The liberals wanted to limit the power of the House of Lords. The King tried to mediate the dispute, but it was still unresolved when he died.

Because most of his subjects were unaware that their monarch's health had been on the decline, King Edward VII's death came as a shock. Bronchial attacks, chronic smoking, overeating and other excesses had taken their cumulative toll upon him.

After suffering several heart attacks on the afternoon of May 6, 1910, King Edward VII died just before midnight, surrounded by his family, close friends and his last mistress, Alice Keppel. It is said that Queen Alexandra informed Mrs. Keppel of the King's grave condition and invited her to say goodbye to him at his deathbed.

E7-223: King Edward VII/Queen Alexandra 1902 Coronation Vase, Goss. $95.—$110.

E7-224: King Edward VII Tile. $175.—$200.

E7-222: King Edward VII 1902 Coronation Dish, Royal Doulton. $155.—$180.

E7-225: "H.R.H. The Prince of Wales Visiting The Tomb of Washington" Pot Lid, Pratt. $275.—$325.

Partial Tea Service for Prince and Princess of Wales 1863 Wedding. E7-209: Plate. $265.—$290. E7-210: Teapot. $535.—$580. E7-211: Creamer and Sugar. $325.—$355. E7-212: Cup and Saucer. $285.—$310.

E7-213: 1887 Manchester Royal Jubilee Exhibition Teapot. $265.—$295. *Courtesy of Anne Minns.*

E7-214: Prince Albert Victor 1886 Royal Visit to Burnley Plate. $395.—$445. *Courtesy of Anne Minns.*

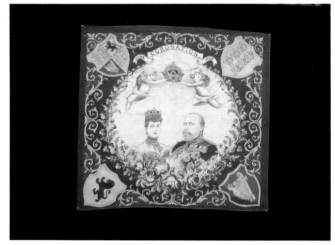

E7-215: King Edward VII and Queen Alexandra 1902 Coronation Handkerchief. $65.—$73. *Courtesy of Anne Minns.*

E7-216: King Edward VII and Queen Alexandra 1902 Coronation Beakers, Royal Doulton. $125.—$155. Each. *Courtesy of Anne Minns.*

E7-217: King Edward VII and Queen Alexandra 1902 Coronation Trio. $250.—$275. *Courtesy of Anne Minns.*

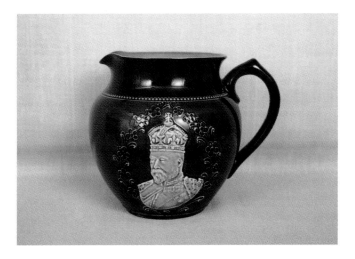

E7-226: King Edward VII/Queen Alexandra 1902 Coronation Jug, MacIntyre. $775.—$815.

Reverse of E7-226 Coronation Jug.

E7-227: King Edward VII 1910 In Memoriam Exemplar, Copeland for Thos. Goode, London. *Deluxe edition limited to 100.* $2650.—$2800.

Reverse of E7-227 Exemplar.

E7-229: Prince of Wales India Visit Mug c.1880's. $290.—$330.

E7-228: King Edward VII 1902 Coronation Jug and Beakers, Minton's Secessionist Ware. $390.—$440.

VI-322: Princess Victoria Plate, from a William Fowler painting, c. 1825. *Courtesy of Dennis Colton.*

VI-323: Queen Victoria 1897 Jubilee Jug. *Courtesy of Anne Minns.*

Chapter 8
Queen Victoria
1837 — 1901

Princess Alexandrina Victoria, the daughter of the Duke and Duchess of Kent, was born May 24, 1819, at Kensington Palace in London. Although her parents wished to name their daughter Victoria, the Prince Regent, later King George IV, demanded she be named after her godfather, Tsar Alexander I of Russia. She was christened Alexandrina Victoria. Until her accession to the throne, close family members called her "Drina."

Twenty-seven days following her eighteenth birthday, Queen Victoria succeeded her uncle, King William IV, to the throne on June 20, 1837.

VI-324: Queen Victoria Metal Bust. $225.—$250.

Left, VI-325: Queen Victoria Proclamation Cup and Saucer. $1390.—$1525. Right, VI-326: Queen Victoria Proclamation Milk and Sugar. $1695.—$1850.

It had been expected that the young queen would be known as Queen Alexandrina. On the day of her succession, she announced that she would be known as Queen Victoria, asserting her new found freedom and authority. Anticipating the accession, a few commemoratives were made with the name Queen Alexandrina. One was a salt glazed flask, and medals were also made.

Seven years earlier her German governess, Baroness Louise Lehzen, produced genealogical tables of the kings and queens of England for Princess Victoria to study. Upon realizing her future destiny, she cried. After regaining her composure, she replied, "I will be good."

At midnight, church bells heralded the initial coronation celebration as thousands started to line the streets of London for a glimpse of their new monarch. Queen Victoria's coronation took place in Westminster Abbey on June 28, 1838.

Queen Victoria's cousin, Prince Albert of Saxe-Coburg, visited London in 1839, and the young monarch fell in love with him; however, his feelings for her were not as immediate. But his strong affection and sense of duty toward Victoria brought an affirmative answer to her proposal of marriage.

On February 10, 1840, in the Royal Chapel at St. James's Palace, Queen Victoria and Prince Albert exchanged their wedding vows.

During the next seventeen years, Queen Victoria and Prince Albert had nine children. Princess Victoria, the Princess Royal, was born in 1840, followed a year later by Albert Edward, the Prince of Wales. In 1843, Princess Alice, and Prince Alfred the following year, increased the family to four children. Princess Helena, born in 1846, was the next child. Two years later, Princess Louise arrived, and Prince Arthur was born in 1850. Prince Leopold (1853) and Princess Beatrice (1857) were the last two children born to Queen Victoria and Prince Albert.

Although Prince Albert's German roots remained strong, he became a British citizen. He was not granted a peerage, but Queen Victoria made him Prince Consort in 1857. He was also a great help to his wife in handling the ever present deluge of papers contained in the Queen's official red boxes. There was almost nothing Prince Albert could not do — from writing music to drawing architectual plans. He was a man of intellect and a great patron of the arts.

Albert introduced the Christmas tree, a German tradition, to England. The Prince Consort's idea for the Crystal Palace Exhibition of 1851 made him a legend. Millions of people turned out to see this international salute to industry and trade. The project produced enough money to purchase thirty acres of land in London's borough of Kensington. This land was to become a shrine to art and science. Today that special area of Kensington is the site of such well-known landmarks as the Victoria and Albert Museum, Royal Albert Hall, the Royal College of Music, and the Imperial College of Science and Technology.

In late November of 1861, the Prince Consort developed typhoid. While sleeplessness and rheumatism caused him constant discomfort and pain, he still performed his duties.

Following Prince Albert's death in December, 1861, tributes in the arts, poetry and music were dedicated to him. Black sashes, ribbons and other expressions of sympathy were worn by mourners. Disraeli's eulogy included a passage which stated, "With Prince Albert we have buried our Sovereign. This German Prince has governed

VI-265: Prince Albert In Memoriam Plates. $395.—$445. Each. *Courtesy of Anne Minns.*

England for twenty-one years with wisdom and energy such as none of our kings has ever shown." A London newspaper, *The Observer*, wrote, "Peace to his ashes! A good husband, a good father, a wise prince, and a safe counselor. England will not look upon his like again!"

Queen Victoria mourned the death of her beloved husband for her remaining years. She spent most of her time in seclusion at Osborne House on the Isle of Wight, Windsor Castle, or Balmoral in Scotland.

Prior to his death, Albert selected John Brown as Queen Victoria's companion and protector. Although this Scottish servant was rough and brash in manner, Queen Victoria held him in high esteem and felt confi-

dent with him. In 1865, the strong- armed, handsome highlander became "The Queen's Highland Servant," as she recorded in her journal. Brown would answer to no one else but the Queen whom she addressed as "wumman." Attending to her every need, the highlander was a combination footman, page, and groom. When her faithful servant died in 1883, Queen Victoria mourned the loss of the man who had become her best and most honest friend.

Queen Victoria had ten prime ministers during her reign. Some historians say Disraeli may have had the greatest influence upon the Queen.

During Jubilee Year (1887), the Prince of Wales was a great comfort and aid to his mother. On June 20th of that year, numerous royals assembled at a luncheon to

Queen Victoria 1887 Beakers, Royal Doulton. Left, VI-003: $95.—$105. Right, VI-266: $95.—$105. *Courtesy of Anne Minns.*

celebrate Queen Victoria's Jubilee. The following day, a Thanksgiving service was held at Westminster Abbey. On June 22, 1887, a tremendous celebration took place in Hyde Park. A bun, milk, and a Jubilee mug were presented to 30,000 school children.

Among the commemoratives on sale at the Strand in London were calendars, photos, mugs and plates. Walking sticks with knobs featuring Victoria's head were also sold. One unusual item for sale was the automatic musical bustle. Each played "God Save the Queen" when the wearer sat down.

Victoria's 1887 Jubilee was lavishly celebrated in London and all over the Empire. The Queen received many gifts, including silver, gold and jewels. Her return gifts had to be more modest. Most were signed photographs.

Ten years later, during her Diamond Jubilee Year, Queen Victoria became the longest reigning monarch in British history. That year, when the Queen traveled from Balmoral to Windsor, thousands of people lined railroad tracks for a glimpse of the royal train. Although they did not expect to see their Queen, men tipped their

VI-267: Queen Victoria 1897 Jubilee "Longest Reign" Mug, William Whiteley. $180.—$200. *Courtesy of Anne Minns.*

Another view of VI-267 Mug. *Courtesy of Anne Minns.*

Queen Victoria died at Osborne House on the Isle of Wight in the sixty-fourth year of her reign. She had brought her people and her country lasting good in an age that encouraged striving for goodness and self-improvement.

A Selection of Queen Victoria 1901 In Memoriam Pieces, Royal Doulton. VI-315: Tray. $260.—$290. VI-316: Creamer. $250.—$265. VI-317: Cup and Saucer. $290.—$320. VI-318: Mug. $320.—$350. *Courtesy of Anne Minns.*

A Selection of Queen Victoria 1901 In Memoriam Pieces, Foley. VI-319: Cup and Saucer. $250.—$275. VI-320: Dish. $90.—$100. *Courtesy of Anne Minns.*

hats, while women waved handkerchiefs. There was no applause for fear of disturbing their sovereign.

Wooden stands were erected along the London Jubilee Parade route on June 22, 1897, stretching from St. Paul's Cathedral to Whitehall and from the National Portrait Gallery to Buckingham Palace. Peddlers sold souvenirs which included Jubilee banners, flags, programs and balloons. Mugs, pictures, place mats, noisemakers and fireworks were also purchased. There were as many tears as there were cheers.

That Diamond Jubilee summer, the Queen received hundreds of tributes and thousands of gifts. A special day was set aside for speeches from the Houses of Lords and Commons, as well as from local governments. A garden party took place at Buckingham Palace; another was held at Windsor for members of Parliament and their families.

VI-268: Queen Victoria 1838 Coronation Framed Silk, E. Vassalon, Designer. $170.—$190. *Courtesy of Anne Minns.*

VI-269: Early Queen Victoria Framed Silk. $170.—$190. *Courtesy of Anne Minns.*

VI-101: Queen Victoria 1838 Coronation Mug, Swansea. $1600.—$1800. *Courtesy of Anne Minns.*

VI-270: Queen Victoria Parian Figure, c. 1838, Minton. *Courtesy of Anne Minns.*

VI-146A: Queen Victoria 1838 Coronation Plate. $1100.—$1225. *Courtesy of Anne Minns.*

VI-100: Queen Victoria 1838 Coronation Mug, Hayter portrait. $1700.—$1875. *Courtesy of Anne Minns.*

VI-272: Queen Victoria 1838 Coronation Cup and Saucer. $1400.—$1550. *Courtesy of Anne Minns.*

Another view of VI-100 Mug, showing Queen Victoria's Mother, the Duchess of Kent. *Courtesy of Anne Minns.*

VI-273: Queen Victoria Platter, c. 1837. *Courtesy of Anne Minns.*

VI-271: Queen Victoria 1838 Coronation Plaque, 3" diameter. $625.—$685. *Courtesy of Anne Minns.*

VI-191: "Victoria 1st Queen of Great Britain and Ireland" Plate. $975.—$1075. *Courtesy of Anne Minns.*

VI-275: Queen Victoria and Prince Albert 1840 Wedding Cup and Saucer. $375.—$450. *Courtesy of Anne Minns.*

VI-276: Queen Victoria Parian Figure, c. 1840. $1275.—$1400. *Courtesy of Anne Minns.*

VI-277: Prince Albert Plate, Swansea, c. 1840. $550.—$610. *Courtesy of Anne Minns.*

VI-278: Queen Victoria and Prince Albert 1840 Wedding Plate. $425.—$495. *Courtesy of Anne Minns.*

VI-279: Queen Victoria and Prince Albert 1840 Wedding Mug. $525.—$600. *Courtesy of Anne Minns.*

VI-280: Queen Victoria and Prince Albert 1840 Wedding Stoneware Jug. $250.—$275. *Courtesy of Anne Minns.*

VI-327: "Marquis & Marchioness of Lorne Landed at Halifax N.S. 25th Novr. 1872" Covered Footed Bowl. Milk glass. $275.—$315.

Reverse of VI-327 Covered Footed Bowl.

VI-329: Queen Victoria 1897 Jubilee Violet Vase with Pierced Handle, Royal Worcester. $795.—$895.

Reverse of VI-329 Vase.

VI-328: Queen Victoria and Prince Albert Ivory Cameos, Framed. $1150.—$1275.

VI-330: Queen Victoria 1887 Jubilee Vase, Doulton Lambeth. Designed by Mark V. Marshall. $2250.—$2475.

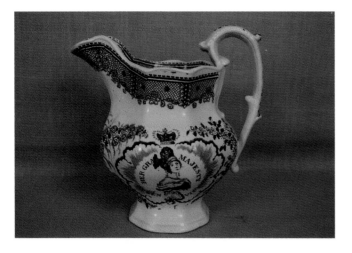

VI-331: Queen Victoria 1838 Coronation Jug. $895.—$995.

VI-334: Queen Victoria Carved Briarwood Pipe. $230.—$255.

VI-332: Queen Victoria 1897 Jubilee Covered Jug. Oriental mark inside lid. $225.—$265.

VI-335: 1860 Volunteers' Jug, Sanford Pottery. $690.—$775.

VI-333: Prince of Wales and Princess Royal Child's Cup and Saucer, Pratt. $240.—$300.

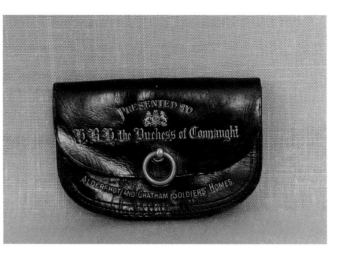

VI-336: "Present to H.R.H. The Duchess of Connaught" (wife of Arthur, Queen Victoria's son) Black Leather Purse. $125.—$155.

VI-290: Queen Victoria Framed
Silk, c. 1851. $150.—$180.
Courtesy of Anne Minns.

VI-291: Princess Alice Framed Silk.
$125.—$150. *Courtesy of Anne Minns.*

VI-292: Queen Victoria and Prince Albert Hand Painted Papier-
Mache Face Shields, c. 1840, Jennens and Bettridge.

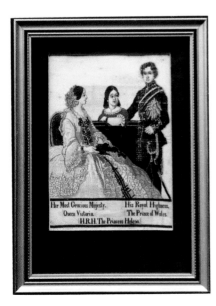

VI-293: Queen Victoria, Prince of Wales and Princess Helen
Framed Silk. $135.—$155. *Courtesy of Anne Minns.*

VI-294: Prince Alfred and The Late Prince Consort Framed Silk.
$130.—$150. *Courtesy of Anne Minns.*

VI-295: Prince Consort In Memoriam Framed Silk, Koechlin of Basle. $165.—$185. *Courtesy of Anne Minns.*

VI-296: Prince Albert In Memoriam Framed Silk, Doulton and Bolton, Coventry. $150.—$170. *Courtesy of Anne Minns.*

VI-075A: Prince Albert In Memoriam Jug. $375.—$415. *Courtesy of Anne Minns.*

VI-297: Princess Alice and Prince of Hesse 1862 Wedding Plate. $780.—$825. *Courtesy of Anne Minns.*

VI-298: Duke and Duchess of Edinburgh 1874 Wedding Mug. $520.—$570. *Courtesy of Anne Minns.*

VI-337: Queen Victoria Jug, Doulton Lambeth. Designed by Emily Partington. "1879" impressed in base. $740.—$825.

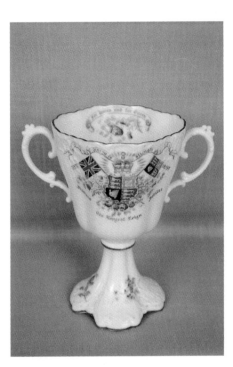

VI-341: Queen Victoria 1897 Jubilee Loving Cup, Aynsley. $750.—$825.

VI-339: Queen Victoria 1901 In Memoriam Jug, Doulton Lambeth. $1150.—$1275.

VI-338: 1901 Australian Federation Jardiniere, Doulton Burslem. $695.—$765.

VI-340: Queen Victoria 1897 Jubilee Jug, Doulton Burslem. $425.—$475.

VI-304: Queen Victoria 1897 Jubilee Mug. Royal Doulton. $265.—$280. *Courtesy of Anne Minns.*

VI-305: Queen Victoria 1887 Jubilee Plates, Minton. $165.—$185. Each. *Courtesy of Anne Minns.*

VI-306: Queen Victoria 1897 Jubilee Enamel Beaker, Queen Victoria with Prince Edward of York. $215.—$240. *Courtesy of Anne Minns.*

Queen Victoria 1897 Jubilee Copeland Mugs. Left, VI-307: $175.—$195. Right, VI-307A: $150.—$170. *Courtesy of Anne Minns.*

VI-308: Queen Victoria 1897 Jubilee Loving Cup, Crown Derby. *Courtesy of Anne Minns.*

VI-309: Queen Victoria 1897 Jubilee Beaker, Minton. $140.—$155. *Courtesy of Anne Minns.*

VI-310: Queen Victoria 1897 Jubilee Plate. $140.—$155.
Courtesy of Anne Minns.

A Selection of Queen Victoria 1897 Jubilee Beakers, Royal Doulton. $165.—$250. *Courtesy of Anne Minns.*

VI-311: Queen Victoria 1897 Jubilee Cup and Saucer. $185.—$205.

VI-312: Queen Victoria 1897 Jubilee Tiled Fire Screen. $650.—$700.

VI-313: Queen Victoria 1897 Jubilee Teapot, Wedgwood & Co. $445.—$485.

VI-314: Queen Victoria 1897 Jubilee Beaker, Royal Doulton. $285.—$315. *Courtesy of Anne Minns.*

CA-016: "Regent Valentine" Jug. Shows King George III presumably denying Queen Caroline access to Princess Charlotte. $1675.—$1800.

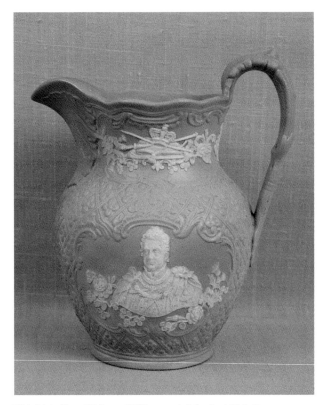

W4-011: King William IV/Queen Adelaide 1831 Coronation Jug, Minton. $825.—$915.

Reverse of CA-016 Jug.

Chapter 9

Pre-Queen Victoria

King George III - 1760—1820

King George III came to the throne in 1760, successor to his grandfather, King George II. His father had died in 1751. He endeavored to take back for the monarchy some of the powers of Parliament and succeeded to some extent in the early years of his reign.

He married Charlotte of Mechlenburg-Strelitz, and she bore him nine sons and six daughters. He showed a great deal of interest in agriculture, and some commemoratives denote this interest.

He supported the war against the American colonies and threatened to abdicate before conceding independence to the rebel country.

After the turn of the century, he was increasingly troubled with physical and mental problems. In 1811, his eldest son, the future King George IV, was made Prince Regent and acted for the King for the remainder of his life.

King George III died on January 29, 1820.

King George IV - 1820—1830

This future king was born on August 12, 1762. He succeeded to the throne upon the death of his father in 1820.

In 1785, he married a Roman Catholic widow, Mrs. Maria Fitzherbert. However, the marriage was not legal. In 1795, he married Princess Caroline of Brunswick, but this was a loveless match. One child, Princess Charlotte, was born of the union.

Princess Charlotte, the heir presumptive, was married to Prince Leopold of Saxe-Coburg in May, 1816. They settled at Claremont. It was at Claremont on November 5, 1817, that she gave birth to a stillborn son. She died early the following morning.

The death of Princess Charlotte presented a dynastic problem, since she was the only legitimate child of any of the sons of King George III. Frederick, Duke of York, had been married over 20 years and was childless. The Duke of Clarence (future King William IV) had ten children by his actress mistress, but was unmarried. Edward, Duke of Kent, also had a long-time mistress. Reluctantly, he agreed to a marriage with Prince Leopold's widowed sister, Princess Victoria of Leiningen. In 1818, following separate weddings, the Duke of Clarence and Princess Adelaide of Saxemeiningen, and the Duke of Kent and Princess Victoria of Leiningen, were married in a double ceremony attended by Queen Charlotte.

The Duke of Clarence's marriage produced two daughters, both of whom did not survive infancy. The Duke of Kent's marriage produced one daughter, the future Queen Victoria. Thus, the line of succession was preserved.

CH-009: Princess Charlotte In Memoriam Plate. $475.—$535. *Courtesy of Anne Minns.*

CH-010: Princess Charlotte In Memoriam Cup and Saucer. $225.—$250. *Courtesy of Anne Minns.*

G4-006: King George IV Figurine. $975.—$1050.

G4-008 King George IV (right) and Queen Caroline (left) Plates. $1985.—$2100. Pair.

The Prince Regent and Princess Caroline were separated in 1796. She was living in Italy when he succeeded to throne and immediately returned to London to claim her position as Queen Consort. King George IV succeeded in keeping her out of Westminster Abbey for the coronation, but was not successful in the notorious Bill of Pains and Penalties which sought to deny her the title and rights of Queen Consort.

A number of commemoratives supporting Queen Caroline were made. During the hearings, evidence against Queen Caroline was brought into the House in a green baize bag. Those who brought it were called the "Green Bag Crew". A verse about them on a jug caused it to become known as the "Green Bag Jug."

CH-011: Princess Charlotte and Prince Leopold with "Goody Bewley" reading her Bible on the grounds of Claremont Cup and Saucer. $590.—$675.

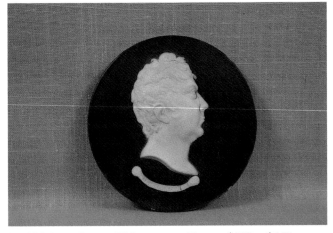

G4-007: King George IV Jasperware Plaque. $420.—$465.

DM-001: Duke of Marlborough Charger, c. 1711. $7500.—$8500.

Shortly after King George IV's coronation, Queen Caroline died on August 7, 1821.

One of the lasting monuments to King George IV's reign is the Royal Pavilion at Brighton.

He died on June 26, 1830, and was succeeded by his brother, the Duke of Clarence as William IV.

G4-009: "George Prince of Wales Chosen Regent of the Imperial Kingdom February 5, 1811" Brass Snuff Box. $190.—$235.

W4-013: King William IV/Queen Adelaide Coronation Jug. $895.—$995.

King William IV - 1830—1837

King William IV was the third son of King George III. The Duke of York, the second son, had died before him in 1827. He married Princess Adelaide of Saxe-Coburg and Meiningen in 1818. They had two daughters, both of whom did not survive infancy.

King William IV's and Queen Adelaide's coronation took place on September 8, 1831, and many commemoratives were made to celebrate the event.

When King William IV ascended the throne, he was 63 years of age, and his reign was short. He died on June 20, 1837, and was succeeded by his niece, the Princess Alexandrina Victoria of Kent.

Reverse of W4-013 Coronation Jug (showing Queen Adelaide.)

Left, VI-342: Queen Victoria in Garden Jug. $815.—$900. Right, W4-012: King William IV/Queen Adelaide Coronation Jug. $1575.—$1750.

Reverse of VI-342 and W4-012 Jugs.

Chapter 10

Autographs

Documents and photographs signed by members of the royal family are not, strictly speaking, commemoratives. However, many commemorative collectors also have an interest in autographs. Therefore, they have been included in this edition.

G6-361: King George VI and Queen Elizabeth 1947-48 Christmas/New Year's Card. Shown with Princesses Elizabeth and Margaret aboard H.M.S. Vanguard entering Cape Town at the start of the 1947 South Africa Tour. $575.—$650.

G6-362: King George VI and Queen Elizabeth 1935-36 Christmas/New Year's Card signed "Elizabeth" and "Albert" as Duke and Duchess of York. Photo of Royal Lodge. $575.—$650.

PC-448: Princess of Wales 1994-95
Christmas/New Year's Card. Shown
with Princes William and Henry.
$3200.—$3700.

E8-218: Card signed "Edward Duke of
Windsor" and "Wallis Windsor" with
photograph. $675.—$775.

PC-449: Prince and Princess or Wales
Signed Photograph dated 1985.
$3000.—$3500.

E2-646: Queen Elizabeth II and Prince Philip 1952 Accession
Year Christmas Card. Shown with Prince Charles and Princess
Anne on steps of Balmoral Castle. This was the first Christmas
card of the yet uncrowned queen. $795.—$895.

G6-363: King George VI and Queen Elizabeth 1943-44 Christmas Card shown with Princesses Elizabeth and Margaret in the
Drawing Room of Buckingham Palace. $575.—$635.

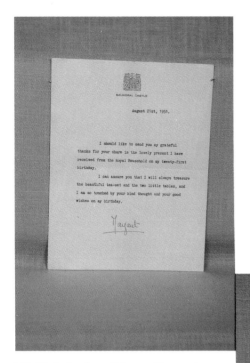

MA-10: Letter from Princess Margaret dated August 21st, 1951, thanking the Royal Household for their gift on her 21st birthday. $235.—$265.

PC-450: Princess of Wales signed photograph, 1993. $3300.—$3800.

E8-220: Duchess of Windsor photograph taken in the Bahamas during World War II when the Duke was Governor General. Signed "Wallis Windsor." $495.—$595.

E8-219: "Edward P. 1922" is the signature on this photograph of the Prince of Wales taken during his world tour in 1922. $875.—$975.

E8-221: Photograph signed "Edward P. 1919" in silver plated frame with Prince of Wales feathers at top. $825.—$925.

VI-343: Photograph signed "Victoria R.I. 1899". $895.—$995.

VI-345: "Victoria R.I." signature on cut paper with Secretary of State Home Department seal. 1887 Jubilee photograph above. $595.—$675.

VI-344: Cut signature "Albert Prince Consort" with engraving by W. Holl. He was Prince Consort from 1857 until his death in 1861. $695.—$775.

G5-338: "George" and "Victoria Mary" cut signatures dated Aug. 15th. Signed when they were Prince and Princess of Wales. $525.—$575.

Left, E7-231: Photograph signed "Albert Edward, R.Y.P. Alice— August 1879." Signed aboard the Royal Yacht Princess Alice. $495.—$575. Right, E7-232: Photograph signed "Alexandra." $445.—$495.

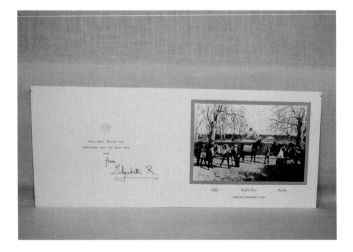

E8-226: Edward, Prince of Wales, signed note on Buckingham Palace card, dated July 8th 1914 and signed "Eddie." $625.—$685.

Reverse of E8-226:

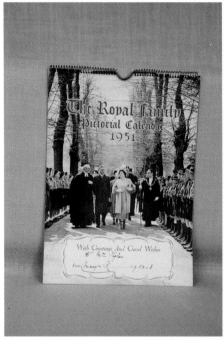

G5-340: 1951 Calendar Royal Family Pictorial Calendar. Signed "Mary R." $265.—$325.

G6-377: Queen Elizabeth, The Queen Mother, 1962 Christmas Card, signed "Elizabeth R." $285.—$335.

MR-011: Princess Mary 1952-53 Christmas Card, signed "Mary." $175.—$195.

Chapter 11
Enamel Boxes

PC-451: 25th Anniversary of Prince Charles's Investiture, Halcyon Days. $185.—$215.

E2-649: Queen Elizabeth II 60th Birthday, Halcyon Days. Limited edition of 1000. $290.—$335.

E2-647: Queen Elizabeth II/Prince Philip 40th Wedding Anniversary, Halcyon Days. Limited edition of 400. $360.—$400.

E2-650: Queen Elizabeth II 40th Anniversary of the Accession, Halcyon Days. $190.—$220.

E2-648: Queen Elizabeth II/Prince Philip 50th Wedding Anniversary, Crummles. $220.—$250.

E2-651: Queen Elizabeth II/Order of the British Empire, Crummles. $255.—$280.

E2-652: Queen Elizabeth II 70th Birthday, Halcyon Days. Limited edition of 500. $320.—$355.

E2-655: Queen Elizabeth II/Prince Philip 50th Wedding Anniversary, Crummles. $160.—$185.

E2-653: Queen Elizabeth II 40th Anniversary of the Accession, Halcyon Days. Limited edition of 250. $320.—$365.

E2-656: Queen Elizabeth II 1977 Silver Jubilee, Halcyon Days. Limited edition of 500. $345.—$395.

E2-654: Queen Elizabeth II/Prince Philip 50th Wedding Anniversary, Halcyon Days. Limited edition of 1000. $370.—$415.

E2-657: Queen Elizabeth II 40th Anniversary of the Coronation, Crummles. $190.—$230.

G6-364: Queen Elizabeth The Queen Mother 90th Birthday, Halcyon Days. $220.—$250.

PC-452: 1982 Prince William Birth, Crummles. $90.—$105.

G6-365: Queen Elizabeth The Queen Mother 85th Birthday, Halcyon Days. Limited edition of 2000. $215.—$245.

E2-659: Queen Elizabeth II First State Visit to Russia by a British Sovereign, Halcyon Days. Limited edition of 100. $260.—$305.

E2-658: Queen Elizabeth II/Prince Philip 50th Wedding Anniversary, Crummles. $160.—$195.

E2-660: Queen Elizabeth II/Prince Philip 50th Wedding Anniversary Musical Box, Halcyon Days. $625.—$695.

G6-366: 1995 Centenary of King George VI's Birth, Halcyon Days. Limited edition of 500. $245.—$280.

G6-367: Queen Elizabeth The Queen Mother 95th Birthday, Halcyon Days. Limited edition of 500. $245.—$280.

MI-006: House of Windsor, Halcyon Days. $180.—$205.

MI-007: House of Hanover, Halcyon Days. $190.—$220.

VI-346: Queen Victoria 150th Anniversary of the Accession and 100th Anniversary of her Golden Jubilee, Halcyon Days. Limited edition of 300. $290.—$335.

VI-347: Centenary of Queen Victoria's Diamond Jubilee, Halcyon Days. Limited edition of 300. $350.—$390.

E2-677: Centenary of Army Rifle Association of which Queen Elizabeth II is a Patron. Crummles. $165.—$185.

E2-678: Queen Elizabeth II and Prince Philip 50th Wedding Anniversary, Crummles. $55.—$65.

MI-011: Buckingham Palace, Crummles. $125.—$140.

MI-012: Windsor Castle, Halcyon Days. $250.—$275.

Left, G6-378: Queen Elizabeth The Queen Mother 90th Birthday, Halcyon Days. $129.—$140. Right, DY-068: Duke and Duchess of York Wedding, 1986, Halcyon Days. $95.—$110.

MI-013: William and Mary, Tercentenary of the "Glorious Revolution" 1688-1689, Halcyon Days. $400.—$450.

Chapter 12
Figurines

Left, VI-348: Queen Victoria and Prince Albert 150th Wedding Anniversary, Royal Doulton. Limited edition of 2500. $990.—$1090. Center, G6-368: Queen Elizabeth The Queen Mother as The Duchess of York, Royal Doulton. Limited edition of 9500. $790.—$900. Right, E2-661: Queen Elizabeth II and Prince Philip 50th Wedding Anniversary, Royal Doulton. Limited edition of 750. $790.—$900.

Left to Right, E2-662: Prince Philip, Duke of Edinburgh, Royal Doulton. Limited edition of 1500. $490.—$550. E2-603: Queen Elizabeth II 20th Anniversary of the Coronation, Royal Doulton. Limited edition of 750. $1695.—$1895. G6-312: Queen Elizabeth The Queen Mother 80th Birthday, Royal Doulton. Limited edition of 1500. $1190.—$1300. E2-664: Queen Elizabeth II 1992 Figurine, Royal Doulton. Limited edition of 5000. $1150.—$1350.

E8-221: "H.R.H. The Prince of Wales—Born June 23rd 1894" Bust, Arcadian. $190.—$225.

E2-665: Queen Elizabeth II Mounted on Imperial Trooping the Color 1957, Beswick. $590.—$675.

PC-453: Prince and Princess of Wales, Royal Doulton. Limited edition of 1500. $1660.—$1800. Pair.

PC-455: Prince and Princess of Wales, Royal Doulton. Limited edition of 1500. $2700.—$2950. Pair.

PC-454: 1981 Royal Wedding Coalport Study of Prince and Princess of Wales. Limited edition of 500 (all sent to Canada). $2350.—$2500.

E8-222: Edward VIII 60th Anniversary of Abdication Toby Jug, Peggy Davies. Limited edition of 350. $280.—$315.

PA-035: Princess Anne 1973 Wedding Bust, Royal Doulton. $265.—$295.

G6-371: Queen Elizabeth The Queen Mother Standing Amidst Rubble of World War II, Royal Doulton. Limited edition of 5000. $775.—$850.

E2-667: Queen Elizabeth II 30th Anniversary of the Coronation, Royal Doulton. Limited edition of 2500. $775.—$850.

G6-313: Queen Elizabeth The Queen Mother 90th Birthday, Royal Doulton. Limited edition of 2500. $665.—$725.

E2-604: Queen Elizabeth II 1992 40th Anniversary of Coronation, Royal Doulton. Limited edition of 3500. $425.—$495.

PC-456: Prince Charles, Coalport. Limited edition of 1000. $275.—$350.

PC-459: Princess of Wales 21st Birthday Bust, Royal Worcester. Limited edition of 100. $725.—$800.

Four Coalport Figurines: Left to Right, VI-349: Queen Victoria 150th Wedding Anniversary. Limited edition of 7500. $575.—$650. PC-457: Prince Charles. Limited edition of 1000. $360.—$400. PC-458: Lady Diana Spencer. Limited edition of 1000. $675.—$750. G6-372: Queen Elizabeth, The Queen Mother, 95th Birthday. Limited edition of 500. $575.—$635.

PC-460: Princess Diana Toby Jug, Kevin Francis Ceramics. Limited edition of 900. $350.—$400.

DY-067: Duchess of York, Royal Doulton. Limited edition of 1500. $775.—$850.

E2-669: Queen Elizabeth II 1953 Coronation Bust, H.W. Lawton China. $85.—$100.

E2-668: Queen Elizabeth II "40th Jubilee Year" Toby Jug, Kevin Francis Ceramics. Limited edition of 400. $300.—$340.

G6-373: Queen Elizabeth The Queen Mother Toby Jug, Kevin Francis Ceramics. Limited edition of 900. $300.—$340.

E8-223: Edward Prince of Wales by Swansea. $390.—$435.

E2-670: Princess Elizabeth Metal Figurine on Musical Base. $650.—$725.

G6-374: Queen Elizabeth, The Queen Mother, 70th Wedding Anniversary, Coalport. Limited edition of 7500. $525.—$585.

VI-350: Queen Victoria from the Queens of England Series by Coalport. Limited edition of 1000. $475.—$525.

E8-224: King Edward VIII Year of Reign 1936, Royal Doulton. $2600.—$2800.

A Selection of Commemoratives for the Coronations of King George VI and Queen Elizabeth in 1937, Queen Elizabeth II in 1953 and the Planned Coronation of King Edward VIII. *Courtesy of Anne Minns.*

A Selection of Commemoratives from 1897 to 1973. *Courtesy of Anne Minns.*

A Selection of Commemoratives for the 1937 Coronation of King George VI and Queen Elizabeth and the Planned Coronation of King Edward VIII. *Courtesy of Anne Minns.*

Chapter 13

Manufacturers

Examples of Commemoratives from Some Different Manufacturers

Caverswall

PC-462: 1982 Prince William Christening Plate. Limited edition of 5000. $95.—$115.

PC-330: Princess of Wales 21st Birthday Plate. Limited edition of 1000. $115.—$130.

Coalport

Left, PC-017: Prince Charles 1969 Investiture Goblet. $138.—$153. Center, PC-156: 1981 Royal Wedding Goblet. Limited edition of 1000. $189.—$225. Right, PC-462: 1981 Royal Wedding Goblet, Limited edition 2000. $179.—$215.

Coalport

E2-409: Queen Elizabeth II 25th Anniversary of Coronation Plate. $130.—$137.

Left, G6-259: Queen Elizabeth, The Queen Mother, 85th Birthday Plate. $98.—$108. Right, E2-245: Queen Elizabeth II Silver Jubilee Loving Cup. $90.—$100.

Crown Devon

Three Musical Pieces. Left, G6-304: King George VI and Queen Elizabeth 1937 Coronation Jug. $675.— $850. Center, G6-101: King George VI and Queen Elizabeth 1937 Coronation Mug. $225.—$275. Right, E8-179: King Edward VIII 1937 Coronation Jug. $750.—$900. *Courtesy of Anne Minns.*

Crown Staffordshire

Left to Right, E8-180: King Edward VIII Coronation Mug. $245.—$275. PA-017: Princess Anne and Captain Mark Phillips 1973 Wedding Mug. $52.—$57. E2-332: Queen Elizabeth II 25th Anniversary of Coronation Mug. $25.—$30. G6-212: Queen Elizabeth, The Queen Mother, 80th Birthday Bell. $65.—$70.

Halcyon Days

Five Enamel Boxes Commemorating First Five Birthdays of Prince William of Wales. *Courtesy of Anne Minns.*

Hammersley

E2-594: Queen Elizabeth II 1953 Coronation Covered Box. $85.—$95.

Left to Right, G6-137: King George VI and Queen Elizabeth 1937 Coronation Tea Plate. $78.—$88. E2-265: Princess Elizabeth and Prince Philip 1951 Canada/USA Royal Tour Mug. $157.—$170. PC-200: Prince and Princess of Wales 1981 Wedding Mug. $48.—$53.

E8-030: King Edward VIII Coronation Cup and Saucer. $110.—$125.

E8-181: King Edward VIII Abdication Loving Cup. $650.—$700.

Commissioned by J. & J. May

Left to Right, DY-066: Princess Beatrice 1988 Birth Mug. $80.—$90. PC-403: Prince and Princess of Wales 1981 Betrothal Mug. $85.—$95. PC-404: Prince and Princess of Wales 1981 Wedding Mug. $80.—$90. PC-378: Prince William of Wales 1982 Birth Mug. $80.—$90.

Three Globes for 1937 Coronation of King George VI and Queen Elizabeth and Planned Coronation of King Edward VIII. *Courtesy of Anne Minns.*

E2-595: Ten Queen's Beasts for Queen Elizabeth II's Coronation in 1953. *Courtesy of Anne Minns.*

Left, E8-023: King Edward VIII 1937 Coronation Covered Box. $295.—$335. Right: G6-305: King George VI and Queen Elizabeth 1937 Coronation Covered Box. $280.—$310. *Courtesy of Anne Minns.*

E2-596: Pair of Queen's Beasts Candlesticks for Queen Elizabeth II's 1977 Silver Jubilee. *Courtesy of Anne Minns.*

G5-339: King George V and Queen Mary 1935 Jubilee Mug, Moorcroft. $725.—$900.

E8-225: King Edward VIII 1937 Coronation Bowl. $250.—$280.

E7-232: King Edward VII and Queen Alexandra 1902 Coronation Teapot, MacIntyre. $395.—$430.

MI-008: World War II Patriotic Series Plate. $595.—$655.

Two Moorcroft Beakers for the Coronation of King George VI and Queen Elizabeth. Left, G6-375: $495.—$540. Right, G6-008: $465.—$525.

Two World War II Patriotic Series Cups and Saucers. Left, MI-009: Prime Minister Winston Churchill. $230.—$265. Right, MI-010: President Roosevelt. $230.—$265.

Three Coronation Loving Cups. Left, E8-183: King Edward VIII. $385.—$425. Center, G6-308: King George VI and Queen Elizabeth. $365.—$395. Right, E2-600: Queen Elizabeth II. $265.—$295. *Courtesy of Anne Minns.*

Three Coronation Nut Dishes. G6-309: King George VI and Queen Elizabeth. $295.—$325. Pair. E8-185: King Edward VIII. $165.—$185. *Courtesy of Anne Minns.*

Royal Crown Derby

Three Loving Cups. Left, E2-601: Queen Elizabeth II 40th Anniversary of Accession. $225.—$245. PC-405: Prince William of Wales Birth. $270.—$295. E2-602: Queen Elizabeth II 60th Birthday. $225.—$245.

Five Miniature Loving Cups. Left to Right, PC-406: Prince William of Wales 1982 Birth. $95.—$115. G5-286: King George V and Queen Mary 1911 Coronation. $290.—$335. G6-310: Queen Elizabeth, The Queen Mother, 90th Birthday. $100.—$115. G5-287: King George V and Queen Mary 1911 Coronation. $250.—$285. PC-407: Prince Henry of Wales 1984 Birth. $90.—$100. *Courtesy of Anne Minns.*

Five Coronation Beakers. First two on left, G6-311: King George VI and Queen Elizabeth. $275.—$300. Each. Center, G5-288: King George V and Queen Mary. $345.—410. Two on Right, E8-185: King Edward VIII. $315.—$340. Each. *Courtesy of Anne Minns.*

Four Figurines. Left to Right, E2-603: Queen Elizabeth II 20th Anniversary of Coronation. $1695.—$1895. G6-312: Queen Elizabeth, The Queen Mother, 80th Birthday. $1190.—$1300. G6-313: Queen Elizabeth, The Queen Mother, 90th Birthday. $665.—$725. E2-604: Queen Elizabeth II 40th Anniversary of Coronation. $425.—$495. *Courtesy of Anne Minns.*

Left, E2-009: Queen Elizabeth II Coronation Beaker. $62.—$73. Right, G5-183: Prince George and Princess May 1893 Wedding Plate. $185.—$205.

Left, G5-130: King George V and Queen Mary 1935 Jubilee Mug. $75.—$82. Center, E8-021: King Edward VIII 1937 Coronation Covered Box with Four Ashtrays. $170.—$190. Right, G6-227: Queen Elizabeth, The Queen Mother, 80th Birthday Loving Cup. $68.—$73.

G5-289: King George V and Queen Mary 1911 Coronation Cup and Saucer. *Courtesy of Anne Minns.*

G5-290: King George V and Queen Mary 1911 Coronation Vase. $675.—$735. *Courtesy of Anne Minns.*

Left, E2-229: Queen Elizabeth II 1953 Coronation Jug, 4½"h. $100.—$110. Right, PC-144: Prince and Princess of Wales 1981 Wedding Dish. $20.—$23.

G5-291: King George V Figurine. $575.—$635. *Courtesy of Anne Minns.*

Rye Pottery

E2-605: Queen Elizabeth II and Prince Philip 25th Wedding Anniversary Tea Plate. $65.—$75.

Shelley

Left, E7-070: King Edward VII and Queen Alexandra 1902 Coronation Jug. $80.—$88. Center, G5-004: King George V and Queen Mary 1910 Coronation Beaker. $70.—$80. Right, G5-180: King George V and Queen Mary 1935 Silver Jubilee Tea Plate. $58.—$63.

Shelley

King George VI and Queen Elizabeth 1937 Coronation Pieces. Top Left, G6-314: Plate with Princesses. $275.—$310. Top Right, G6-315: Plate with King and Queen. $250.—$275. Bottom, Left to Right, G6-316: Loving Cup. $300.—$335. Center, G6-317: Loving Cup. $680.—$740. Right, G6-318: Loving Cup. $385.— $425. *Courtesy of Anne Minns.*

Spode

Four Loving Cups. Top Left, G5-292: King George V and Queen Mary 1935 Silver Jubilee. $1500.—$1675. Top Right, VI-097: Queen Victoria Transvaal War 1899—1900. $1975.—$2075. Bottom Left, E8-186: King Edward VIII 1936 Abdication. $1600.—$1800. Bottom Right, G6-319: King George VI and Queen Elizabeth 1937 Coronation. $1500.—$1675. *Courtesy of Anne Minns.*

Spode

Top Left to Right, E8-102: King Edward VIII 1937 Coronation Mug. $85.—$95. G5-293: King George V and Queen Mary 1935 Silver Jubilee Mug. $105.—$115. G5-294: King George V and Queen Mary 1911 Coronation Beaker. $125.—$140. G6-102: King George VI and Queen Elizabeth 1937 Coronation Mug. $77.—$85. G6-097: King George VI and Queen Elizabeth 1937 Coronation Mug. $85.—$95. Bottom Left to Right, G6-320: King George VI and Queen Elizabeth 1937 Coronation Oversized Mug. $270.—$295. G5-295: King George V and Queen Mary 1935 Silver Jubilee Platter. $85.—$95. E7-199: King Edward VII and Queen Alexandra 1902 Coronation Goblet. $275.—$325. *Courtesy of Anne Minns.*

Tuscan

Plates, Left to Right, E8-187: King Edward VIII 1937 Coronation. $175.—$200. E2-606: Queen Elizabeth II 1959 St. Lawrence Seaway Opening. $130.—$145. VI-321: Queen Victoria 1897 Jubilee. $185.—$210. E2-369: Queen Elizabeth II 1953 Coronation. $69.—$75. Bottom, Left to Right, G6-321: King George VI and Queen Elizabeth 1937 Coronation Cup and Saucer. $70.—$78. G6-322: King George VI and Queen Elizabeth 1937 Coronation Loving Cup. $275.—$300. E8-188: King Edward VIII 1936 Abdication Cup and Saucer. $200.—$225. *Courtesy of Anne Minns.*

G6-376: Queen Elizabeth The Queen Mother 80th Birthday Framed Plaque. Limited edition of 250. $370.—$415.

E2-671: Queen Elizabeth II 60th Birthday Framed Plaque. Limited edition of 250. $375.—$425.

E2-672: Queen Elizabeth II 1976 Royal Visit to Washington Plate. Limited edition of 12. $1125.—$1250.

Wedgwood

E2-673: Queen Elizabeth II 1977 Silver Jubilee Diced Goblet. Limited edition of 750. $875.—$975.

E2-674: Queen Elizabeth II 1977 Silver Jubilee Lidded Jug. Limited edition of 400. $270.—$310.

112

Britain's Royal Family

George III
m.
Charlotte

George IV m. Caroline	**William IV** m. Adelaide	Edward, Duke of Kent m. Victoria	(Twelve other Sons and Daughters)

Charlotte m. Leopold of Saxe-Coburg

Victoria m. Albert of Saxe-Coberg-Gotha

Victoria, Pss. Royal m. Frederick III	**Edward VII** m. Alexandra of Denmark	Alice m. Louis IV of Hesse	Alfred, Duke of Edinburgh m. Marie of Russia	Helena m. Pr. Christian of Schleswig-Holstein	Louise m. Duke of Argyll	Arthur, Duke of Connaught m. Louise of Prussia	Leopold, Duke of Albany m. Helena of Waldeck	Beatrice m. Henry of Battenberg

Albert Victor, Duke of Clarence d. 1892	**George V** m. May of Teck	Louise, Pss. Royal m. Duke of Fife	Victoria	Maud m. Haakon VII of Norway

Edward VIII m. Wallis Warfield Simpson	**George VI** m. Elizabeth Bowes-Lyon	Mary, Pss. Royal m. Viscount Lascelles	Henry, Duke of Gloucester m. Alice Montagu-Douglas-Scott	George, Duke of Kent m. Marina of Greece	John

Elizabeth II m. Philip, Duke of Edinburgh	Margaret m. Anthony Armstrong-Jones (div. 1978)

Charles, Pr. of Wales m. Diana Spencer (div. 1996)	Andrew, Duke of York m. Sarah Ferguson (div. 1996)	Anne, Pss. Royal m. Mark Phillips (div. 1992) m. Tim Laurence	Edward

William of Wales	Henry of Wales

Calendar

Major Royal Events Commemorated 1800 — Present

King George III

1820 - Death

King George IV

1816 - Wedding of Princess Charlotte to Prince Leopold
1817 - Death of Princess Charlotte
1821 - Coronation
1821 - Queen Caroline - Support in Bill of Pains and
   Penalties
1821 - Queen Caroline - Death
1830 - Death of King George IV

King William IV and Queen Adelaide

1831 - Coronation
1837 - Death of King William IV

Queen Victoria

1837 - Accession and Proclamation
1838 - Coronation
1840 - Wedding to Prince Albert
1861 - Death of Prince Albert
1887 - Golden Jubilee
1897 - Diamond Jubilee
1901 - Death

King Edward VII

1863 - Wedding to Princess Alexandra
1888 - Silver Wedding Anniversary
1901 - Accession
1902 - Coronation
1910 - Death

King George V

1893 - Wedding to Princess May of Teck
1910 - Accession
1911 - Coronation
1935 - Silver Jubilee
1936 - Death

King Edward VIII

1911 - Investiture as Prince of Wales
1936 - Accession and Abdication
1937 - Coronation (Planned)
1937 - Wedding to Mrs. Wallis Simpson
1972 - Death

King George VI

1923 - Wedding to Lady Elizabeth Bowes-Lyon
1936 - Accession
1937 - Coronation

Queen Elizabeth, The Queen Mother

1980 - 80th Birthday
1990 - 90th Birthday
1995 - 95th Birthday

Queen Elizabeth II

1947 - Wedding to Prince Philip
1952 - Accession
1953 - Coronation
1960 - Wedding of Princess Margaret
1972 - Silver Wedding Anniversary
1973 - Wedding of Princess Anne
1977 - Silver Jubilee
1978 - 25th Anniversary of Coronation
1986 - 60th Birthday
1986 - Wedding of Prince Andrew
1987 - 40th (Ruby) Wedding Anniversary
1992 - 40th Anniversary of Accession
1993 - 40th Anniversary of Coronation
1996 - 70th Birthday
1996 - Prince Andrew's Divorce
1997 - 50th (Golden) Wedding Anniversary

Prince Charles

1969 - Investiture as Prince of Wales
1981 - Wedding to Lady Diana Spencer
1982 - Birth of Prince William of Wales
1984 - Birth of Prince Henry of Wales
1992 - Separation from Princess of Wales
1996 - Divorce from Princess of Wales
1997 - Death of Princess of Wales

Value Guide

Values of commemoratives vary from one part of the country — or world — to another. Values are also affected by the condition of the commemorative as well as its rarity. In this guide, the values shown assume that the piece is in good to excellent condition. One must be a little more forgiving in the case of very old commemoratives.

A few pieces, such as portraits, are not true commemoratives by the strictest definition. However, they have been included because of their popularity with commemorative collectors. Size relationships cannot be determined from the photographs which are taken close-up for greater clarity.

The values shown are based on the authors' experience and knowledge and are intended as a general guide only. They should not be used for establishing selling prices. The authors and the publisher assume no responsibility for problems arising from the use of these suggested values.

How to Use The Value Guide

Arrangement

The guide is arranged alphabetically by monarch or royal person's name. Sons and daughters of monarchs are shown under the monarch's name until age 21. Within each major section commemoratives are arranged alphabetically by event and then alphabetically by type of piece such as mug, plate, etc.

The guide consists of the following major sections:

Andrew
Anne
Charles
Edward VII
Edward VIII
Elizabeth II
George V
George VI
Elizabeth, The Queen Mother
Princesses Elizabeth and Margaret
Miscellaneous and Mixed Monarchs
Pre-Victoria
Victoria

Abbreviations Used in the Guide

BC: Bone China
B&W: Black and White
d.: diameter
h.: height
Kg.: King
LE: Limited Edition
Qn.: Queen
Pr.: Prince
Pss.: Princess

Prince Andrew — Duke of York

Prince Andrew's 21st Birthday

DY-001 - Mug, miniature. Sepia portrait. Commemoration on reverse. Gold trim. 2"h. Coronet BC. $25.—$28.

DY-002 - Mug. Sepia portrait. Color decoration. Gold trim. 3½"h. Caverswall BC. $79.—$85.

DY-003 - Plate. Sepia portrait. Color decoration. Gold rim. LE 500. 10½"d. Caverswall bone china. $110.— $125.

1986 Wedding to Miss Sarah Ferguson

DY-004 - Bell, miniature. Color portraits. Gold trim. 2"h. Finsbury BC. $15.—$18.

DY-005 - Bell. Color decoration. Gold trim. Family trees on reverse. 5"h. 3½"d. at base. Aynsley BC. $51.—$57.

DY-006 - Bell. Blue silhouettes front. Blue commemoration reverse. Gold decoration. 4"h. 3"d. Royal Worcester BC. $49.—$55.

DY-007 - Bell. Color portraits and decoration. Gold trim. 5½"h. 3"d. at base. Herbert Pottery. $28.—$33.

DY-008 - Booklet. Royal Wedding Official Souvenir. 32 pages. Color photographs. 11½"x8¼". $12—$15.

DY-009 - Bowl, footed. Color decoration with gold trim. Family trees below arms. 2"h. 5½"d. Aynsley BC. $47.—$52.

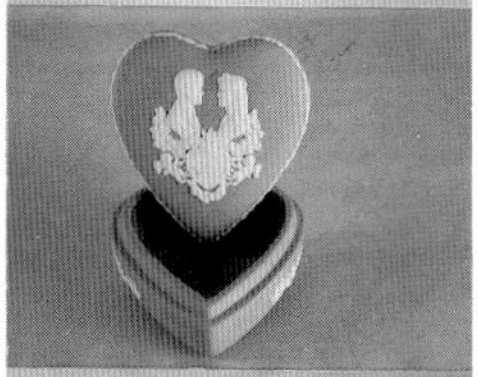

DY-010 - Box. White on light blue jasperware. 1¼"h.x2¼"x2¼". Wedgwood. $35.—$39.

DY-011 - Box, enamel. Color decoration on white lid. Red base. Gold tone trim. 2¼"d. 1" deep. Crummles. $110.—$115.

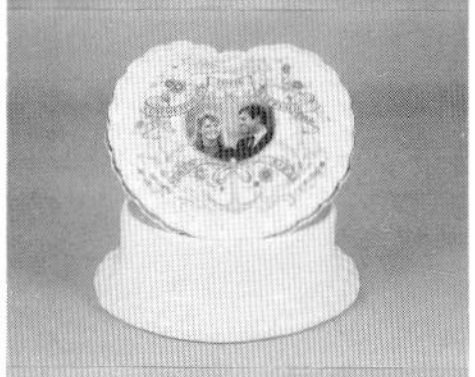

DY-012 Box. Color portrait and decoration. Gold trim. 1¾"h.x4"x4". Bone china. $26.—$29.

DY-013 - Cup and Saucer. Color portrait and decoration. Colclough bone china. $29.—$33.

DY-014 - Cup and Saucer. Color portraits and decoration. Color floral band inside rim. Gold trim. Coalport bone china. $50.—$55.

DY-015 - Cup and Saucer. White on pale blue jasperware. Wedding bells on cup's reverse. Wedgwood. $59.—$64.

DY-016 - Dish. White on pale blue jasperware. 4½"d. Wedgwood. $27.—$30.

DY-017 - Dish. Color portrait and decoration. Gold rim. 4½"d. Royal Albert bone china. $21.—$24.

DY-018 - Egg Cup. Caricature egg cups in white pottery. Each 4¼"h. $59.—$64. Pair.

DY-019 - Egg Cup. Color portrait. Bells, flowers and date on reverse. Gold trim. 2"h. Coronet BC. $14.—$17.

DY-020 - Jigsaw Puzzle. In tin. Color portraits and decoration. Puzzle is 19"x 14". Tin is 10½"x8"x 2¼". Waddingtons. $42.—$47.

DY-021 - Jigsaw Puzzle. "A Royal Occasion". 500 cardboard pieces. 19"x14". Hestair. $28.—$32.

DY-022 - Loving Cup. Gold/bronze tone portraits and decoration. Blue flowers. LE 1000. 3"h. 5"across. Royal Crown Derby. $299.—$315.

DY-023 Loving Cup, Royal Betrothal. Color portrait and decoration. 3¼"h. 5¼"across. Sutherland BC. $128.—$135.

DY-024 - Loving Cup. Color decoration. Gold lion handles and trim. Color arms and date on reverse. 3¼"h. 5½"across. Paragon. $99.—$112.

DY-025 - Loving Cup. Color portrait. "The Duke and Duchess of York" under portrait. Gold trim. 3"h. 4¾" across. Fenton BC. $53.—$57.

DY-026 Money Box. Colorful Bunnykins design. Commemoration on reverse. 3"h. 3¼"d. Royal Doulton. $27.—$31.

DY-027 - Mug. Color portrait and decoration. Gold trim. "A-S" and flowers inside rim. 3¾"h. Royal Albert bone china. $39.—$43.

DY-028 - Mug. Color portrait and decoration. Gold trim. 3¾"h. Colclough bone china. $30.—$34.

DY-029 - Mug. Gold and bright color decoration. LE 5000. 3½"h. Mason's Ironstone. $91.—$97.

DY-030 - Mug. Color decoration. Family trees on reverse. 3¾"h. 3"d. Aynsley BC. $61.—$66.

Prince Andrew — Duke of York

1986 Wedding to Miss Sarah Ferguson

DY-031 - Mug. Gold on white decoration. Same design reverse. Doves and bells opposite handle. 3"h. Wedgwood BC.
$66.—$71.

DY-032 - Mug. Color portrait and decoration. Gold trim. 3½"h. 3¼d. Johnson Brothers BC.
$21.—$23.

DY-033 - Mug. Color portrait. Gold trim. Other Dukes of York listed on reverse. 3¼"h. Coronet BC.
$26.—$30.

DY-034 - Mug. Color silhouettes and decoration. Gold trim. 3½"h. 3"d. LE 1500. Caverswall BC
$46.—$51.

DY-035 - Mug. Black and white portraits. Copper tone decoration. 3½"h. Kiln Craft Pottery.
$25.—$29.

DY-036 - Mug. Wedding and Conferment of Dukedom of York. R. Guyatt design. LE 1000. 4"h. 4"d. Wedgwood.
$199.—$214.

DY-037 - Mug. Musical. Color portraits and decoration. Music activated by light. 3¼"h.
$25.—$29.

DY-038 - Mug. Wedding and Conferment of Dukedom of York. Gold on white. Arms, date reverse. 3"h. Wedgwood BC.
$72.—$77.

DY-039 - Mug. Colorful Bunnykins design. 3"h. Royal Doulton.
$23.—$26.

DY-040 - Mug. Corgis carry wedding train. Greys and black on pink background. 3¼"h. 3"d. Kiln Craft Pottery.
$31.—$35.

DY-041 - Plate. Westminster Abbey in sepia. Gold overlay on blue border. LE 2500 numbered. 10½"d. Royal Doulton BC.
$129.—$139.

DY-042 - Plate. Color and gold decoration. Gold trim. Vivid reds and blues with gold highlights. 8"d. Mason's Ironstone.
$92.—$98.

DY-043 - Plate. Color portraits and decoration. Bells, initials, national flowers. Gold trim. 7¼"d. Coalport bone china.
$51.—$56.

DY-044 - Plate. Color portrait and decoration. Gold rim. Commemoration on reverse. 10½"d. Colclough BC.
$36.—$40.

DY-045 - Plate. Color portraits and decoration. Gold rim. 8"d. Johnson Brothers BC.
$25.—$29.

DY-046 - Plate. Color silhouettes and decoration. Gold trim. Westminster Abbey. 8½"d. Caverswall BC.
$61.—$66.

DY-047 - Plate. Color arms and family trees. Gold rim. 10½"d. Aynsley BC.
$79.—$84.

DY-048 - Plate. Color portrait. Names of previous Dukes of York. Gold trim. 7¼"d. Coronet BC.
$41.—$46.

DY-049 - Plate. Color portraits and decoration. Commemoration on reverse. 8¼"d. Royal Albert BC.
$47.—$51.

DY-050 - Plate. White decoration on light blue jasperware. 7"d. Wedgwood.
$42.—$46.

DY-051 - Playing Cards. Color portraits and decoration. Double deck in box. Waddington's.
$27.—$31.

DY-052 - Tea Towel. Color decoration. 18"x 29". Linen. Ulster.
$13.—$16.

DY-053 - Tea Towel. Black and white portraits. Color decoration. 19"x29". Blue background. Cotton.
$12.—$15.

DY-054 - Tin. Color portraits. Blue background. 8"d. 2"deep.
$22.—$25.

DY-055 - Tin. Color portrait and decoration. Medium blue background. 2¼"h.x 9"x 8½". Crawford's.
$31.—$35.

DY-056 - Tin. Color portraits. Dark red background. Silver trim. 6"h. 4½"d.
$22.—$25.

DY-057 - Tray. Metal. Color portrait. Blue printing and trim on white background. 12"d. 1"deep.
$22.—$25.

Princess Beatric's Birth — 1988

DY-058 - Dish. Gold silhouettes and decoration. Commemoration in gold on base. 4½"d. Coalport bone china.
$25.—$29.

DY-059 - Mug. Gold decoration. LE 2000. Richard Guyatt design. 2¾"h. 2¾"d. Wedgwood BC.
$78.—$83.

DY-060 - Plate. Pale blue silhouette portraits. Color decoration. Gold rim. S. Barnsley design. 8½"d. Caverswall BC.
$61.—$66.

1973 Wedding to Captain Mark Phillips

PA-001 - Bell. Color portraits and decoration. Horseshoe and bells reverse. Gold handle and trim. 5"h. 3½"d. Aynsley BC. $64.—$69.

PA-004 - Bowl, footed. Color portraits and decoration. Gold trim. 1¾"h. 5½"d. Aynsley bone china. $53.—$58.

PA-007 - Dish. Raised design. Blue border on white. 4½"d. Rye Pottery. $17.—$20.

PA-010 - Dish, crystal. "A" and "M" with hearts, crown and flowers etched in well with commemoration. 6¼"d. $51.—$56.

PA-013 - Loving Cup. Shades of blue on white background. 5"h. 6½"across. Rye Pottery. $98.—$105.

PA-016 - Mug. Black and white profiles in gold frames. Reverse shows them on horseback. 3½"h. 3"d. Staffordshire Potteries. $34.—$38.

PA-019 - Mug. Color and gold decoration. Richard Guyatt design. 4"h. 4"d. Wedgwood. $69.—$74.

PA-022 - Mug. Betrothal. Their birth dates. Color decoration. Gold rim. Wilson's Paignton Devon. Pottery. $46.—$51.

PA-025 - Plaque. White on pale blue jasperware. Commemoration in gold on reverse. LE 2000. 4½"x3¼". Wedgwood. $139.—$149.

PA-028 - Plate. Color portraits and decoration. Greek key border. 8"d. Crown Staffordshire BC. $54.—$60.

PA-002 - Box. Color decoration. color commemoration inside. Gold trim. 2"h. 4"d. Crown Staffordshire bone china. $50.—$55.

PA-005 - Bowl. Color decoration. Gold rim. 1½"deep. 6"d. Crown Staffordshire BC. $47.—$52.

PA-008 - Dish. White on pale blue jasperware. 4½"d. Wedgwood. $28.—$31.

PA-011 - Goblet. White on light blue jasperware medallion. Blue body. Clear base. 5"h. 4"d. at top. Wedgwood. $128.—$136.

PA-014 - Mug. Color portraits and decoration. Bells, flowers, horseshoe. "A&M". 3½"h. Aynsley BC. $54.—$61.

PA-017 - Mug. Color decoration. Gold trim. 4½"h. Crown Staffordshire bone china. $52.—$57.

PA-020 - Mug. Sepia portraits. Westminster Abbey on reverse. Gold trim. 3½"d. at top. Wilson's Paignton Devon BC. $47.—$52.

PA-023 - Mug. Beige profiles in green wreath. Bells, ribbons, horseshoe. Gold trim. 3¾"h. 3¼"d. Crown Staffordshire BC. $57.—$61.

PA-026 - Plate. Color decoration. Gold overlay border. Gold rim. 10¼"d. Crown Staffordshire BC. $71.—$78.

PA-029 - Playing Cards. Color portraits and decoration. Silver and gold borders. Double deck in plastic case. Worshipful Co. $62.—$67.

PA-003 - Box, footed. Color decoration. Gold riding crop and hat form finial. LE 1000. 6"h. 4½"d. at top. Coalport BC. $98.—$103.

PA-006 - Bust. Black basalt. Gold commemoration. 11"h. 6½" across at shoulders. LE 750. Royal Doulton. $285.—$310.

PA-009 - Dish. Color crown. Black commemoration around edge. Gold rim. 4½"d. Queen Anne bone china. $28.—$33.

PA-012 - Horseshoe. Sterling silver. LE 750 numbered. 3½"x 3½". Made by Barker Ellis for Antique Collectors Guild. In case. $160.—$175.

PA-015 - Mug. Black and white portraits in bronze tone frames. Horse between. 3½"h. 3"d. Staffordshire Potteries. $34.—$38.

PA-018 - Mug. Gold decoration on black background. 4"h. 3"d. Portmeirion Pottery. $28.—$32.

PA-021 - Mug. Sepia portraits. Color decoration. Gold trim. 3½"h. 3½"d. at top. Wilson's Paignton Devon BC. $44.—$49.

PA-024 - Mug, miniature. Sepia portrait. Gold trim. 2"h. Coronet BC. $18.—$21.

PA-027 - Plate. Color portraits. Gold on white border. 10½"d. Aynsley BC. $70.—$76. $77.—$82. Blue border.

PA-030 - Tea Towel. Shades of blue and gold and white decoration. 30"x19". Ulster linen. $19.—$23.

PC-001 - Bell. Red and gold dragons and lions. Purple and gold coronet. LE 500 numbered. 8"h. 3¾"d. Royal Crown Derby. $645.—$695.

PC-002 - Bowl. Color decoration. Gold trim. Two handles. 3"h. 5" across. Sheriden BC. $70.—$75.

PC-003 - Bowl, footed. Previous Princes of Wales listed. Color decoration. Gold trim. 2"h. 5¼"d. Aynsley bone china. $51.—$56.

PC-004 - Box. Color decoration. Gold trim. Unglazed. 1½"h.x5"x4". Wood & Sons. $31.—$35.

PC-005 - Cup and Saucer. Feathers, national flowers, flags on Caernarvon Castle background. Gold trim. Bone china. $50.—$55.

PC-006 - Cup and Saucer. Red Welsh dragon. Gold trim. Liverpool Road Pottery bone china. $49.—$54.

PC-007 - Decanter. "King's Gate Caernarvon Castle". Color decoration. Signed B. Jones Owen. 8"h. x 6¼"x3½"h. Keystone. $128.—$143.

PC-008 - Decanter. Black with amber tumbler. 10½"h. Made by Wedgwood for Sandeman. $71.—$76.

PC-009 - Dish. Sepia portrait. Color decoration. Gold rim. 4½"d. Coronet BC. $34.—$38.

PC-010 - Dish. Color decoration. Gold rim. Heart shape. 4¾"x4½". H. J. Wood Ltd. $19.—$23.

PC-011 - Dish. Gold and black decoration. Gold trim. 4½"d. Crown Ducal. $17.—$21.

PC-012 - Dish. Color decoration. Gold band. 4¾"d. Bone china. $30.—$35.

PC-013 - First Day Cover. Postmarked Birmingham. 8½"x4¼". $11.—$14.

PC-014 - Goblet, crystal. Feathers etched on one. Welsh dragon on other. 6"h. 3"d. Signed Stephen Richard 1969. $98.—$108. Pair.

PC-015 - Goblet, crystal. Etched with feathers and "1969" below. Signed W. Wilson. 6"h. 3"d. $50.—$55.

PC-016 - Goblet. Color and gold decoration. 4¾"h. 3¼"d. at top. Made by Royal Crown Derby for Harrods. $785.—$820. Pair.

PC-017 - Goblet. Gold on white. "Charles Prince of Wales 1969". 4½"h. 4"d. at top. Coalport BC. $138.—$153.

PC-018 - Goblet. Black on white. Aqua background. Gold trim. 4½"h. 2½"d. Grosvenor BC. $47.—$52.

PC-019 - Locket, photo. Welsh dragon on reverse. Hinged on eyelet. Sterling silver. 1¼"d. $68.—$73.

PC-020 - Medal. Caernarvon Castle and commemoration on reverse. 2"d. Boxed. $31.—$36.

PC-021 - Money Box. Gold on black basalt. Hexagonal. 3¼"x3¼" x3¼". Wedgwood. $61.—$65.

PC-022 - Money Box. Red on green. White trim. Dragon, feathers, commemoration in Welsh. 3¼"x3¼"x3¼". Wedgwood. $49.—$53.

PC-023 - Money Box. White on green jasperware. Gold lettering. Hexagonal. 3¼"x3¼"x3¼". Wedgwood. $66.—$71.

PC-024 - Money Box "Piggy Bank". Color decoration. 3"h. 4½" long. Devon Pottery. $54.—$59.

PC-025 - Mug. B&W Caernarvon Castle by Carl Toms. From 19th century view drawn by Gastineau. 4½"h. Wedgwood. $70.—$75.

PC-026 - Mug. Red Welsh dragon. Red and green decoration. Commemorative band inside. 3¼"h. 3"d. Adams Ironstone. $31.—$35.

PC-027 - Mug. Red Welsh dragon on green national flowers. Gold trim. 3"h. 2¾"d. Liverpool Road Pottery. $39.—$43.

PC-028 - Mug. Gold on white decoration. 3½"h. Staffordshire Potteries. $36.—$40.

PC-029 - Mug. Color daffodil and leek design. Commemoration inside rim. 3¼"h. 3"d. Lord Nelson Pottery. $40.—$45.

PC-030 - Mug. Colorful design by Marianne Zara and Kenneth Wright for Lord Nelson Pottery. 3¼"h. 3"d. $40.—$45.

PC-031 - Mug. Caernarvon Castle, feathers, flowers. Treacle brown. Gold trim. 3"h. 3"d. Lord Nelson Pottery. $25.—$29.

PC-032 - Mug. Red Welsh dragon. Caernarvon Castle. Color decoration. Gold trim. 3"h. 3"d. Hammersley bone china. $77.—$82.

PC-033 - Mug, shaving. Color decoration. Gold trim. 3½"h. 6"across. No mark. Pottery. $44.—$48.

PC-034 - Mug. Color decoration. Gold trim. Wales' arms on reverse. 3"h. 3"d. Hammersley BC. $77.—$82.

PC-035 - Mug. Gold on black basalt. Normal Wilson design. Feathers in wreath on reverse. 4½"h. Wedgwood. $80.—$85.

PC-036 - Mug. White raised feathers. "Croeso '69" beneath. Deep green background. White inside. 2¾"h. 2¾"d. Wales. $47.—$51.

PC-037 - Mug. Gold on black. John Cuffley design. Gold feathers and commemoration on reverse. 3¾"h. Portmeirion Pottery. $54.—$59.

PC-038 - Mug. Embossed feathers opposite handle. Black. Incised "1969". 4"h. Rye Pottery. $71.—$76.

PC-039 - Mug. Gold decoration. Purple trim. Black drawings. 4½"h. 3¼"d. Royal Windsor bone china. $44.—$48.

PC-040 - Mug. Black and white feathers, castle, Welsh dragon. Gold trim. 3½"h. Royal Worcester BC. $95.—$101.

PC-041 - Mug. Orange on yellow. Welsh dragon and commemoration. 3¾"h. Marked "England". Pottery. $20.—$25.

PC-042 - Mug. Black on white. Handle opposite feathers. Gold trim. Commemoration around inside rim. 3¾"h. Grosvenor. $64.—$69.

PC-043 - Mug. Gold/bronze tone silhouette. Color decoration. Gold trim. 3"h. Falconware Pottery. $58.—$63.

PC-044 - Mug. Sepia profile. Color decoration. Gold trim. Feathers on reverse. Coronet bone china. $61.—$66.

PC-045 - Mug. Raised profile and feathers. Charcoal grey. Date and Caernarvon Castle on reverse. 4½"h. Holkham Pottery Ltd. $34.—$38.

PC-046 - Mug. Shades of brown and beige. Commemoration on base. 5"h. 2½"d. Haverfordwest Pottery, Wales. $59.—$64.

PC-047 - Mug. Gold and black decoration. Gold trim. Design approved by College of Arms London. 3½"h. Crown Ducal. $39.—$43.

PC-048 - Mug. Black and gold decoration by Richard Guyatt. Commemoration inside rim and on base. 4"h. 4"d. Wedgwood. $113.—$121.

PC-049 - Mug. Color decoration. Gold trim. Previous Princes of Wales listed. Commemorative band inside rim. 3½"h. Aynsley bone china. $75.—$80.

PC-050 - Mug. Red Welsh dragon in front of Caernarvon Castle. Color decoration. Gold trim. 4"h. Pottery. Marked "England". $24.—$28.

PC-051 - Pin. Metal pinback. Red, white and blue feathers on white and green background. 1"d. $11.—$14.

PC-052 - Plaque. White with gold rim. Gold commemoration on reverse. LE 200. 8"d. Coalport. $235.—$250.

PC-053 - Plaque, stand alone. Red Welsh dragon. Gold border. Commemoration below dragon. 4¼"h. 4¼"d. Liverpool Pottery. $40.—$44.

PC-054 - Plaque, wooden. Color portrait, Caernarvon Castle. Metallic seal. 15"x3¾". Hand made on Isle of Anglesey. $25.—$29.

PC-055 - Plate. Color arms. Gold on white border. 10½"d. Aynsley bone china. $79.—$85. $81.—$87. Gold on green border.

PC-056 - Plate. Gold and black decoration. Gold rim. 7"d. ¾"deep. Crown Ducal Pottery. $45.—$49.

PC-057 - Plate. B&W portrait Pr. Charles and Lord Mayor Cardiff. Green/orange, gold overlay. 10½"d. Mercian China. $133.—$141.

PC-058 - Plate. Color Caernarvon Castle. Includes investiture as Earl of Chester. Gold rim. 10½". Royal Worcester BC. $143.—$153.

PC-059 - Plate. Gold/copper silhouette portrait. Cobalt blue border. Gold trim. Color decoration. 6½"d. Falconware. $60.—$65.

PC-060 - Plate. Sepia portrait. Color decoration. Gold trim. Gold overlay around border. 7¾"d. Coronet bone china. $64.—$69.

PC-061 - Plate. Sepia portrait. Color decoration. Gold trim. 8"d. Coronet BC. $60.—$64.

PC-062 - Plate. Blue on white decoration. 6½"d. Rye Pottery. $51.—$55.

PC-063 - Plate. Lavish gold and color decoration. Gold commemoration on reverse. 10½"d. Spode BC. $90.—$96.

PC-064 - Plate. Commemoration in Welsh, English on reverse. Red feathers and border. 6¾"d. Creigiau, Wales. $55.—$60.

PC-065 - Plate. Red Welsh dragon. Color decoration. Gold trim. Embossed border. 8½"d. Lord Nelson Pottery. $45.—$49.

PC-066 - Plate. Color decoration. Gold overlay on maroon border. 10½"d. Edwardian bone china. $34.—$38.

PC-067 - Pomander. Red Welsh dragon in front of Caernarvon Castle. Gold trim. 1¾"h. 4"d. Pottery. $28.—$33.

PC-068 - Purse, leather. Red, white and green. Center design in black. Metal frame and snap. Red lining. 4½"x3¼". $22.—$26.

PC-069 - Spoon, tea caddy. Sterling silver. Bowl 1½"d. Overall 2¾"long. $67.—$72.

PC-070 - Spoon. Feathers in bowl. 6" long. Sterling Silver. In case. J.D. Beardmore. $193.—$208.

PC-071 - Tile. Red Welsh dragon. 4¼"d. Richards Group. $26.—$30.

PC-072 - Tin. Color decoration. Prince's Inescutcheon of Wales on sides. Red hinged lid. 4¼"x5"x3". Brook Bond PG Tips. $33.—$38.

PC-073 - Tin, Color portrait. Color decoration. Red on gold hinged lid. 3½"h.x4¼"x3". $47.—$54.

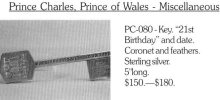

PC-074 - Tray, metal. Color decoration on purple background. 12"d. Avon Tin. $36.—$41.

PC-075 - Tray, metal. Red, green, yellow and black on copper tone background. 13½"d. 1"deep. $33.—$38.

PC-076 - Tray, metal. Red, yellow and white on purple background. 12½"d. 1"deep. $36.—$41.

PC-077 - Vase. Red Welsh dragon. Plain on reverse. 3½"h. 7¼"wide. 2"deep. Pottery. $40.—$44.

PC-078 - Vase. Color and gold arms. Earlier Princes of Wales listed. LE 250. 8½"h. Spode bone china. $535.—$555.

Prince Charles, Prince of Wales - Miscellaneous

PC-079 - Dish. "Charles, Prince of Wales 1958". Commemorates his creation as Prince of Wales. 4¼"d. $125.—$140.

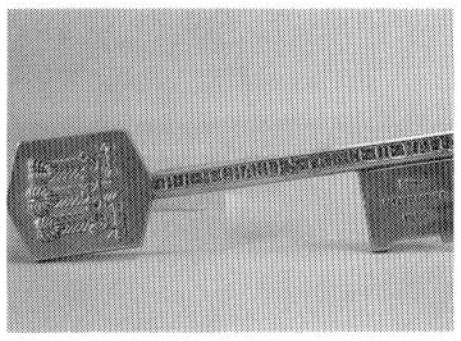

PC-080 - Key. "21st Birthday" and date. Coronet and feathers. Sterling silver. 5"long. $150.—$180.

PC-081 - Mug, 30th Birthday. Sepia portrait. Color decoration. Gold trim. LE 500. 4¼"h. Panorama Studios BC. $40.—$44.

Prince Charles, Prince of Wales — 1981 Wedding to Lady Diana Spencer

PC-082 - Beaker, enamel. Black profile portraits. Pale color decoration. Light green interior. 3½"h. 3"d. Halcyon Days. $215.—$230.

PC-083 - Beaker. Sepia portraits. Color decoration. Feathers, doves, flowers, arms on reverse. 4"h. 3"d. Caverswall BC. $70.—$75.

PC-084 - Beaker, Betrothal. Color portraits. Color and gold decoration. 4"h. 3"d. Caverswall BC. $81.—$86.

PC-085 - Beaker. Brown tone portraits and decoration. Feathers, arms, bells on reverse. 3¾"h. 3¼"d. Royal Doulton. $42.—$47.

PC-086 - Beaker. Gold silhouettes and St. Paul's dome on blue. Gold handle and trim. 3¾"h. 2½"d. Highland BC, Scotland. $79.—$84.

PC-087 - Bell. Color decoration. Family trees on reverse. Gold trim. 4¼"h. 3½"d. at base. Aynsley BC. $57.—$61.

PC-088 - Bell. Color portraits and decoration. Gold trim. Feathers and national flowers. 5¼"h. 2½"d. Crown Staffordshire. $50.—$55.

PC-089 - Bell. Engagement and Wedding bells. Blue on white. Gold band. 2½"h. 2"d. at base. Highland BC, Scotland. $55.—$60. Pair.

PC-090 - Bell. Color portrait and decoration. Gold trim. 6½"h. 3¼"d. at base. Hexagon Studios. $25.—$29.

PC—091 - Bell. Sepia portraits. Color decoration. Gold trim. 4"h. 3"d. at base. Sutherland BC. $21.—$25.

PC-092 - Bell. Color portraits and decoration. Gold trim. 4¼"h. 2¼"d. at base. Fenton bone china. $21.—$25.

PC-093 - Bell. White on pale blue jasperware. 3¼"h. 2½"d. at base. Wedgwood. $59.—$64.

PC-094 - Bell. Color portraits, one on each bell. Color decoration. Gold trim. 3¼"h. 3"d. at base. Royal Albert bone china. $61.—$66. Pair.

PC-095 - Bell, crystal. Profile portraits within their initials with St. Paul's between. Date below. 6"h. 3"d. LE 1000. Schott Glass. $95.—$103.

PC-096 - Bell. Color decoration. "C" and "D" on bells. St. Paul's on reverse. Gold trim. 4¼"h. 2¾"d. Royal Worcester BC. $41.—$45.

PC-097 - Booklet. Royal Wedding Official Souvenir. Color illustrations. 32 pages. Royal Jubilee Trust. $11.—$14.

PC-098 - Bookmark. Feathers, dove, wedding bells. Pale blue background. Jacquard woven. 8"x2". J. & J. Cash. $21.—$24.

PC-099 - Bowl. Color portraits and decoration. Gold trim.. 7½"x 6¼"x1½"deep. Coalport bone china. $48.—$53.

PC-100 - Bowl, footed. Family trees. Color decoration. Gold trim. 2"h. 5½"d. Aynsley bone china. $35.—$39.

PC-101 - Box, enamel. Color decoration. Commemoration inside. 1½"d. 1"deep. Crummles. $93.—$98.

PC-102 - Box. Sepia portraits. Color decoration. Gold trim. 1¾"h. 4"d. H. Aynsley Co. Ltd. $26.—$30.

PC-103 - Box, locking. Color portraits and flowers on lid. Gold trim. LE 2000 numbered. 3"d. 1"deep. Coalport BC. $43.—$47.

PC-104 - Box. Raised gold profile portraits on lid. Gold trim. 1¾"h. 3¾"d. Commemoration on base. Coalport BC. $35.—$39.

PC-105 - Box. Sepia portraits. Color decoration. Gold trim. 1¾"h. x3½"3". Spode bone china. $26.—$30.

PC-106 - Box. Color portrait and decoration. 2¼"h.x 3¼"x3". James Kent. $25.—$29.

PC-107 - Box. Black and white portraits. Color decoration. St. Paul's, Buckingham Palace on sides. 2½"h. 3¼"d. Sadler Pottery. $26.—$30.

PC-108 - Box. Red and blue bands and ribbons. Black feathers. Gold trim. 3¾"d. 2"deep. Royal Worcester BC. $51.—$56.

PC-109 - Box. Color portrait and decoration. Gold trim. 2"h.x 4½"x3½". Croft China bone china. $35.—$39.

PC-110 - Box, miniature. Gold feathers. Red initials. Gold commemorative band. ¾"h.x1¼"x1¼". Spode BC. $30.—$34.

PC-111 - Box, miniature. Lacquered. Color portrait. Black background. ¾"h.x2"x2". $19.—$23.

PC-112 - Box, cardboard. Color portrait. Dark blue background. 2½"h. 4¼"d. Charbonnet Chocolates. $16.—$19.

PC-113 - Bus. Silver with color decoration. Doors open. "St. Paul's" on front. 2¼"h. 4½"long. Matchbox. $17.—$20.

PC-114 - Bust. Hand painted. LE 1000. 6"h. 3¼"across at shoulders. Coalport bone china. $83.—$88.

PC-115 - Bust. White. Each 4½"h. 3½" across. No mark but believed to be made by Coalport. BC. $74.—$79. Pair.

PC-116 - Bust. White with blue below. Gold trim. 4½"h. 3½"across. Coalport bone china. $89.—$95. Pair.

PC-117 - Coaster. Black and white portraits. Color decoration. Cork backing. 3½"d. Pottery. $9.—$11.

PC-118 - Coaster. Black and white portraits. Cork backing. 3½"d. Set of 6. Maw & Co. $24.—$27.

PC-119 - Coin. Crown. Silver tone metal. Queen Elizabeth II on reverse. 1½"d. $4.—$5.

PC-120 - Compact. Color portrait. Gold tone finish. 3"d. $17.—$20.

PC-121 - Coronet. Purple and gold. White below. 2"h. 1¾"d. Caverswall bone china. $59.—$65.

PC-122 - Cup and Saucer. Sepia portraits. Color decoration. Gold trim. Red Welsh dragon inside cup. BC. $31.—$35.

PC-123 - Cup and Saucer. Black and white portraits. Color decoration. Gold trim. Royal Albert BC. $32.—$36.

PC-124 - Cup and Saucer, milk glass. Color decoration. Arcopal France. $26.—$30.

PC-125 - Cup and Saucer. Black and white portraits. Color decoration. Gold trim. Argyle BC. $25.—$29.

PC-126 - Cup and Saucer, miniature. Color and gold decoration. Gold trim. Saucer 2½"d. Cup 1"h. Spode BC. $67.—$72.

PC-127 - Cup and Saucer. Color portraits. Color arms on reverse. Gold trim. Crown Staffordshire bone china. $39.—$43.

PC-128 - Dish, glass. Black decoration. 4½"x3¾". Pettis Studio. $13.—$15.

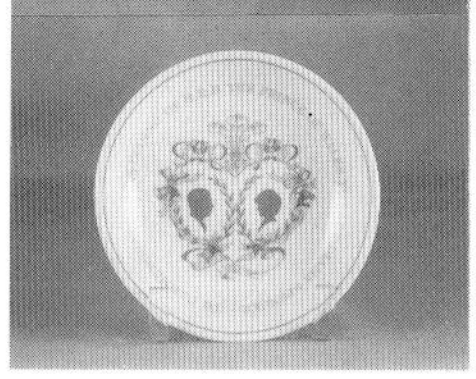

PC-129 - Dish. Silver grey silhouettes. Pastel blue and yellow decor-ation. Blue band. 4"d. Royal Tuscan BC. $29.—$33.

PC-130 - Dish. Color portraits and decoration. Embossing around gold rim. 5"d. 1"deep. H. Aynsley & Co. Ltd. $25.—$28.

PC-131 - Dish. Color portrait. Gold rim. 4½"d. Royal Grafton bone china. $21.—$24. $22.—$25. Shell Shape 5"x4½".

PC-132 - Dish. White on pale blue jasperware. 6"x3¼"x½"deep. Wedgwood. $62.—$67.

PC-133 - Dish. Sterling silver. Raised portraits in well with feathers. 3"d. ½"deep. St. James House Co. London. $117.—$123.

PC-134 - Dish. Sepia portraits. Pastel color decoration. 5"d. ½"deep. Pottery. $16.—$19.

PC-135 - Dish. Color portraits and decoration. Gold rim. Commemoration on reverse. 4"d. Crown Staffordshire BC. $19.—$22.

PC-136 - Dish. Color portraits and decoration. Gold rim. Commemoration on reverse. 4"d. Coalport bone china. $19.—$22.

PC-137 - Dish. Color portraits and decoration. Gold rim. Commemoration on reverse. 4¾"d. Royal Winton Ironstone. $19.—$22.

PC-138 - Dish. Sepia portraits. Pastel color decoration. Gold rim. 4"d. Royal Overhouse Pottery. $24.—$27. Pair.

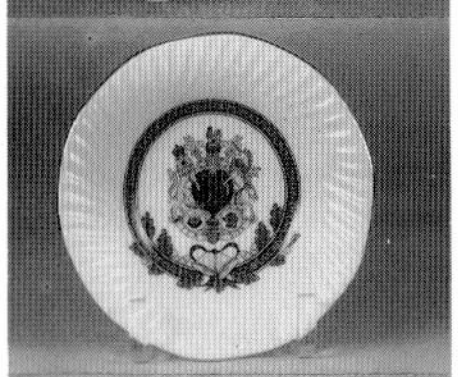

PC-139 - Dish. Color decoration. Gold rim. Brown silhouettes and commemoration on reverse. 4¾"d. 1"deep. Elizabethan BC. $24.—$27.

PC-140 - Dish. Color portraits and decoration. Green rim. Commemoration on reverse. 7¾"x5¼"x1" deep. Pottery. $50.—$54.

PC-141 - Dish. Color flowers. Gold decoration and lettering. 4½"d. Royal Crown Derby bone china. $46.—$51.

PC-142 - Dish. Color portraits. Gold rim. 4¾"d. Royal Albert bone china. $38.—$42. Pair.

PC-143 - Dish. Blue on white decoration. 5¾"d. 1"deep. Rye Pottery. $24.—$28.

PC-144 - Dish. Black feathers. Red and blue bands. 4½"d. ¾"deep. Royal Worcester BC. $20.—$23.

PC-145 - Dish. White portraits and feathers on pale blue jasperware. 4"d. Wedgwood. $30.—$34.

PC-146 - Dish. White portraits and decoration on pale blue jasperware. 4¼"d. Wedgwood. $53.—$58. Pair.

PC-147 - Dish. Black and white portraits. 4½"d. Jason Works bone china. $17.—$20.

PC-148 - Dish. Blue on white decoration. 3"d. Adams. $35.—$39. Pair.

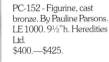

PC-149 - Dish. Color portraits and decoration. 4½"d. James Kent. $17.—$20.

PC-150 - Doll. Navy blue velvet uniform. Porcelain head, hands and feet. LE 2500. 16"h. Boxed. $56.—$61.

PC-151 - Egg Cup. Color and sepia portraits and bells. Commemorative band and "Congratulations". 2¾"h. Pottery. $23.—$26.

PC-152 - Figurine, cast bronze. By Pauline Parsons. LE 1000. 9½"h. Heredities Ltd. $400.—$425.

PC-153 - Figurine, plastic. Pr. Charles in uniform. Pss. of Wales in dark blue gown. 4"h. on 3½"x3" red base. Dapol. $32.—$37.

PC-154 - First Day Cover. 6½"x3½". Canceled St. Paul's "29 Jul 1981". $12.—$14.

PC-155 - Goblet. Gold on white. Gold and color arms on reverse. 5"h. 3½"d. at top. Royal Worcester BC. $74.—$79.

PC-156 - Goblet. Color portraits. Gold trim. St. Paul's and horse drawn carriage, flowers. LE 1000. 4¾"h. Coalport BC. $189.—$225.

PC-157 - Goblet. Gold on cobalt blue. White base and inside. Gold trim. 4¾"h. 4"d. LE 2000. Coalport BC. $138.—$153.

PC-158 - Goblet. Color and gold decoration. St. Paul's in gold on reverse. 5"h. 3½"d. at top. Royal Worcester bone china. $82.—$90.

PC-159 - Goblet. Prince of Wales feathers. Sterling silver. 5"h. 2¼"d. at top. In case. $266.—$281.

PC-160 - Goblet. Black and white portraits. Color decoration. Gold trim. Red dragon, flowers on reverse. 3¾"h. 3"d. $18.—$21.

PC-161 - Goblet, glass. Black and white portraits. Color and gold decoration. 6"h. 3¼"d. at top. $17.—$20.

PC-162 - Goblet. White on pale blue jasperware medallion. Amethyst glass body. Clear base. 6"h. 4"d. at top. Wedgwood. $185.—$195.

PC-163 - Jar, ginger. Black and white portraits. Color decoration. 5¼"h. 4½"d. at center. Carlton Ware Pottery. $36.—$41.

PC-164 - Jar, ginger. Color portraits and decoration. Feathers and "Ich Dien" on sides. 5¼"h. 4¼"d. Sadler Pottery. $36.—$41.

PC-165 - Jardiniere. Sepia portraits. Color decoration. Green band around top. 5¼"h. 6½"d. at top. Pottery. $46.—$51.

PC-166 - Jigsaw Puzzle in tin. Color portrait. Puzzle 19"x 14". Blue and gold tin 10½"x7¾" x2"deep. 500 pieces. Waddingtons. $41.—$46.

PC-167 - Jigsaw Puzzle. Color engagement portrait. 300 cardboard pieces. 15"x11¼". $24.—$28.

PC-168 - Jigsaw Puzzle. Color portrait. About 500 cardboard pieces. 19"x14". Waddington's. $32.—$36.

PC-169 - Jigsaw Puzzle. Color portrait. About 500 cardboard pieces. 20"x13¼". Falcon. $24.—$28.

PC-170 - Jigsaw Puzzle. Color portrait. 300 cardboard pieces. 15"x11¼". $24.—$28.

PC-171 - Jigsaw Puzzle. Color group wedding picture. About 300 cardboard pieces. 11¼"x15". $23.—$27.

PC-172 - Jug. Sepia portraits. Color decoration. Gold trim. Welsh dragon reverse. 4½"h. 6"across. Price Kensington Pottery. $36.—$41.

PC-173 - Jug. Color portraits and decoration. 3½"h. 5½" across. James Kent Pottery. $33.—$37.

PC-174 - Jug. Black and white portraits. Color decoration. Color and gold arms. 7½"h. 5"d. Mason's. $57.—$62.

PC-175 - Jug, milk. Color portraits and decoration. "Duke of Cornwall" on reverse. 6¼"h. 3½"d. A.E. Rodda, Cornwall. $69.—$74.

PC-176 - Jug, milk. Brown profiles. Color and gold decoration. "Duke of Cornwall" reverse. 6¼"h. 3½"d. A.E. Rodda. $69.—$74.

PC-177 - Kneeler. Color needlepoint stitched on medium blue background. Blue leatherette on reverse. 3"h.x15"x10½". $150.—$160.

PC-178 - Lace Panel. 18"x13½". Nottingham lace. $31.—$36.

PC-179 - Lamp Base. Raised color portraits. Color decoration. 8½"h.x4"x4½" at base. Derek Fowler Studios. $127.—$134.

PC-180 - Lamp Base. Sepia portraits. Color decoration mainly medium brown. 8½"h.x4"x4½" at base. Derek Fowler Studios. $114.—$119.

PC-181 - Loving Cup. Color decoration. Gold lion handles. Gold trim. 3"h. 5¼" across. Paragon BC. $94.—$99.

PC-182 - Loving Cup. Color decoration. Family trees reverse. Gold trim. 3½"h. 5½" across. Aynsley BC. $47.—$51.

PC-183 - Loving Cup. Color portrait and decoration. Gold trim. 3¾"h. 5½" across. Caverswall BC. $70.—$75.

PC-184 - Loving Cup. Black and white portraits. Color decoration. Gold trim. 4¼"h. 6¾"across. Hammersley BC. $98.—$108.

PC-185 - Loving Cup. Brown tone portraits. Gold and color decoration. Names inside rim. 3"h. LE 5000. Royal Doulton BC. $83.—$89.

PC-186 - Loving Cup, miniature. "C" and "D" in red. Remainder of decoration is gold. 1"h. 1¾"across. Spode bone china. $67.—$72.

PC-187 - Loving Cup, Betrothal. Color portrait. Her hand with ring reverse. 3½"h. 5½"across. Caverswall BC. $98.—$108.

PC-188 - Loving Cup. Gold on cobalt blue. White background. LE 1500 numbered. 3"h. 5" across. Royal Crown Derby BC. $280.—$295.

PC-189 - Loving Cup. Sepia portraits. Bright color and gold decoration on cobalt blue and white. 5½"h. 6¾" across. Mason's. $155.—$165.

PC-190 - Loving Cup. Color portraits and decoration. Gold trim. 3½"h. 5½"across. Royal Stafford BC. $63.—$68.

PC-191 - Loving Cup. Color portrait and decoration. Gold trim. Color bells inside. 3½"h. 5"across. Bone china. $49.—$53.

PC-192 - Loving Cup, 3-handled. Color portraits and decoration. Gold trim. 6¼"h. LE 500. Caverswall BC. $305.—$320.

PC-193 - Loving Cup. Color portraits and decoration. Gold trim. 3½"h. 5¾"across. Elizabethan BC. $51.—$55.

PC-194 - Loving Cup. Color portraits and decoration. 4½"h. 6½"across. James Kent Pottery. $56.—$61.

PC-195 - Loving Cup. Color portraits and decoration. Gold trim. 3¼"h. 5¼"across. Crown Staffordshire bone china. $59.—$64.

PC-196 - Loving Cup. Color portraits and decoration. Color feathers inside. 4"h. 6" across. Scarborough Pottery. $47.-$52.

PC-197 - Loving Cup, miniature. Gold silhouette portraits and decoration. 2"h. 3¼"across. Wade. $10.—$12.

PC-198 - Money Box. Blue on white decoration. 3"h. 3¼"d. Adams. $27.—$30.

PC-199 - Money Box. Black and white portraits. Color decoration on blue background. Hexagonal. 3¼"d. Wedgwood. $41.—$45.

PC-200 - Mug. Sepia portraits. Color decoration. Gold trim. 4¾"h. Hammersley bone china. $48.—$53.

PC-201 - Mug. Color portraits. Color decoration. Arms on reverse. Gold trim. 4½"h. 3"d. Crown Staffordshire BC. $42.—$46.

PC-202 - Mug. Color portrait. Feathers and date on reverse. Gold trim. 3½"h. 3¼"d. at top. Pall Mall BC. $28.—$32.

PC-203 - Mug, milk glass. Color portraits. Feathers and commemoration reverse. 3½"h. 2¼"d. at top. Arcopal France. $21.—$24.

PC-204 - Mug. Black and white portraits. Pastel color decoration. Silver trim. 5¼"h. 3½"d. Sylva Ceramics. $27.—$31.

PC-205 - Mug. Color portraits and decoration. Gold trim. Feathers and arms on reverse. 3¼"h. 3"d. Coalport BC. $72.—$77.

PC-206 - Mug. Color and gold decoration. 4"h. 4"d. Heart of England BC. $33.—$37.

PC-207 - Mug. Purple decoration. Gold trim. St. Paul's on reverse with names and date. 3½"h. 3"d. at top. Royal Worcester BC. $36.—$40.

PC-208 - Mug. Color decoration. Gold trim. 4¾"h. 3½"d. at top. Wood and Sons. $29.—$33.

PC-209 - Mug. Color decoration. Gold trim. Family trees reverse. Commemoration inside rim. 3¼"h. Aynsley bone china. $38.—$42.

PC-210 - Mug. Blue on white decoration. 3"h. 3"d. at base. Rye Pottery. $26.—$30.

PC-211 - Mug. Light blue decoration. Designed y Carl Toms/Lord Snowdon. LE 5000. 4¾"h. 3¾"d. Wedgwood. $67.—$72.

PC-212 - Mug. Blue on mottled grey. 4"h. 3"d. Dunoon Pottery. $30.—$34.

PC-213 - Mug. Black on white. 3"h. 3"d. Carlton Ware. $55.—$65.

PC-214 - Mug. Color portraits and decoration on blue background. Gold tim. LE 5000. 3¼"h. 3½"d. Coalport BC. $85.—$92.

PC-215 - Mug. Black and white portrait. Richard Guyatt/ Jenkins design. 4"h. 4"d. Crown Staffordshire BC. $60.—$65.

PC-216 - Mug. Lidded. Color portraits and decoration. 4"h. 3¼"d. Pottery. $29.—$33.

PC-217 - Mug. Color portraits and decoration. Gold trim. 3½"h. 3¼"d. Bone china. $29.—$33.

PC-218 - Mug. Color arms. Gold trim. 3"h. 3"d. Wood & Sons. $16.—$19.

PC-219 - Mug. Shades of blue. Silver trim. Richard Guyatt design. LE 3000. 4¼"h. 4¼"d. Wedgwood. $75.—$85.

PC-220 - Mug. Sepia portraits. Pss. of Wales on reverse. Color decoration. 3¾"h. 3¼"d. Royal Overhouse Pottery. $28.—$32.

PC-221 - Mug. Red, blue and black decoration. 3½"h. 3"d. Sunshine Ceramics. $31.—$35.

PC-222 - Mug. Color decoration. Designed by Hornsea Primary School children. 3½"h. Hornsea Pottery. $36.—$40.

PC-223 - Mug. Color and gold decoration. Feathers on reverse. old rim. 3½"h. 3"d. Made for National Trust by Boncath. $32.—$36.

PC-224 - Mug. Gold silhouettes. St. Paul's dome and arms on blue background. Gold handle and trim. 3¾"h. Highland BC Scotland. $81.—$86.

PC-225 - Mug. White silhouettes. Color decoration. Commemoration on reverse. Bells opposite handle. 3½"h. Denby. $29.—$33.

PC-226 - Mug. Gold decoration on white. 3¼"h. 3"d. Oakley China Ltd. BC. $39.—$43.

PC-227 - Mug. Color portraits on reverse. Color decoration. Gold trim. 3"h. LE 2500. Coalport BC. $69.—$74.

PC-228 - Mug. Their names on front and reverse. Feathers and date opposite handle. 2½"h. 3¼"d. at base. $29.—$33.

PC-229 - Mug, Sepia portraits. Brown decoration. Gold rim. 3½"h. 3¼"d. Poole. $24.—$29.

PC-230 - Mug. Sepia portraits. Color decoration. Gold trim. 3½"h. Spode BC. $42.—$46.

PC-231 Mug. Raised profile portraits. Commemoration on reverse. Blue. 4¼"h. 3¾"d. Holkham Pottery. $39.—$44.

PC-232 - Mug. Gold design on black basalt. Feathers in wreath on reverse. LE 2500. 4¾"h. 3"d. at top. Wedgwood. $71.—$76.

PC-233 - Mug. White on pale blue jasperware. St. Paul's on reverse. 4½"h. 3¼"d. Wedgwood. $87.—$92.

PC-234 - Mug, Engagement. Black and white portraits. Black with some red decoration. 3½"h. 3"d. Pottery. "England." $23.—$27.

PC-235 - Mug. Gold on black design. White inside. 3¾"h. 3"d. Lancaster. $24.—$28.

PC-236 - Mug. Color portraits and decoration. Gold trim. 3¾"h. 3¼"d. Royal Kent BC. $35.—$39.

PC-237 - Mug. Black and white portrait. Color decoration. 3¼"h. 3¼"d. Wedgwood. $42.—$46.

PC-238 - Mug. Black and white portraits. Color decoration on purple background. 3½"h. 3"d. Made in England. $15.—$19.

PC-239 - Mug. Color portraits and decoration. Gold trim. 3½"h. 3¼"d. Royal Grafton bone china. $21.—$25.

PC-240 - Paperweight. Etched portraits and feathers. 4"x2¼"x¾". $26.—$29.

PC-241 - Paperweight. Etched design on purple background. LE 750. 3"d. Caithness. $82.—$87.

PC-242 - Paperweight. Welsh dragon. "29 July 1981" on base. Pressed glass. 1"h. 3¼"d. $24.—$28.

PC-243 - Paperweight. Black and white portraits in heart encircled by wedding band. Blue background. ¾"h. 2¾"d. $23.—$27.

PC-244 - Picture. Framed color portrait. Felt back. 5½"x4¾". $52.—$57.

PC-245 - Picture. Portraits reverse painted on glass. Black, gold and bronze. Black and gold frame. 11¾"x8¼". $68.—$73.

PC-246 - Picture. Color engagement portrait in brass frame. Portrait 3½"d. Frame 5¼"d. Hanger. $18.—$21.

PC-247 - Plaque, miniature. White on pale blue jasperware. Goldtone frames with feathers. LE 500. 2¾"x2". Wedgwood. $285.—$300. Pair.

PC-248 - Plaque. White on pale blue jasperware. Dated 1981. LE 3000. 4¼"x3¼". Wedgwood. $95.—$100.

PC-249 - Plaque. Color portrait. Gold rim. Commemoration on reverse. 7½"d. Crown Staffordshire bone china. $47.—$51.

PC-250 - Plaque. Black and white portraits. Color decoration. 9½"x5"d. Britannia Pottery Ltd. $36.—$40.

PC-251 - Plaque, stand alone. Color portrait and decoration. Gold trim. 4"x4". Canadian Classics. $24.—$28.

PC-252 - Plate. Gold decoration on cobalt blue. Gold commemoration reverse. LE 9500 numbered. 8½"d. Fleetwood Collection. $125.—$139.

PC-253 - Plate. Gold on cobalt blue. White behind fretwork. LE 2500. Gold commemoration reverse. 10¼"d. Bing and Grondahl. $130.—$142.

PC-254 - Plate. Red and blue bands. Gold rim. 7"d. Royal Worcester BC. $28.—$32.

PC-255 - Plate. Color decoration. Blue rim. 10"d. 1"deep. Denby Pottery. $47.—$51.

PC-256 - Plate. Color portraits. Caernarvon Castle in center. Castles around border. LE 1000 numbered. 10¾"d. Coalport BC. $87.—$94.

PC-257 - Plate. Royal residences around border. Doves, bells, crowns between. LE 5000 numbered. 10¼"d. Caverswall BC. $75.—$80.

PC-258 - Plate. White on pale blue jasperware. 6"d. Wedgwood. $69.—$74.

PC-259 - Plate. Color portraits. Blue border. 8¼"d. Royal Albert bone china. $73.—$80. Pair.

PC-260 - Plate. Gold and brown tone portraits. Gold and blue decoration. Embossed gold border. LE 1000 10½"d. Minton BC. $350.—$365.

PC-261 - Plate. Sepia portrait. Silver rim. 8¼"d. Centre Gallery. Ltd. bone china. $30.—$34.

PC-262 - Plate. Color portraits and decoration. Royal residences on border. Gold trim. 8¼"d. Caverswall BC. $66.—$71.

PC-263 - Plate. Brown tone portraits. Color flowers and bells. Gold overlay. LE 5000 numbered. 10½"d. Royal Doulton. $125.—$135.

PC-264 - Plate. Color portraits and decoration. Gold overlay on blue border. 8¾"d. Weatherby. $26.—$30.

PC-265 - Plate. Color portraits and decoration. Gold rim. LE 500. 10½"d. Coalport bone china. $125.—$135.

PC-266 - Plate. Black and white portraits. Color decoration. 6"d. Wedgwood. $26.—$30.

PC-267 - Plate. Black and white portraits. Color decoration. 10"d. Wedgwood. $44.—$49.

PC-268 - Plate. Color portraits and decoration. Blue bands around border. 8¼"d. Midwinter Fine Tableware Staffordshire. $38.—$42.

PC-269 - Plate. Color portraits and decoration. Gold rim. 6½"d. Duchess bone china. $20.—$24.

PC-270 - Plate. Black and white portraits. Color decoration. Gold rim. 6½"d. Queen Anne BC. $17.—$20.

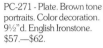

PC-271 - Plate. Brown tone portraits. Color decoration. 9½"d. English Ironstone. $57.—$62.

PC-272 - Plate. Color portraits and decoration. Gold trim. 10"d. LE 3000 numbered. Paragon BC. $110.—$120.

PC-273 - Plate. Burnished gold profiles. Color decoration. Gold overlay on red border. 9¾"d. Royal Falcon Pottery. $45.—$49.

PC-274 - Plate. Black and white portraits. Color decoration. Two gold bands. 8¼"d. Queen Anne BC. $22.—$26.

PC-275 - Plate. Color portrait. Gold rim. LE 10,000. 7½"d. Crown Staffordshire. $51.—$55.

PC-276 - Plate. Color portrait and decoration. Gold trim. Attendants around border. LE 5000. 8¼"d. Caverswall BC. $62.—$77.

PC-277 - Plate. Sepia portraits. Color decoration. Gold overlay on deep red border. 6¼" d. Weatherby. $18.—$21.

PC-278 - Plate. Sepia portraits. Color decoration. Gold trim. 8"d. Bone china. $30.—$34.

PC-279 - Plate. Sepia and color portraits. Color feathers, arms, dragon. Gold decoration. LE 3000. 10½"d. Royal Worcester BC. $225.—$240.

PC-280 - Plate. Color portrait and decoration. Commemoration on reverse. Embossed border. 10"d. $70.—$75.

PC-281 - Plate. Sepia portraits. Color decoration. Blue banded border with gold trim. 9"d. Royal Overhouse Pottery. $39.—$43.

PC-282 - Plate. Color portraits and decoration. Gold rim. 10¾"d. Coalport bone china. $79.—$84.

PC-283 - Plate. Sepia portraits. Color decoration. Gold trim. 10¾"d. Crown Staffordshire BC. $58.—$63.

PC-284 - Plate. Black and white portraits. Color decoration. Gold trim. 10½"d. Bone china. $45.—$49.

PC-285 - Plate, ribbon. Color portraits. Gold rims. Blue ribbons. 8"d. Pottery. $79.—$84. Pair.

PC-286 - Plate. Black and white portraits. Color decoration. 8"d. Bone china. $35.—$39.

PC-287 - Plate. Sepia portraits. Color decoration. 9½"d. Ashley bone china. $75.—$80.

PC-288 - Plate. Black and white portraits. Color decoration. Gold trim. 9"d. Royal Worcester BC. $50.—$55.

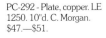

PC-289 - Plate. Blue on white. Silver band. Embossed border. 10½"d. Adams. $22.—$26.

PC-290 - Plate, glass. Black decoration on smoke glass. Commemoration on border. 10"d. $33.—$37.

PC-291 - Plate. Color and gold decoration. LE 1000 numbered. 10¾"d. Aynsley BC. $230.—$240.

PC-292 - Plate, copper. LE 1250. 10"d. C. Morgan. $47.—$51.

PC-293 - Playing Cards. Their portraits on the jokers. Double deck in clear plastic presentation box. $32.—$36.

PC-294 - Pocket Knife. Sepia portraits. Color flowers. Gold commemoration. Two blades. 3¼"long. $25.—$29.

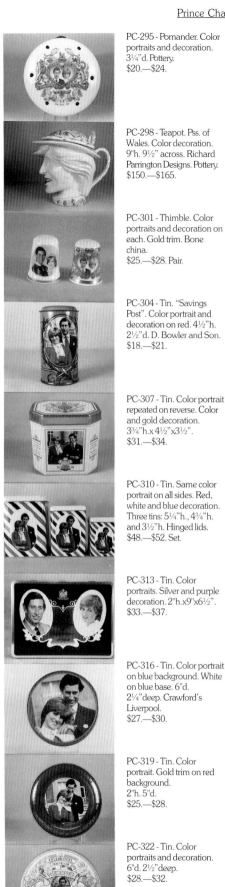

PC-295 - Pomander. Color portraits and decoration. 3¼"d. Pottery. $20.—$24.

PC-298 - Teapot. Pss. of Wales. Color decoration. 9"h. 9½" across. Richard Parrington Designs. Pottery. $150.—$165.

PC-301 - Thimble. Color portraits and decoration on each. Gold trim. Bone china. $25.—$28. Pair.

PC-304 - Tin. "Savings Post". Color portrait and decoration on red. 4½"h. 2½"d. D. Bowler and Son. $18.—$21.

PC-307 - Tin. Color portrait repeated on reverse. Color and gold decoration. 3¾"h. x 4½"x3½". $31.—$34.

PC-310 - Tin. Same color portrait on all sides. Red, white and blue decoration. Three tins: 5¼"h., 4¾"h. and 3½"h. Hinged lids. $48.—$52. Set.

PC-313 - Tin. Color portraits. Silver and purple decoration. 2"h.x9"x6½". $33.—$37.

PC-316 - Tin. Color portrait on blue background. White on blue base. 6"d. 2¼"deep. Crawford's Liverpool. $27.—$30.

PC-319 - Tin. Color portrait. Gold trim on red background. 2"h. 5"d. $25.—$28.

PC-322 - Tin. Color portraits and decoration. 6"d. 2½"deep. $28.—$32.

PC-296 - Teapot. Sepia portraits. Color decoration. Portraits repeated on reverse. 4½"h. 6¾"across. Pottery. $59.—$64.

PC-299 - Tea Towel. "A Princess for Wales". Color portrait on light blue. 28½"x18½". Ulster linen. $22.—$26.

PC-302 - Tin. Four different color portraits on dark blue background. 5¼"h. 3"d. $34.—$38.

PC-305 - Color portrait repeated on reverse. Dark blue background. 7"h. 4"d. Regency Ware. $30.—$33.

PC-308 - Tin. Color portraits front and reverse. Color and gold decoration on ivory. 4¼"h.x3¼"x3¼". Ridgways Tea. $28.—$31.

PC-311 - Tin. Color portraits and decoration. 5¼"h.x3¾"x1¾". Edward Sharp & Sons. $23.—$26.

PC-314 - Tin. Color portrait of Prince Charles. Gold tone base. 3¼"x2¼"x1"deep. $24.—$27.

PC-317 - Tin. Color portrait. Color portraits Qn. Elizabeth II and Pr. Philip on sides. 3"h. 6¼"d. Luxury Dundee Cake. $33.—$36.

PC-320 - Tin. Color portraits on medium blue background. Gold tone base. ¾"h. 2¼"d. Edward Sharp & Sons Ltd. $20.—$23.

PC-323 - Tray. Gold design on blue background. Plastic. 11¾"d. Invicta Plastics Ltd. $20.—$23.

PC-297 - Teapot. Sepia portraits. Color decoration. Gold trim. 5"h. 7"across. Price Kensington. Pottery. $57.—$61.

PC-300 - Thimble. White profiles on pale blue jasperware. Wedgwood. Boxed. $25.—$29. Pair.

PC-303 - Tin. Three different color portraits. Color decoration on blue. 5¾"h. 5¾"d. Commemoration on lid. $30.—$34.

PC-306 - Tin. Color portrait on lid. Separate portraits on sides. St. Paul's on one side. 4¼"h.x4½"x 4". London Tea Co. $28.—$32.

PC-309 - Tin. Color portraits and feathers. Dark blue background. 6"h. 4½"d. $28.—$31.

PC-312 - Tin. Color portraits on two sides. Commemoration other two. Red background. 4½"h.x3½"x3½". Overseas Trading Co. $33.—$37.

PC-315 - Tin. Color portrait. Commemoration in gold on blue background around sides. 8"d. 2"deep. Huntley & Palmers. $35.—$39.

PC-318 - Tin. Color portrait. Gold on medium blue background. 2¼"h. 5"d. $26.—$29.

PC-321 - Tin. Color portraits in gold frames. Dark red background. Gold sides. 3¾"d. 1½" deep. Smith Kendon Ltd. $22.—$25.

PC-324 - Vase. Sepia portraits and color decoration on front and reverse. 5½"h. 2½"d. Mason's Ironstone. $33.—$40.

Prince Charles — Prince and Princess of Wales

PC-325 - First Day Cover, Pss. of Wales' 21st Birthday. Falk-land Island Dependencies. 8½"x4½". Postmarked "7 Sep 82". $15.—$19.

PC-326 - Loving Cup, First Visit to Wales. Color portrait in wedding attire. Gold trim. 3½"h. 5½"across. LE 250. Coronet BC. $74.—$79.

PC-327 - Mug, Australia/ New Zealand 1983 Visit. Color portrait. Gold trim. 3¾"h. 3"d. Caverswall BC. $31.—$35.

PC-328 - Mug, Australia/ New Zealand 1983 Visit. Miniature Color portrait. 1"h. Caverswall BC. $10.—$13.

PC-329 - Mug, Pss. of Wales' 21st Birthday. Color portrait and decoration. Gold trim. 3½"h. Caverswall BC. $90.—$105.

PC-330 - Plate, Pss. of Wales' 21st Birthday. Color portrait and decoration. Gold trim. LE 1000. Caverswall bone china. $115.—$130.

Prince Henry of Wales

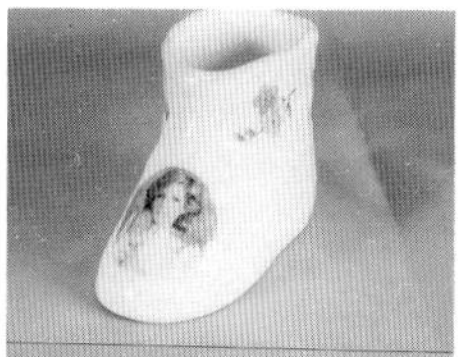

PC-331 - Bootee, Birth. Color portrait Pss. of Wales holding Pr. Henry. 1¾"h. 2¾" long. Coronet BC. $20.—$23.

PC-332 - Box, Birth. Color picture of Balmoral Castle. Commemoration inside lid. 4"d. 2"deep. Aynsley bone china. $36.—$40.

PC-333 - Dish, Birth. White decoration on pale blue jasperware. 4"d. Wedgwood. $27.—$30.

PC-334 - Egg Cup, Birth. Color portrait with Pss. of Wales. Gold trim. 2¼"h. Coronet BC. $18.—$21.

PC-335 - Egg Cup, Birth. Color portrait with Pss. of Wales. Gold trim. 2¼"h. Coronet BC. $18.—$21.

PC-336 - Loving Cup, Birth. Color decoration. Gold lion handles. 3¼"h. 5" across. Paragon BC. $110.—$120.

PC-337 - Loving Cup, Birth. Miniature. Color decoration. Gold trim. 1½"h. 2¼" across. Sutherland bone china. $22.—$26.

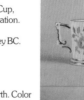

PC-338 - Loving Cup, Birth and Christening. Color portrait. Gold trim. 3¾"h. 5½"across. Coronet BC. $49.—$53.

PC-339 - Loving Cup, Birth. Color and gold decoration. LE 750 numbered. 3"h. 4¾" across. Royal Crown Derby bone china. $260.—$275.

PC-340 - Loving Cup, Birth. Colorful Bunnykins design. 3"h. 5"across. Royal Doulton pottery. $30.—$33.

PC-341 - Loving Cup, Birth. Color decoration. Gold trim. 2½"h. 3¾"across. Aynsley BC. $38.—$42.

PC-342 - Loving Cup, Birth. Miniature. Pink roses with gold leaves. Gold trim. 1½"h. 2¼" across. Royal Crown Derby BC. $100.—$110.

PC-343 - Money Box, Birth. Colorful Bunnykins design. Book shape. Royal Doulton. 4¼"h.x 3¼"x2½". $40.—$44.

PC-344 - Mug, Birth. Color portrait by Lord Snowdon. 3¼"h. 3"d. Coronet BC. $26.—$30.

PC-345 - Mug, Birth and Christening. Color family portrait. Gold trim. 3"h. 2¾"d. Coronet BC. $33.—$37.

C-346 - Mug, Birth and Christening. Color portrait with Pss. of Wales. 3"h. 2¾"d. Coronet BC. $32.—$36.

PC-347 - Mug, Birth. Color decoration. Gold trim. LE 1000 numbered. 3½"h. 3"d. Caverswall BC. $52.—$57.

PC-348 - Mug, Birth. Richard Guyatt design in gold on white. 2¾"h. Wedgwood bone china. $65.—$70.

PC-349 - Plate, Birth. Color flowers frame commemoration. Gold trim. 8½"d. Royal Albert BC. $31.—$35.

PC-350 - Thimble, Birth. Color portrait with Pss. of Wales. Gold band. Finsbury bone china. $15.—$18.

PC-351 - Thimble, Birth. Color decoration. Gold rim. St. George BC. $12.—$15.

Prince William of Wales

PC-352 - Beaker, Birth.. Color and gold decoration. Gold lion head handles. LE 1000. 4½"h. 3¼"d. at top. Caverswall BC. $67.—$73.

PC-353 - Bell, Birth. Color picture of Windsor Castle. Gold trim. 3¼"h. Aynsley bone china. $29.—$33.

PC-354 - Bell, Birth. Color portraits and decoration. 5¼"h. Crown Staffordshire bone china. $41.—$46.

Prince William of Wales

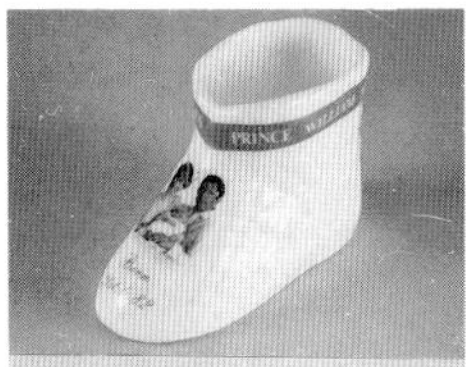

PC-355 - Bootee, Birth. Color Lord Snowdon portrait. 1¾"h. 2¾"long. Coronet BC. $25.—$30.

PC-356 - Bowl, Birth. Color portrait and decoration. Gold trim. 6"d. 1¾"deep. Coalport bone china. $28.—$32.

PC-357 - Bowl, Birth. Blue on white design. 5¾"d. 1¼"deep. Rye Pottery. $24.—$28.

PC-358 - Box, Birth. Enamel. Color decoration on lid. Blue base. 1½"d. 1"deep. Crummles. $95.—$100.

PC-359 - Box, Birth. White decoration on pale blue jasperware. 1¼"h.x2½"x2½". Wedgwood. $68.—$73.

PC-360 - Box, Birth. Locking. Color portrait and decoration. Gold trim. ¾"h. 3"d. LE 2000. Coalport BC. $48.—$53.

PC-361 - Cradle, Birth. Light blue and gold decoration. 2"h. 2½"long. Caverswall bone china. $35.—$40.

PC-362 - Cup and Saucer, Birth. Color portrait and decoration. Gold trim. Color design inside cup. Finsbury BC. $37.—$41.

PC-363 - Cup and Saucer, Birth. Miniature. Color portrait and decoration. Saucer 2"d. Cup 1¼"d. at top. Caverswall BC. $40.—$44.

PC-364 - Cup and Saucer, Birth. Miniature. Color portrait. Gold trim. Saucer 2¾"d. Cup 1½"h. Coronet BC. $28.—$32.

PC-365 - Dish, Birth. Color portrait and decoration. Gold rim. 4"d. Crown Staffordshire BC. $22.—$25.

PC-366 - Egg Cup, Birth. Color portrait. Gold trim. 2½"h. Coronet BC. $22.—$25.

PC-367 - Egg Cup, First Birthday. Color portrait. Gold trim. 2½"h. Coronet BC. $22.—$26.

PC-368 - Loving Cup, Birth. Color decoration. Gold trim. 2¼"h. 4"across. Aynsley BC. $40.—$45.

PC-369 - Loving Cup, Birth. Color decoration. Gold lion handles. 3¼"h. 5" across. Paragon BC. $125.—$135.

PC-370 - Loving Cup, Birth. Medium blue/grey decoration. 2¾"h. 5"across. Rye Pottery. $63.—$68.

PC-371 - Loving Cup, Birth. Color and gold decoration. Gold trim. LE 500 numbered. 3½"h. 5¼"across. Victoria BC. $120.—$133.

PC-372 - Loving Cup, Birth. Colorful Bunnykins design. 3"h. 5"across. Royal Doulton. Pottery. $33.—$37.

PC-373 - Loving Cup, Birth and Christening. Color Snowdon portrait. Gold trim. 3¾"h. 5½"across. Coronet bone china. $59.—$65.

PC-374 - Loving Cup, Christening. Color portrait and decoration. 3½"h. 5½"across. Caverswall BC. $74.—$78.

PC-375 - Loving Cup, First Birthday. Color portrait. Gold trim. 3"h. 5"across. Coronet bone china. $47.—$51.

PC-376 - Money Box, Birth. Colorful Bunnykins design. Book shape. Royal Doulton. 4¼"h.x 3¼"x2½". $44.—$48.

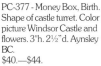

PC-377 - Money Box, Birth. Shape of castle turret. Color picture Windsor Castle and flowers. 3"h. 2½"d. Aynsley BC. $40.—$44.

PC-378 - Mug, Birth. Black, purple and gold decoration. Gold trim. 3½"h. 3"d. J&J May. Bone china. $72.—$77.

PC-379 - Mug, Birth. Gold decoration. LE 500. 3¼"h. 3¼"d. Ironbridge Gorge Museum Trust by Coalport. BC. $105.—$110.

PC-380 - Mug, Birth. Gold decoration and trim. 3½"h. 3"d. Royal Worcester BC. $55.—$60.

PC-381 - Mug, Birth. Pastel color decoration mostly pink and blue. 3½"h. 3"d. Arthur Wood Pottery. $35.—$39.

PC-382 - Mug, Birth. Color decoration. Order of succession. 3¼"h. 3"d. Caverswall bone china. $32.—$36.

PC-383 - Mug, Birth and Christening. Color Snowdon portrait. Gold trim. 4"h. 3"d. Coronet BC. $34.—$38.

PC-384 - Mug, Birth. Color drawings by Hornsea Primary School children. 3"h. 3"d. Hornsea Pottery. $37.—$41.

Prince William of Wales

PC-385 - Mug, Birth. Color portrait and decoration. Gold trim. Commemoration on reverse. 4¾"h. 3"d. Crown Staffordshire. $39.—$43.

PC-386 - Mug, Birth. Gold on white. Richard Guyatt design. 3"h. 3"d. Wedgwood bone china. $70.—$75.

PC-387 - Mug, Birth. Miniature. Color portrait and decoration. Gold trim. 1¾"h. 1½"d. Coalport BC. $40.—$44.

PC-388 - Mug, Birth. Color portrait and decoration. 2¾"h. Coalport BC. $43.—$48.

PC-389 - Mug, Birth. Miniature. Color portrait. Gold trim. 1½"h. St. George BC. $18.—$22.

PC-390 - Mug, Pr. William's 3rd Birthday, Pr. Henry's 1st. B&W portraits. Gold trim. 2½"h. LE 150. Dorincourt BC. $55.—$60.

PC-391 - Plaque, Birth. Framed. Color decoration. Mounted on blue velvet. Gold frame. Plaque is 3"d. Crown Staffordshire. $39.—$43.

PC-392 - Plaque, Birth. Stand alone. Color portrait by Lord Snowdon. Gold trim. 4"h. 3¾"d. Coronet bone china. $26.—$30.

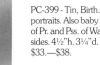

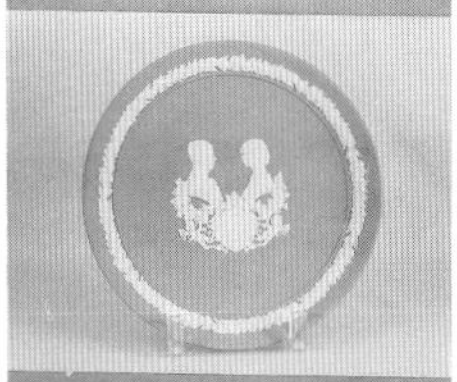

PC-393 - Plate, Birth. White decoration on pale blue jasperware. 6½"d. Wedgwood. $51.—$56.

PC-394 - Plate, Birth. Gold commemoration and crown in center. Blue latticework with gold trim. LE 3000. 8"d. Royal Doulton. $110.—$120.

PC-395 - Plate, Birth. Color decoration. Gold family silhouettes. Gold trim. 10¾"d. Caverswall BC. $79.—$85.

PC-396 - Plate, Birth. Gold on white. Brushed gold silhouettes. 7"d. Royal Worcester BC. $49.—$54.

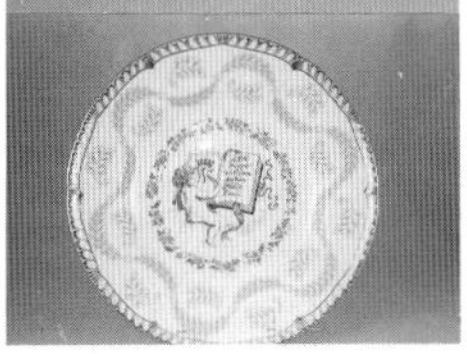

PC-397 - Plate, Birth and Christening. Color and gold decoration. LE 500 numbered. 8¼"d. Royal Crown Derby BC. $185.—$200.

PC-398 - Thimble, Birth. Gold crown on one. Gold profile of Pss. of Wales on the other. Caverswall bone china. $25.—$29. Pair.

PC-399 - Tin, Birth. Color portraits. Also baby pictures of Pr. and Pss. of Wales on sides. 4½"h. 3¼"d. $33.—$38.

King Edward VII and Queen Alexandra

E7-001 Ashtray, Coronation. Color decoration mostly hand painted. Gold rim. 4½"d. Wedgwood. $50.—$55.

E7-002 - Beaker, Coronation. Blue on white. 4½"h. Mortlock's Ltd., Oxford St., London. $95.—$110.

E7-003 - Beaker, Coronation. Applied busts and crown. Color decoration on ivory. 4½"h. Watcombe, Torquay. $165.—$180.

E7-004 - Beaker, Coronation. Sepia portraits. Color decoration. Gold rim. 3¼"h. 2¼"d. at top. Foley BC. $95.—$105.

E7-005 - Beaker, Coronation. Raised portraits and decoration. Westminster, Houses of Parliament. 3½"h. Pewter. $90.—$100.

E7-006 - Beaker, Coronation. Color decoration partially hand painted. Fluted. Gold rim. 4"h. Foley bone china. $95.—$105.

E7-007 - Beaker, Coronation. Color portraits. Gold rim. 3¾"h. 2½"d. at top. Bone china. $83.—$90.

E7-008 - Beaker, Coronation. Color portraits and decoration. Enamel on tin. 3½"h. 3"d. at top. $98.—$108.

E7-009 - Beaker, Coronation. Green on white. Coronation Dinner. 3¾"h. Royal Doulton. $67.—$74.

E7-010 - Beaker, Coronation. Sepia portraits. Gold bands. Borough Bournemouth. 3½"h. 2¾"d. Bone china. $73.—$80.

E7-011 - Beaker, Coronation. Color portraits and decoration. Enamel on tin. 3¼"h. 3¼"d. at top. $105.—$115.

E7-012 - Beaker, Lithophane. King Edward VII in coronation robes seen when held to light. 3"h. Bone china. $110.—$120.

E7-013 - Beaker, Lithophane. King Edward VII's likeness seen in bottom when held to light. 4½"h. Bone china. $100.—$110.

E7-014 - Bowl, Coronation. Color decoration partially hand painted. Gold rim. 2¼"h. 4"d. Foley bone china. $64.—$70.

E7-015 - Bowl, Coronation. Color portraits and decoration. Gold rim. Embossing. 2½"h. 4½"d. at top. BC. $60.—$67.

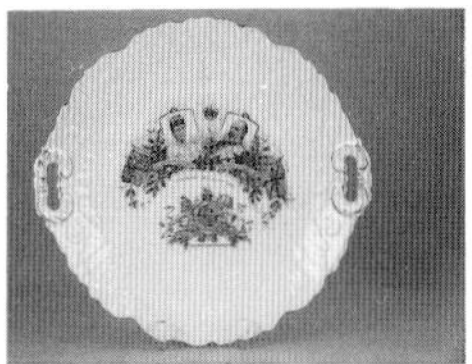

E7-016 - Bowl, Coronation. Color portraits and decoration. Gold trim. Embossing. 9½"x9"x 1¼"deep. Bone china. $94.—$99.

E7-017 - Bowl, Silver Wedding Anniversary. Glass. 9"d. 2¼"deep. $100.—$110.

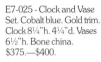

E7-018 - Box, Enamel. Color arms, "ER" and "Edward VII" on lid. Silver plate. 1¼"d. ½"deep. $54.—$59.

E7-019 - Bust, Accession. Miniature. Gold color. 2¼"h. 1¾" across. Britain's metal. $48.—$53.

E7-020 - Bust, In Memoriam. Brown unglazed. Blue/grey glazed base. "1910 Edward VII". 10"h. Doulton Lambeth. $275.—$300.

E7-021 - Busts, Pr. and Pss. of Wales made at time of their wedding. White bisque. Each 4¼"h. 3"across at shoulders. $415.—$445. Pair.

E7-022 - Candlestick Holder, Coronation. Color portraits and decoration. Place for matches. 2½"h. 6½"d. Bone china. $130.—$145.

E7-023 - Chair, Coronation. Sterling silver. 2¼"h.x1"x¾". $110.—$120.

E7-024 - Cigarette Case. Color portrait of King Edward VII. Simulated leather. 3½"x2½"x¾". $39.—$44.

E7-025 - Clock and Vase Set. Cobalt blue. Gold trim. Clock 8¼"h. 4¼"d. Vases 6½"h. Bone china. $375.—$400.

E7-026 - Creamer and Sugar, Coronation. Color portraits. Color decoration. Gold trim. Creamer 3¾"h. Sugar 4½"d. 2"deep. BC. $100.—$110.

E7-027 - Creamer and Sugar, Coronation. Color portraits. Gold trim. Creamer 2½"h. Sugar 3¼"d. 2"deep. Royal Doulton BC. $125.—$135.

E7-028 - Cup and Saucer. Color decoration partially hand painted. Gold trim. Foley BC. $65.—$71.

E7-029 - Cup and Saucer, Coronation. Sepia portraits. Color decoration. Gold trim. Crown mark. BC. $100.—$110.

E7-030 - Cup and Saucer, Coronation. Color portraits. Color decoration. Gold trim. Chapman bone china. $79.—$89.

E7-031 - Cup and Saucer, Coronation. Color portraits. Color decoration. Gold trim. Bone china. $74.—$81.

E7-032 - Cup and Saucer, Coronation. Color decoration. Gold trim. Color flowers inside cup. Regent bone china. $79.—$86.

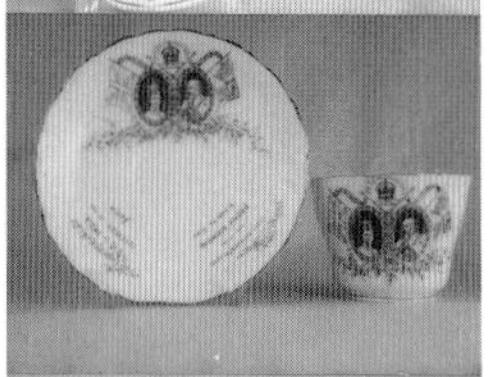

E7-033 - Cup and Saucer, Coronation. Sepia portraits. Color decoration. Gold trim. Aynsley for William Whiteley Ltd. BC. $105.—$115.

E7-034 - Cup and Saucer, Coronation. Color decoration partially hand painted. Gold trim. No mark. Bone china. $84.—$93.

E7-035 - Cup and Saucer, Coronation. Color portraits. Gold trim. Royal Doulton bone china. $110.—$120.

E7-036 - Cup and Saucer, Coronation. Color portraits and decoration on blue. Metal. Cup 2¼"h. $98.—$108.

E7-037 - Cup and Saucer, Coronation. Color portraits. Color floral decoration. Gold trim. Bisto BC. $89.—$97.

E7-038 - Cup and Saucer, Coronation. Color decoration partially hand painted. Gold trim. Wreathed crown in cup. BC. $68.—$73.

E7-039 - Cup and Saucer, Coronation. Correct coronation date. Color portraits. Floral decoration in cup. Gold trim. BC. $185.—$205.

E7-040 - Cup and Saucer, Coronation. Lithophane. Their likenesses seen in cups when held to light. Bone china. $285.—$310. Pair.

E7-041 - Cup and Saucer, Queen Alexandra. Lithophane. Her likeness seen in bottom of cup when held to light. $200.—$220.

E7-042 - Cup and Saucer, Silver Wedding Anniversary. Color decoration. Gold trim. BC. $173.—$189.

E7-043 - Cup and Saucer, Wedding. Lavender tone portraits and decoration. A&C. $225.—$255.

E7-044 - Dish, Coronation. Amber glass. 5½"x4¼"x 1" deep. $63.—$69.

E7-045 - Dish, Coronation. Pressed glass. Crown in center. 5"d. ¾"deep. $55.—$60.

E7-046 - Dish, Coronation. Color decoration. Gold Rim. 5"x4½"x¾"deep. Regent bone china. $49.—$54.

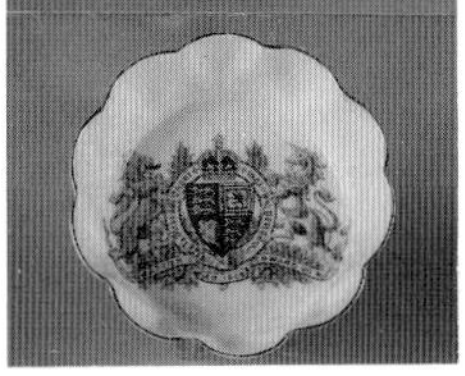

E7-047 - Dish, Coronation. Color decoration. Gold Rim. 4¼"d. 1¼"deep. Regent bone china. $49.—$54.

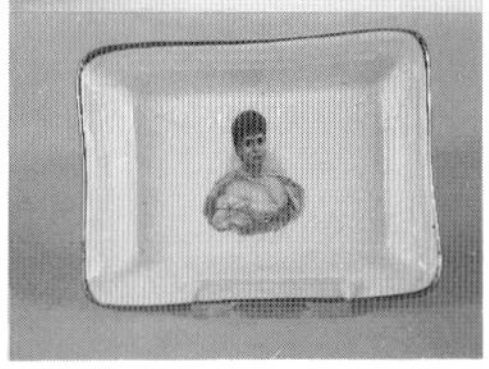

E7-048 - Dish, Coronation. Color Alexandra. Gold rim. 3½"x2½"x¾" deep. Royal Doulton. $50.—$55.

E7-049 - Dish, Coronation. Color portraits. Color decoration. Gold rim. 3¼"d. Royal Doulton bone china. $50.—$55.

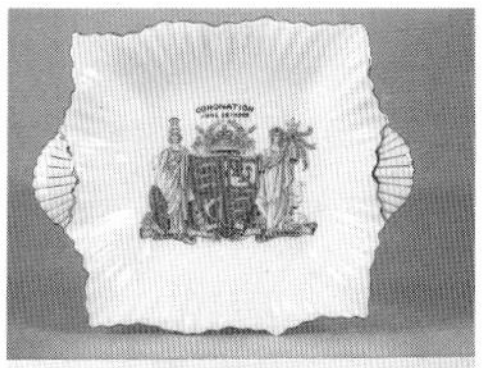

E7-050 - Dish, Coronation. Color decoration partially hand painted. Gold trim. 6¾"x6". Foley bone china. $70.—$77.

E7-051 - Dish, Coronation. Gold decoration on cobalt blue background. 4¼"x3½". Coalport bone china. $135.—$145.

E7-052 - Dish, In Memoriam. Color portrait. Purple bunting. Color decoration. Gold rim. 6½"d. Foley BC. $105.—$115.

E7-053 - Dish, In Memoriam. Brass. Birth, accession and death dates. "Edward The Peacemaker". 5½"x3¾". $65.—$72.

E7-054 - Dish, "HRH Albert Edward Prince of Wales" around his profile. Brass. 3½"d. $53.—$58.

E7-055 - Dish, Silver Wedding Anniversary. Blue pressed glass. 6½" handle to handle. 1¼" deep. $80.—$87.

E7-056 - Dish, Silver Wedding Anniversary. Color decoration. Gold trim. Green background. 6¼"d. Bone china. $80.—$87.

E7-057 - Egg Cup, Coronation. Color portrait. 2½"h. Bone china. $48.—$53.

E7-058 - Egg Cup, Coronation. Color portrait Queen in mourning veil (for Queen Victoria's death). 2½"h. BC. $48.—$53.

E7-059 - Egg Cup, Coronation. Color portrait in gold frame on puce background. 2½"h. Bone china. $48.—$53.

E7-060 - Figurine, Coronation. Flatback. Hand painted color and gold decoration. 8¼"h. 5"across. $310.—$335.

E7-061 - Figurines, Staffordshire. Gold highlights. Names on bases. 12¼"h. 4½"x3½" base. $525.—$575. Pair.

E7-062 - Figurines, Staffordshire. Marked Prince of Wales and Princess of Wales. Each 12½"h.x9". $965.—$1015. Pair.

E7-063 - Hat, Coronation. Color decoration. 1½"h. 2½"d. at brim. Foley bone china. $43.—$49.

E7-064 - Jar, Coronation. Brown decoration. 2½"h. Coleman's Mustard. Pottery. Minton. $43.—$48.

E7-065 - Jar, Coronation. Footed jam. Color decoration partially hand painted. Gold trim. 4"h. Base 4½"d. Hammersley $147.—$162.

E7-066 - Jar, Coronation. Hand painted cypher, arms, Pr. of Wales feathers. 6"h. 4½"d. Wedgwood. $205.—$225.

E7-067 - Jug, Coronation. Color decoration. Gold trim. 2"h. 3"across. Alfred Dunn, Birmingham. Bone china. $80.—$88.

E7-068 - Jug, Coronation. Color decoration. Gold trim. 2¼"h. 1¾"across. W.H. Goss BC. $44.—$49.

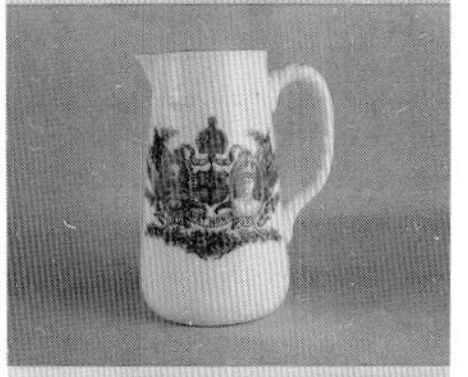

E7-069 - Jug, Coronation. Color portraits. Color decoration. Gold trim. 4½"h. 3½"across. R.H. & S.L. Plant BC. $95.—$108.

E7-070 - Jug, Coronation. Color decoration. Gold trim. 6¼"h. Foley BC. $80.—$88.

E7-071 - Jug, Coronation. Color portraits and decoration. Gold trim. 5¼"h. Austrian BC. $150.—$165.

E7-072 - Jug, Coronation. Gold, silver, color design. Gold lion handle. LE 500. 7½"h. 6¾"across. Crown Staffordshire. $680.—$725.

E7-073 - Jug, Coronation. Color portraits. Gold decoration. 4½"h. Bone china. $69.—$76.

E7-074 - Jug, Coronation. Color portraits and decoration. Gold trim. "Present from Windsor Canada". 3¼"h. BC. $95.—$103.

E7-075 - Jug, Coronation. Color portraits and decoration. Gold trim. 5¾"h. 5¾" across. BC. $115.—$130.

E7-076 - Jug, In Memoriam. Brown shading to green base. Birth and death dates. 6¼"h. Pottery. $90.—$100.

E7-077 - Jug, In Memoriam. Color portrait and decoration. Gold trim. 8"h. 6½"across. Bone china. $153.—$169.

E7-078 - Jug, Silver Wedding Anniversary. Color portraits. Gold trim. 5"h. 5"across. Bone china. $111.—$130.

E7-079 - Jug, Wedding 1863. Light purple tone portraits and decoration. Arms and crown on reverse. 3¾"h. 4½"across. $355.—$390.

E7-080 - Jug, Wedding 1863. Blue tone portraits. Princess Alexandra on reverse. 8½"h. 5¾"across. J. & M.P.Bell, Glasgow. $395.—$430.

E7-081 - Jug, Wedding 1863. Raised white profiles. Princess Alexandra on reverse. 6½"h. 6"across. J. & M.P.Bell, Glasgow. $820.—$880.

E7-082 - Loving Cup, Coronation. Color portraits and decoration. Gold rim. 4½"h. 6¼"across. Foley Faience. $175.—$200.

E7-083 - Loving Cup, In Memoriam. Three handles. Birth, accession, death dates. 3¼"h. W. H. Goss bone china. $100.—$110.

E7-084 - Loving Cup, Lithophane. Three handles. King Edward VII seen when held to light. 2¼"h. 2"d. Gold trim. Bone china. $100.—$110.

E7-085 - Match Safe, Coronation. Profile portrait. 1¾"h.x1¼"x ½". "Long Live the King" on reverse. Silver plate. $58.—$63.

E7-086 - Medal, Accession and Coronation. Coronation scene on reverse. 1¾"d. Silver tone metal. $23.—$28.

E7-087 - Mug, Accession and Coronation. Sepia portraits. Color decoration. 3¼"h. R.H. & S.L. Plant. $113.—$123.

E7-088 - Mug, Coronation. Color decoration partially hand painted. Gold trim. 3"h. 3"d. Hammersley BC. $106.—$116.

E7-089 - Mug, Coronation. Pink on white. Coronation chair and House of Lords' throne on sides. 3"h. Aynsley. $125.—$135.

E7-090 - Mug, Coronation. Color decoration. Gold trim. 3"h. 3"d. Foley BC. $100.—$110.

E7-091 - Mug, Coronation. Color decoration mostly hand painted. Gold trim. 3"h. 2½"d. at top. Bone china. $90.—$100.

E7-092 - Mug, Coronation. Colorful design is opposite handle. 3"h. 3"d. Johnson Brothers. $89.—$99.

E7-093 - Mug, Coronation. Miniature pair. Color portraits. 2"h. 1¾"d. Made in Germany. Bone china. $86.—$94. Pair.

E7-094 - Mug, Coronation. Color portraits and decoration. Gold trim. 3"h. 3"d. $90.—$100.

E7-095 - Mug, Coronation. Sepia portraits. Color decoration. 3¾"h. 3"d. at top. Bone china. $110.—$120.

E7-096 - Mug, Coronation. Color portraits and decoration. Harrod's. Pottery. $90.—$98.

E7-097 - Mug, Coronation. Color portraits and decoration. Gold trim. 3"h. 3"d. Pottery. $90.—$98.

E7-098 - Mug, Coronation. Green decoration on white. 4"h. 4"d. Royal Doulton. $130.—$135.

E7-099 - Mug, Coronation. Color portraits and decoration. Gold trim. 2¾"h. 2¾"d. Pottery. $74.—$81.

E7-100 - Mug, Coronation. Sepia portraits and decoration. Gold trim. 3"h. Aynsley for Wm. Whiteley. BC. $90.—$99.

E7-101 - Mug, Coronation. Enamel on tin. Sepia portraits. Color decoration. Handle opposite portraits. 3"h. 3"d. $70.—$76.

E7-102 - Mug, Coronation. Color portraits and decoration. Gold trim. Foley. $100.—$110.

E7-103 - Mug, Coronation. Blue tone portraits and decoration. Gold trim. 3¼"h. 3¼"d. W.H. Schofield, Brighton. Pottery. $75.—$81.

E7-104 - Mug, Coronation. Brown tone portraits and decoration. 2½"h. 2½"d. Pottery. $70.—$75.

E7-105 - Mug, Coronation. Color portraits and decoration. Gold trim. Handle opposite portraits. 3¼"h. $95.—$105.

E7-106 - Mug, Coronation. Color portraits and decoration. Wide gold band on rim. 3"h. Bone china. $79.—$86.

E7-107 - Mug, Coronation. Brown tone portraits and decoration. 3"h. W.T. Copeland & Sons. Pottery. $111.—$121.

E7-108 - Mug, Coronation. Color portraits. Coronation postponement notation. 3½"h. Royal Doulton BC. $135.—$149.

E7-109 - Mug, Coronation. Color decoration partially hand painted. Flowers on reverse. Gold trim. 3"h. Aynsley BC. $96.—$105.

E7-110 - Mug, Coronation. Sepia portraits in gold beaded frames. Color decoration. Gold trim. 3¼"h. Wm. Lowe. BC. $121.—$137.

E7-111 - Mug, Coronation. Shaving. Color portraits. Gold trim. 3¾"h. 5¼"across. Bone china. $100.—$115.

E7-112 - Mug, Coronation. Raised color decoration on deep blue. 4"h. 3"d. at top. Royal Doulton stoneware. $275.—$300.

E7-113 - Mug, Coronation. White on blue glass. Handle opposite commemoration. 3¼"h. 2¼"d. $100.—$110.

E7-114 - Mug, Coronation. Lithophane. King's likeness seen when held to light. Color decoration. 2¾"h. BC. $100.—$110.

E7-115 - Mug, Silver Wedding Anniversary. Color and gold decoration on light blue. Gold rim. 3"h. Bone china. $100.—$110.

E7-116 - Needle Case. Sepia wedding portraits under glass. 2¾"x1¾"x½". Velvet edge. $150.—$165.

E7-117 - Paperweight. 1902 Penny and coin with King Edward VII's likeness. 2½"d.x1". $55.—$60.

E7-118 - Picture, Coronation Souvenir. B&W picture changes to King in coronation robes when tab is pulled. 5½"x3". $40.—$45.

E7-119 - Postcard. Three-dimensional color portrait cards with sparkles and "jewels". By Bas-Relief. $22.—$25. Pair.

E7-120 - Picture. Framed sepia portrait of Queen Alexandra. Portrait is 3"d. Wooden frame is 5"d. $39.—$44.

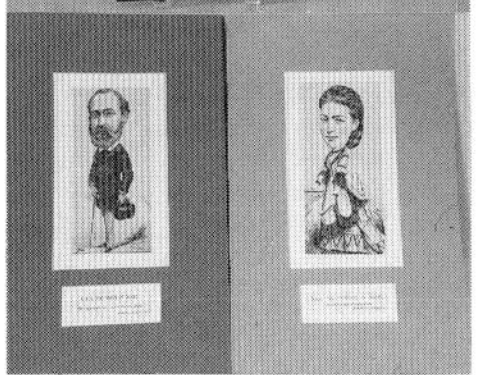

E7-121 - Picture. Pr. and Pss. of Wales color prints matted. Prints are 5¾"x3". Matting is 12"x8". Faustin. $49.—$56. Pair.

E7-122 - Pin. "VII-E-Edward". Red and blue enamel bar pin. 1½"across. Gold tone. $36.—$41.

E7-123 - Plaque, Coronation. B&W portraits. Queen Alexandra in mourning veil. Color decoration. 8½"x7½". $120.—$133.

E7-124 - Plaque, Coronation. Color portraits and decoration. Gold on green border. 12"x11". $205.—$225.

E7-125 - Plaque. "Edward VII" is under his raised portrait. White on medium blue background. 5½"x4¾". $90.—$100.

E7-126 - Plaque. Color portraits mounted on deep green. Plaques are 5¾"x4½". Black frames are 7¼"x6¾". $180.—$195. Pair.

E7-127 - Plaque. "Princess Alexandra". White raised profile portrait. Frame is 7"d. Bauerrichter & Co. $245.—$270.

E7-128 - Plaque, Silver Wedding Anniversary. Miniature. Sepia portraits and decoration. 2½"h. 4"across. Copeland Spode. $175.—$195.

E7-129 - Plate, Accession. Color portraits and decoration. Gold trim. 8¼"d. Bone china. $118.—$128.

E7-130 - Plate, Coronation. Sepia portraits and decoration. Mayor/Mayoress of Worcester. 9¼"d. Royal Worcester. $138.—$153.

E7-131 - Plate, Coronation. Brown tone portraits and decoration. 6½"d. $75.—$81.

E7-132 - Plate, Coronation. Green on white with gold highlights. Gold rim. 6¾"d. Blair's bone china. $85.—$95.

E7-133 - Plate, Coronation. Sepia portrait. Color decoration partially hand painted. 9½"d. Wedgwood. $150.—$165.

E7-134 - Plate, Coronation. Color portraits. Gold rims. 6½"d. Royal Doulton bone china. $140.—$155. Pair.

E7-135 - Plate, Coronation. Color portraits. Gold crown, cypher, commemoration and rim. 7"d. Royal Doulton BC. $78.—$88.

E7-136 - Plate, Coronation. Color decoration. Gold rim. Embossing. 7"d. Aynsley bone china. $70.—$77.

E7-137 - Plate, Coronation. Color decoration partially hand painted. Gold rim. 6¼"d. Regent bone china. $60.—$66.

E7-138 - Plate, Coronation. Blue on white decoration. 6¾"d. Royal Copenhagen bone china. $205.—$225.

E7-139 - Plate, Coronation. Gold cypher, crown and date. Gold rim. 5¾"d. Royal Doulton BC. $50.—$55.

E7-140 - Plate, Coronation. Color portrait framed in heavy gold embossing. Gold on cobalt blue. 8¾"d. Hammersley. $190.—$210.

E7-141 - Plate, Coronation. Color decoration partially hand painted. Color cypher and crown. 9¼"d. Foley BC. $50.—$55.

E7-142 - Plate, Coronation. Blue and white portraits and decoration. Embossing. 10"d. No mark. $228.—$239.

E7-143 - Plate, Coronation. Blue and white portraits and decoration. 10¼"d. Coalport bone china. $148.—$163.

E7-144 - Plate, Coronation. Postponement notation. Sepia portraits. Color decoration. City of Leeds. 7"d. Newcastle. $85.—$93.

E7-145 - Plate, Coronation. Color portraits. Gold rim. 8¾"d. Made in Austria. Bone china. $70.—$77.

E7-146 - Plate, Coronation. Color portraits. Queen Alexandra in mourning veil. Gold trim. 8½"d. BC. $110.—$120.

E7-147 - Plate, Coronation. Color portraits and decoration. Gold trim. 8½"d. Bone china. $95.—$105.

E7-148 - Plate, Coronation. Color portrait. Gold rim. 8½"d. Bone china. $65.—$72.

E7-149 - Plate, Coronation. Color portraits and decoration. Cobalt blue border. 6½"d. Bone china. $90.—$100.

E7-150 - Plate, Coronation. Color portraits and decoration. Gold rim. 7"d. Bone china. $58.—$63.

E7-151 - Plate, Coronation. Color portraits. Pastel flowers. Gold rim. 7¼"d. Bisto BC. $68.—$75.

E7-152 - Plate, Coronation. Color portraits and decoration. Gold rim. 7"d. Foley bone china. $75.—$81.

E7-153 - Plate, Coronation. Sepia portraits. Color decoration partially hand painted. 7"d. Wm. Whiteley BC. $80.—$88.

E7-154 - Plate, Coronation. Correct date. Color portraits and decoration. Gold rim. 6"d. Bone china. $95.—$105.

E7-155 - Plate, Coronation. Color portraits. Brown decoration. Gold rim. 8"d. Royal Doulton bone china. $170.—$185.

E7-156 - Plate, Coronation. Color portraits and decoration. Gold rim. 9¼"d. Pottery. $105.—$115.

E7-157 - Plate, In Memoriam. Blue on white. Birth and death dates. Embossing. 10"d. Pottery. $112.—$122.

E7-158 - Plate, In Memoriam. Birth, accession, and death dates. Color portrait and decoration. Gold rim. 5¾"d. Clifton BC. $130.—$145.

E7-159 - Plate. Pr. and Pss. of Wales. Metal. Raised portraits. Alphabet around rim. No paint remaining. 4¼"d. $265.—$290.

E7-160 - Plate, Queen Alexandra. Color portrait. Gold trim. Reticulated border. Puce background. 8¾"d. Bone china. $70.—$77.

E7-161 - Plate, Queen Alexandra's 70th Birthday. Blue on white. 8"d. Royal Copenhagen BC. $225.—$250.

E7-162 - Postcard, Coronation. Color portraits and decoration. $13.—$16.

E7-163 - Tape Measure. Sepia portraits. 1½"d.x½". Chas. Leonard & Sons, Gen. Drapers. $50.—$61.

E7-164 - Tape Measure. Sepia portrait of Edward, Prince of Wales c. 1860's. Mirror on reverse. 1¼"d. $85.—$90.

E7-165 - Teapot, Coronation. Color portrait and decoration. Gold trim. 5"h. 7"across. Bone china. $170.—$185.

E7-166 - Teapot, Coronation. Color portraits and decoration. Gold trim. 4½"h. 7"across. BC. $160.—$175.

E7-167 - Teapot, Coronation. Color portrait. Gold trim. Embossing. 5¾"h. 7" across. Bone china. $148.—$163.

E7-168 - Teapot, Color decoration partially hand painted. 3½"h. 7"across. Hammersley bone china. $190.—$210.

E7-169 - Teapot, Coronation. B&W portraits. Puce background. 5"h. 7" across. Bone china. $132.—$147.

E7-170 - Teapot, Coronation. Color portraits and decoration. Gold trim. 5¼"h. 7¼"across. Bone china. $143.—$158.

E7-171 - Teapot, Coronation. Color portraits and decoration. Gold trim. 4¼"h. 6½"across. Bone china. $128.—$143.

E7-172 - Teapot Stand, Coronation. Color portraits and decoration. 7"d. Pottery. $85.—$95.

E7-173 - Tin, Bristol Dock Opening 1908. Color portraits. Color and gold decoration. 6"x3½"x1"deep. J.S. Fry & Sons. $40.—$45.

E7-174 - Tin, Cardiff Visit 1907. Color portraits. Gold trim. 6"x3½"x¾"deep. J.S. Fry & Sons. $55.—$60.

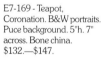

E7-175 - Tin, Coronation. Color portraits and decoration. 3"x2"x 1"deep. $38.—$43.

E7-176 - Tin, "Coronation Souvenir from Queen Alexandra." Color portrait. 5"x2"x¼"deep. Rowntree. $50.—$55.

E7-177 - Tin, Coronation. Raised profiles. 2¼"d. ¼"deep. Mazawattee Chocolate. $39.—$43.

E7-178 - Tin, Coronation. Sepia portraits. Color decoration. Balmoral and Windsor reverse. 8"x3"x4"deep. $210.—$230.

E7-179 - Tin, Coronation. Color portraits and decoration. 5"h.x 5"x3½". Ridgways Ltd. Merchants. $92.—$102.

E7-180 - Tin, Coronation. B&W portraits on color background. 2¼"x1½"x ¾"deep. Rowntree. $45.—$50.

E7-181 - Tin, Coronation. Color portraits. Red border, yellow background. 5"x2"x½"deep. Rowntree. $37.—$43.

E7-182 - Tin, Coronation. Color portraits. Manchester. Front and reverse shown. 3¼"h. 1½"d. Rowntree. $45.—$50.

E7-183 - Tin, Coronation. Color portraits. (Geo. V and Edw. VIII on ends). Coronation scene. 7½"h.x8½"x5½". $120.—$135.

E7-184 - Tin, Coronation. Color portraits and decoration. 4¼"h.x 6¼"x4¼". $115.—$130.

E7-185 - Tin, Coronation. Color portraits. (Geo. V, Qn. Mary, Edw. VIII on sides). 6¾"h.x6¾". $120.—$135.

E7-186 - Tin, Coronation. Color portraits and decoration. 5"x2"x ½"deep. Rowntree. $37.—$43.

E7-187 - Tin, Coronation. Color portraits and decoration. Glasgow Celebrations. 4"x3"x 2"deep. $50.—$56.

E7-188 - Tin, Coronation. Color portraits and decoration. 3¼"x 2"x¼"deep. Cadbury Brothers. $28.—$32.

E7-189 - Tin, Coronation. Color portraits. (Geo. V and Edw. VIII on ends). Coronation scene. 7½"h.x8½"x5½". $120.—$135.

E7-190 - Tin, In Memoriam. B&W portraits and design on purple. Queen Alexandra reverse. 6"h.x4½"x3". $58.—$65.

E7-191 - Tin, In Memoriam. Sepia portrait. (Portrait is on card inserted in lid.) 6½"x4"x1½" deep. Rowntree's Cocoa. $75.—$85.

E7-192 - Tin, King Edward VII. Sepia portraits. Queen Alexandra on reverse. Color decoration. 2"h. 1½"d. Reeve's. $115.—$130.

E7-193 - Tin, King Edward VII. Embossed profile. Color decoration. 7½"x4½"x2½" deep. Mazawattee. $38.—$43.

E7-194 - Tin, Pss. of Wales. Blue/Black portrait and decoration. Pss. visiting wards on sides. 4"x2½"deep. $125.—$140.

E7-195 -Tin, Queen Alexandra. Color portrait and decoration. Red base. 2½"x2¼"x¾"deep. $65.—$72.

E7-196 - Tumbler, Coronation. Silver decoration on glass. Names, crown and flowers. 4¼"h. 3¼"d. $42.—$47.

E7-197 - Vase, In Memoriam. B&W profile. Birth, accession and death dates. Green leaves. 3½"h. Goss BC. $105.—$115.

E7-198 - Vase, Queen Alexandra in mourning veil (for Queen Victoria). Color portrait and decoration. 5½"h. BC. $48.—$53.

King Edward VIII

E8-001 - Ashtray, Coronation. Color portrait and decoration. Gold rim. 4¾"d. Grindley. $40.—$45.

E8-002 - Ashtray, Coronation. Blue on white portrait and decoration. 5"d. Copeland Spode. $65.—$75.

E8-003 - Beaker, Abdication. Sepia portrait. Color decoration. Gold trim. 4"h. 3"d. $90.—$97.

E8-004 - Beaker, Coronation. Color portrait framed in gold. LE 2000. "1937" and crowns embossed in gold. 4"h. Minton. $335.—$375.

E8-005 - Beaker, Coronation. B&W portrait on blue background. 4"h. 2¾"d. at top. Wedgwood & Co. Ltd. $82.—$90.

E8-006 - Beaker, Coronation. Sepia portrait. Color decoration. 4"h. 3"d. at top. Shelley bone china. $70.—$77.

E8-007 - Beaker, Coronation. Sepia portrait. Color decoration. Gold rim. 3¾"h. Pottery. $43.—$48.

E8-008 - Beaker, Coronation. Sepia portrait. Color decoration. Gold rim. 3½"h. 2¾"d. at top. Empire. $43.—$48.

E8-009 - Beaker, Coronation. Sepia portrait. Color decoration. 3½"h. Pottery. $38.—$43.

E8-010 - Beaker, Coronation. Sepia portrait. Color decoration. Gold rim. 4"h. 2¾"d. at top. Aynsley BC. $68.—$75.

E8-011 - Beaker, Coronation. Sepia profile on red. Color decoration. 4¼"h. 3"d. at top. Pottery. Copeland Spode. $42.—$47.

E8-012 - Biscuit Bucket, Coronation. Sepia portrait. Color decoration. Metal handle. 4½"h. 5¾"d. Pottery. $120.—$135.

E8-013 - Biscuit Bucket, Coronation. Brown tone portrait. Color decoration. Blue rattan handle. 5¼"h. 4½"d. Pottery. $125 —$140.

E8-016 - Bowl, Coronation. Charlotte Rhead hand painted orange, blue, gold design. Hat shape. 6¼"d. Crown Ducal. $130.—$145.

E8-019 - Bowl, Coronation. Color decoration. Gold trim and handles. 6¾"x5¼"x 1"deep. Paragon BC. $80.—$88.

E8-022 - Box, Coronation. Sepia portrait. Color decoration. Gold trim. 2½"h.x3½"x3". Aynsley bone china. $95.—$105.

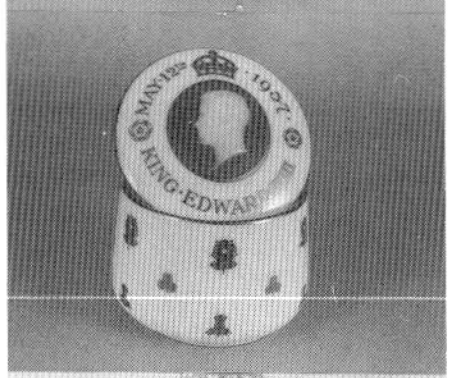

E8-025 - Box, Prince of Wales. Cardboard. Sepia portrait. Orange background. Fabric ribbon. 5"x3½"x2"deep. $24.—$29.

E8-028 - Creamer and Sugar, Coronation. Sepia portrait. Color decoration. Gold trim. Creamer 3"h. Sugar 3½"d. Kensington. $78.—$88.

E8-031 - Cup and Saucer, Coronation. Color portrait wearing robes. Color decoration. Royal Doulton bone china. $85.—$95.

E8-034 - Cup and Saucer, Coronation. Sepia portrait. Color decoration partially hand painted. Gold trim. Tuscan BC. $80.—$89.

E8-037 - Dish, Coronation. Brown tone portrait. Color decoration. Gold rim. 5¾"x4"x¾"deep. J&G Meakin. Pottery. $40.—$45.

E8-040 - Dish, Coronation. Also visit to Cox's Cave during its centenary 1937. Sepia portrait. 4½"d. 1"deep. Grafton BC. $95.—$105.

E8-043 - Dish, Coronation. Sepia portrait. Gold decoration on cobalt blue. 5¼"x5¼"x1"deep. Crown Staffordshire. $130.—$145.

E8-014 - Bowl, Coronation. Color portrait and decoration. Gold rim. 6½"d. 1¼" deep. Grindley. $45.—$50.

E8-017 - Bowl, Coronation. Charlotte Rhead hand painted orange, black, gold design. 5¼"d. Crown Ducal. Pottery. $120.—$135.

E8-020 - Box, Coronation. Green, yellow and white. Sceptre and orb on sides. 5¾"h. 5½"d. Moorcroft Pottery. $950.—$1000.

E8-023 - Box, Coronation. White profile on blue. Gold trim. LE 300. 2"h. 2½"d. By Minton for W.H. Plummer. BC. $295.—$335.

E8-026 - Brooch, Coronation. Red, white and blue ribbon. 1¾"across. On original card. $30.—$35.

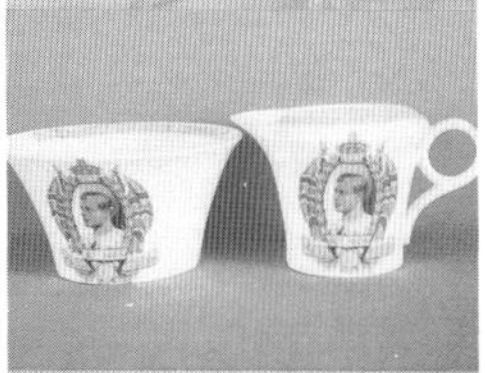

E8-029 - Cup and Saucer, Coronation. Sepia portrait. Color decoration. Floral border. Gold trim. Aynsley BC. $115.—$130.

E8-032 - Cup and Saucer, Coronation. Sepia portrait. Color decoration. Gold trim. Phoenix Ware. $60.—$66.

E8-035 - Cup and Saucer, Coronation. Sepia portrait. Color decoration. Shelley bone china. $80.—$90.

E8-038 - Dish, Coronation. Sepia portrait. Color decoration. 4½"d. Shelley BC. $45.—$50.

E8-041 - Dish, Coronation. Blue on white portrait and decoration. 4½"d. 1"deep. Copeland Spode. $89.—$99.

E8-044 - Dish, Coronation. Color portrait and decoration. Gold rim. 5"d. Grindley Creampetal. $45.—$50.

E8-015 - Bowl, Coronation. Sepia portrait. Color decoration. Blue rim with gold band below. 6½"d. Sutherland BC. $50.—$56.

E8-018 - Bowl, Coronation. Sepia portrait. Color decoration. Floral band inside well. 9"d. C.W.S. Pottery. $61.—$68.

E8-021 - Box, Coronation. Cigarette box with four ashtrays. Color portrait and decoration. 5"x3½"x 2". Royal Doulton. $170.—$190.

E8-024 - Box, Portrait. Black plastic with white raised profile portrait. 4"d. 1½"deep. Beetleware. $40.—$45.

E8-027 - Creamer and Sugar, Coronation. Sepia portrait. Color decoration. Each 2½"h. Shelley BC. $100.—$110.

E8-030 - Cup and Saucer, Coronation. Accession date also shown. Color decoration partially hand painted. Hammersley. $110.—$125.

E8-033 - Cup and Saucer, Coronation. Color portrait wearing crown. Color decoration. Gold trim. Grindley Creampetal. $70.—$77.

E8-036 - Dish, Abdication. Sepia portrait. Color decoration partially hand painted. 5½"d. Tuscan BC. $90.—$100.

E8-039 - Dish, Coronation. Sepia portrait. Color decoration. Yellow trim and handles. 6"x4¾". Shelley BC. $50.—$55.

E8-042 - Dish, Coronation. Color decoration partially hand painted. Gold rim. 4¾"x3¾". Hammersley BC. $75.—$85.

E8-045 - Dish, Coronation. Sepia portrait. Gold decoration on cream. 3¾"d. 1"deep. Crown Staffordshire BC. $68.—$75.

E8-046 - Dish, Coronation. Sepia portrait. Color decoration. Red and blue trim. 4¾"x4"x ½"deep. T&K BC. $42.—$47.

E8-047 - Dish, Coronation. Sepia portrait. Color decoration. Gold rim. 5"d. Center well is 3"d. ¾"deep. BC. $42.—$47.

E8-048 - Dish, Coronation. Sepia portrait. Color decoration. Gold rim. 4½"x4½"x1"deep. Empire. $43.—$48.

E8-049 - Dish, Coronation. Sepia portrait. Color decoration. Gold trim. 5¼"x4½". Aynsley BC. $44.—$49.

E8-050 - Dish, Prince of Wales. B&W portrait (with cigarette in his mouth) on blue. Color decoration. Gold rim. 4"d. $45.—$50.

E8-051 - Dish, Prince of Wales. Sepia portrait in Army uniform. Gold rim. 4"d. Pottery. $45.—$50.

E8-052 - Door Knocker, Accession. Brass. Crown at top. "Edward VIII" and "1936". 4¼"x2" at shoulders. 1"deep. $120.—$135.

E8-053 - Egg Cup, Coronation. Sepia portrait. Color decoration. Gold band around rim. 2½"h. Pottery. $35.—$40.

E8-054 - Egg Cup, Coronation. Brown tone portrait. Color decoration. Gold rim. 2½"h. Pottery. $34.—$40.

E8-055 - Fabric, Coronation. Color portrait. Coronation scene, procession, Westminster, etc. 36"wide. Cotton chintz. $40.—$45. yard.

E8-056 - First Day Cover, Wedding. B&W photographic portrait. Canceled Monts 3.6.37. 5"x6". Mount 8"x10". $200.—$220.

E8-057 - Flag, Coronation. Black and white portrait. Color decoration. 8½"x12½". Cotton. $22.—$25.

E8-058 - Flag, Coronation. Black and white portrait. Red, white and blue flag. 5½"x3¼". $17.—$19.

E8-059 - Globe, Coronation. Commemoration around base. Color decoration. Gold trim. 3¼"h. 3"d. Melba BC. $235.—$255.

E8-060 - Handkerchief, Coronation. Profile, commemoration and date. Red or blue. 10½"x8½". $26.—$30.

E8-061 - Handkerchief, Coronation. Black and white portrait. Color decoration. 10"x10". Rayon. $20.—$24.

E8-062 - Handkerchief, Coronation. "Edward" is formed by flying airplane. Red, white and blue. 12"x12". Rayon. $18.—$22.

E8-063 - Jar, Coronation. Cookie. Sepia portrait. Red and blue trim. 9"h.x 6½"x4¼". Pottery. $200.—$220.

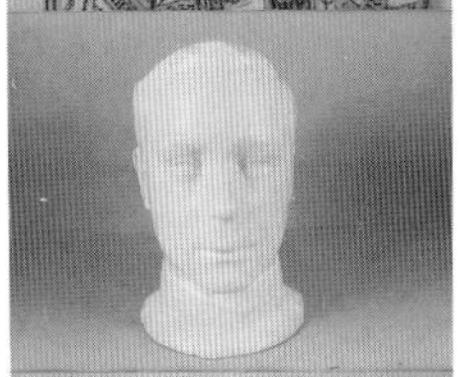

E8-064 - Jug, Character. Musical. Plays "God Save The King". Ivory color pottery. 8¼"h. 7"across. Bretby. $200.—$225.

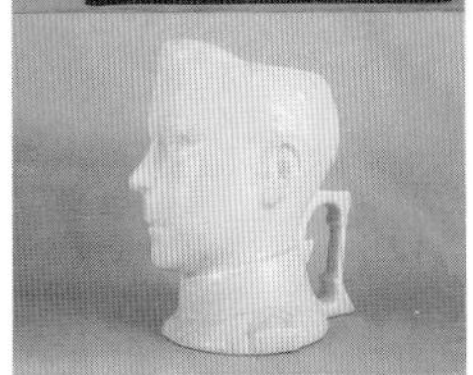

E8-065 - Jug, Character. "E" handle. Ivory color pottery. 8¼"h. 7"across. Bretby. $120.—$135.

E8-066 - Jug, Character. Lion handle. White pottery. 5½"h. 6"across. $110.—$120.

E8-067 - Jug, Coronation. Sepia portrait. Color decoration. Blue trim. 4"h. 5"across. Pottery. $67.—$73.

E8-068 - Jug, Coronation. Sepia portrait on blue. Red and blue bands. Color decoration. 5½"h. 3½"d. Wadeheath. $70.—$77.

E8-069 - Jug, Coronation. White raised profile on blue. 5"h. 6"across. Johnson Brothers. Pottery. $55.—$60.

E8-070 - Jug, Coronation. Sepia portrait. Color decoration. 5½"h. 6"d. Parrott & Co. $65.—$70.

E8-071 - Jug, Coronation. Hand painted Charlotte Rhead design in red, gold, blue on white. 7½"h. Pottery. $210.—$230.

E8-072 - Jug, Coronation. Sepia portrait. Color decoration. 3½"h. 5¾"across. Square shape. Pottery. $53.—$58.

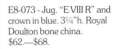

E8-073 - Jug. "E VIII R" and crown in blue. 3¼"h. Royal Doulton bone china. $62.—$68.

E8-074 - Jug, Prince of Wales. Color portrait. Color flowers on reverse. Gold trim. 5"h. 4¼"across. BC. $120.—$135.

E8-075 - Loving Cup, Year of Reign. Hand painted. Prince of Wales' portrait on reverse. LE 2000. 6¾"h. 7" across. Royal Doulton. $1100.—$1350.

E8-076 - Loving Cup, Coronation. Beige tone portrait on blue. Color decoration. Crowns on handles. 3"h. Radford's BC. $78.—$88.

E8-077 - Loving Cup, Coronation. Beige tone portrait. Color decoration. Beige trim. 5"h. 6"across. Shelley. $125.—$140.

E8-078 - Loving Cup, Coronation. Sepia portrait. Hand painted flags to sides. Gold decoration on red. 5"h. Aynsley BC. $365.—$410.

E8-079 - Loving Cup, Coronation. Brown tone portrait. Color decoration. Gold bands and trim. 4½"h. 7"across. Shelley BC. $550.—$600.

E8-080 - Loving Cup Coronation. Sepia portrait both sides. Color decoration. Gold trim. 3"h. 5¼" across. Anchor BC. $115.—$130.

E8-081 - Loving Cup, Coronation. Raised portrait and color decoration. 6"h. 7" across. Pottery. $190.—$210.

E8-082 - Loving Cup, Coronation. Color and gold decoration. Gold lion handles. LE 1000 numbered. 5¼"h. 8½" across. Paragon BC. $495.—$545.

E8-083 - Medal, Coronation. Crown topped bar holds red, white, blue ribbon. Bronze medal 1"d. Original card and box. $45.—$50.

E8-084 - Medal, Prince of Wales. 1928. Raised profile portrait. Bronze. Sun rays and sailing scene on reverse. 1½"d. $39.—$44.

E8-085 - Mug, Abdication. Sepia portrait. Color decoration. Gold trim. 4"h. 2¾"d. Crownford Burslem. $100.—$110.

E8-086 - Mug, Coronation. Crown above cypher. Light green slipware. Pottery. 3"h. $63.—$69.

E8-087 - Mug, Coronation. Color decoration partially hand painted. Gold trim. 3"h. 3"d. Hammersley BC. $110.—$125.

E8-088 - Mug, Coronation. Color Dame Laura Knight circus design. 3¼"h. 3"d. at top. Pottery. $68.—$75.

E8-089 - Mug, Coronation. Color Dame Laura Knight circus design. Deluxe edition with certificate. 3¼"h. 3"d.. $115.—$130.

E8-090 - Mug, Coronation. Musical. Plays "God Save The King". Raised portrait and design. 5"h. 5"d. Pottery. $180.—$200.

E8-091 - Mug, Coronation. Raised white profile on pale blue. 3½"h. 3"d. at top. Johnson Brothers. $42.—$47.

E8-092 - Mug, Coronation. Raised profile portrait with crown above. Mottled green/rust finish. 4½"h. Arthur Wood. $95.—$105.

E8-093 - Mug, Coronation. White profile portrait on royal blue jasperware. White inside. 4"h. 4"d. Wedgwood. $370.—$410.

E8-094 - Mug, Coronation. Sepia portrait. Color decoration. Gold trim. 3½"h. 3"d. at top. Delphine BC. $60.—$66.

E8-095 - Mug, Coronation. Color portrait. Color decoration. Gold trim. 3½"h. 2¾"d. Morley, Fox & Co. $48.—$53.

E8-096 - Mug, Coronation. Sepia portrait. Color decoration. Crown, orb, sceptre on handle. Gold trim. 4"h. 3"d. $78.—$85.

E8-097 - Mug, Coronation. Color portrait and decoration. Gold rim. 3"h. 3"d. Pottery. $40.—$45.

E8-098 - Mug, Coronation. Sepia portrait. Color decoration. Lion and crown on reverse. 4"h. 3¼"d. Alma Ware. $53.—$58.

E8-099 - Mug, Coronation. Sepia profile portrait. Color flowers. Blue trim. 3¾"h. 3¼"d. G.W.S. Longton. $57.—$62.

E8-100 - Mug, Coronation. Sepia portrait. Color decoration. Red and blue "ER" handle. 3"h. 3¼"d. at top. $90.—$99.

E8-101 - Mug, Coronation. Matching cover. Sepia portrait. Color decoration. Gold trim. 4½"h. Cover 3¾"d. Tuscan. $115.—$125.

E8-102 - Mug, Coronation. Color portrait and decoration. Lion handle. 3½"h. By Copeland for Thos. Goode. $85.—$95.

E8-103 - Mug, Coronation. Sepia portrait. Color decoration. Gold trim. 2¾"h. 2¾"d. Melba Ware. $42.—$47.

E8-104 - Mug, Coronation. Sepia portrait. Color decoration. Floral handle. Gold rim. 4"h. 2¾"d. Aynsley BC. $72.—$79.

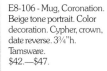

E8-105 - Mug, Coronation. Sepia portrait. Color decoration. Blue trim. 4"h. J&G Meakin. $47.—$52.

E8-106 - Mug, Coronation. Beige tone portrait. Color decoration. Cypher, crown, date reverse. 3¾"h. Tamsware. $42.—$47.

E8-107 - Mug, Coronation. Sepia portrait. Color decoration. Gold trim. 3"h. Falconware by Hanley. $42.—$47.

E8-108 - Mug, Coronation. Green glass. Raised profile and design. 3¾"h. 3"d. at top. $52.—$57.

E8-109 - Mug, Coronation. Crystal. Etched crown, cypher and commemoration. 5¼"h. 3"d. Thomas Goode. $135.—$150.

E8-110 - Mug, Coronation. Color portrait and decoration. 3"h. 2¾"d. at top. Royal Doulton bone china. $83.—$92.

E8-111 - Mug, Coronation. Shaving. Sepia portrait. Color decoration. 4"h. 6¼" across. Pottery. $78.—$85.

E8-112 - Mug, In Memoriam. Their birth, marriage, death dates. Black and purple decoration. 3¾"h. Dorincourt BC. $85.—$95.

E8-113 - Mug, King Edward VIII. Sepia portrait. Gold Rim. 3"h. Morley, Fox & Co. Ltd. $55.—$60.

E8-114 - Mug, Prince of Wales. Sepia portrait. Gold trim. 3¾"h. 3½"d. at top. Pottery. $77.—$85.

E8-115 - Needle Case, Coronation. Sepia portrait. Gold tone case. 2"long. ½"d. $59.—$64.

E8-116 - Paperweight. Black and white portrait. Color and glitter added. 1"h.x4¼"x2". Glass with felt base. $27.—$31.

E8-117 - Pendant, King Edward VIII. Color portrait on mother of pearl. Color "jewels". 1¾"x1". Silver tone. $38.—$43.

E8-118 - Pin, Coronation. B&W portrait. Red, white and blue pinback. 1¼"d. Metal. $15.—$18. Each.

E8-119 - Plaque, Coronation. Signed F. Garbutt. Commemoration on reverse. Ivory color. 8½"x5¾". Soho Pottery. $100.—$110.

E8-120 - Plaque, In Memoriam. Profile portrait. From 1924 portrait. Black basalt. LE 2000 numbered. 4¼"x3¼". Wedgwood. $115.—$130.

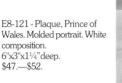

E8-121 - Plaque, Prince of Wales. Molded portrait. White composition. 6"x3"x1¼" deep. $47.—$52.

E8-122 - Plaque, Portrait. Stand alone. Gold color plastic. 7"x5½". $22.—$25.

E8-123 - Plate, Abdication. Sepia portrait. Color decoration. Proclamation, abdication dates. 9"d. Stanley BC. $100.—$110.

E8-124 - Plate, Accession. Color portrait and decoration. Blue band on embossed rim. 9"d. Ruwaha, Belgium. $180.—$200.

E8-125 - Plate, Coronation. Beige tone portrait. Color decoration. 6½"d. Shelley BC. $63.—$69.

E8-126 - Plate, Coronation. Color portrait wearing crown. Color decoration. Gold rim. 9"d. Grindley Creampetal. $80.—$90.

E8-127 - Plate, Coronation. Sepia portrait. Color decoration. Gold rim. 7"d. Aynsley BC. $73.—$80.

E8-128 - Plate, Coronation. Sepia portrait. Color decoration. Red and blue trim. 8¼"d. C.W.S. BC. $68.—$75.

E8-129 - Plate, Coronation. Black and white portrait. Blue decoration. 8½"d. Wedgwood & Co. Ltd. $85.—$95.

E8-130 - Plate, Coronation. Color decoration partially hand painted. Gold trim. Embossing. 10½"d. Paragon BC. $200.—$225.

E8-131 - Plate, Coronation. Blue portrait and decoration. 8¼"d. Copeland Spode. $132.—$147.

E8-132 - Plate, Coronation. Sepia portrait. Color decoration. Silver rim. 7"d. Pottery. $42.—$47.

E8-133 - Plate, Coronation. Blue portrait and decoration. 10½"d. By Copeland Spode for Lawley's, Regent St. $152.—$165.

E8-134 - Plate, Coronation. Sepia portrait. Color decoration. Gold trim. 6¼"d. Tuscan BC. $50.—$55.

E8-135 - Plate, Coronation. Sepia portrait. Hand painted flags. Gold rim. 10½"d. Cauldon BC. $177.—$197.

E8-136 - Plate, Coronation. Sepia portrait. Color decoration. Gold rim. 6"d. T.L.& K. BC. $43.—$48.

E8-137 - Plate, Coronation. Sepia portrait. Color decoration. Gold rim. 5"d. Alma Ware. $37.—$42.

E8-138 - Plate, Coronation. Color portrait and decoration. Red and blue bands. Floral border. 9"d. Royal Ivory. $58.—$65.

E8-139 - Plate, Coronation. Sepia portrait. Color decoration. Gold rim. 9¼"d. Sovereign Potters. $53.—$58.

E8-140 - Plate, In Memoriam. Gold profiles and decoration. Puce border. LE 1000 numbered. 10½"d. Coalport BC. $190.—$210.

E8-141 - Playing Cards. "Hello Canada". Made for 1919 Visit. Single deck. C. Goodall & Son. $89.—$99.

E8-142 - Ribbon, Coronation. Blue and white portrait. Red commemoration. 3½"x1¼. $42.—$47.

E8-143 - Sugar, Coronation. White on royal blue jasperware. 4"h. 5½"across. Wedgwood. $195.—$215.

E8-144 - Tape Measure, Prince of Wales. Tape comes out of neck on reverse. 2¼"h. 1½"d. at base. "Ivorine". $69.—$78.

E8-145 - Teapot, Coronation. Sepia portrait. Color decoration. Recessed lid. 3¼"h. 7"across. Grindley. $90.—$100.

E8-146 - Teapot, Coronation. Sepia portrait. Color decoration. Gold trim. 5½"across. 8"across. Lancasters Ltd. $110.—$120.

E8-147 - Teapot, Coronation. 3¼"h. 6½"across. Swan brand chromium plated. $60.—$67.

E8-148 - Teapot, Coronation. Color decoration. Gold trim. 5½"h. 9"across. Paragon BC. $410.—$445.

E8-149 - Teapot, Coronation. Sepia portrait. Color decoration. Gold trim. 5"h. 9"across. Includes 5¼"d. stand. $155.—$170.

E8-150 - Tin, Accession. Color portrait and decoration. Wm. IV 1836 on reverse. 5¾"h.x 4¾"x3¼". Ridgway. $120.—$135.

E8-151 - Tin, Accession. Color portrait and decoration. Gold trim. 6½"x4½"x3½"deep. $80.—$90.

E8-152 - Tin, British Empire Exhibition Wembley 1924. Color portrait and decoration. 4"h.x4"x3". $82.—$92.

E8-153 - Tin, Coronation. Color portrait. Windsor, Buckingham Palace on sides. Purple background 4¼"h. 4"d. $58.—$65.

E8-154 - Tin, Coronation. Color portrait. Windsor and Fort Belvedere on sides. Blue background. 6¼"h. 4¼"d. $79.—$89.

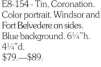

E8-155 - Tin, Coronation. Gold medallion profile on top. Coin slot. Gold decoration on red. 3¼"x4¼"x2". Oxo. $40.—$45.

E8-156 - Tin, Coronation. Color portrait. Red and blue decoration on silver. Coin slot. 2¼"h.x 4"x2½". $49.—$53.

E8-157 - Tin, Coronation. Sepia Vandyk portrait. Blue on gold decoration. 8"x5"x3"deep. Cremona Toffee. $53.—$58.

E8-158 - Tin, Coronation. Color portrait and decoration. 6¼"x 4¾"x2½"deep. Peek, Freen & Co. Biscuits. $56.—$66.

E8-159 - Tin, Coronation. Color portrait also on reverse. Red background. 6¼"h. 4"d. $83.—$90.

E8-160 - Tin, Coronation. Color portrait. Color and gold decoration. 6½"h. 3½"d. Hudson Scott & Sons Ltd. $49.—$54.

E8-161 - Tin, Coronation. Sepia portrait and decoration. Windsor Castle on sides. 6"h.x4"x4". E.I. & Co. Ltd. $48.—$53.

E8-162 - Tin, Coronation. Blue tone portrait. Gold frame. Color and gold decoration. 6"d. 2"deep. Walter's Palm Toffee. $57.—$62.

E8-163 - Tin, Coronation. Sepia portrait. Color decoration. Orange background. 6"d. 2¼" deep. Walter's Toffee. $57.—$62.

E8-164 - Tin, Coronation. Color portrait and decoration. Windsor or Buckingham Palace. 5¾"x 3¾"x1¼"deep. $65.—$75.

E8-165 - Tin, Coronation. Color portrait and decoration on blue. 5¾"x3¾"x2½"deep. Riley's Toffee. $48.—$53.

E8-166 - Tin, Coronation. Color portrait on red. Important dates listed on base. 5¼"x4"x 1½"deep. $50.—$55.

E8-167 - Tin, Coronation. Color portrait. Gold decoration on red. 7"x 5¾"x3"deep. $53.—$58.

E8-168 - Tin, Morley Ind. Coop. Society Ltd. Visit 1933. Color portrait. Blue and gold background. 5¾"x4¼"x1¾"deep. $48.—$53.

E8-169 - Tin, North East Coast Exhibit at Newcastle-Upon-Tyne 1929. Color portrait. 5"x3"x1"deep. Cremona. $52.—$57.

E8-170 - Tin, Portrait. Color portrait. Black on gold sides. 5"d. 3"deep. $53.—$58.

E8-171 - Tin, Prince of Wales. Sepia portrait. Dark brown background. 9"d. 3½" deep. $48.—$53.

E8-172 - Tin, Prince of Wales. Color portrait and decoration with gold are on inside lid. 9"x7¼"x 3¼"deep. Sovereign. $75.—$85.

E8-173 - Tin, Prince of Wales. Color portrait and decoration on red. 4"x2½"x1½"deep. Thorne's Toffee. $45.—$50.

E8-174 - Tin, Prince of Wales. Color portrait. Gold on red background. 4¼"x2½"x 1½"deep. Thorne's Toffee. $45.—$50.

E8-175 - Tin, Prince of Wales. Color portrait. Gold decoration on red. Scenes from 1920's tours. 5¼"x5¼"x2"deep. $97.—$107.

E8-176 - Tin, Prince of Wales' 21st Birthday. Color portrait. Dark blue background. 4½"h. 3½"d. $95.—$105.

E8-177 - Tumbler, Coronation. Sepia portrait. Color decoration. Ribbon commemoration. Glass. 4¼"h. $27.—$29.

E2-001 - Album. Coronation. Fold-out photo album on pin. Black and white photos. Gold tone. 1"x1". $28.—$33.

E2-004 - Ashtray, Coronation. Pressed glass. Queen's profile and "Elizabeth R. 1953". 4¼"d. ¼" deep. $18.—$22.

E2-007 - Beaker, Coronation. Cypher and crown. Embossed gold on white. 4"h. Minton bone china. $230.—$250.

E2-010 - Beaker, Coronation. Sepia portrait. Color decoration. 4¼"h. Copeland Spode. $36.—$44.

E2-013 - Beaker, 60th Birthday. Color portrait and decoration. Gold handles. LE 250. 4½"h. Caverswall. $50.—$58.

E2-016 - Bell, Silver Jubilee. Raised flowers. Silver trim. 5¼"h. Crown Staffordshire BC. $32.—$38.

E2-019 - Bell, Silver Jubilee. Black and white portrait. Color decoration. Wooden handle. 7½"h. Royal Grafton. $60.—$66.

E2-022 - Bowl, Coronation. Brown decoration in center. 7¼"d. 1½" deep. Poole Pottery. $47.—$56.

E2-025 - Bowl, Coronation. Pressed glass. Crown and "EIIR" in well. 8"d. at top. 4¼"d. at base. 4" deep. $58.—$68.

E2-028 - Bowl, Silver Jubilee. Footed. Lists Kings and Queens of England. 5½"d. Aynsley BC. $36.—$45.

E2-031 - Bowl, 60th Birthday. Color decoration. Words of "God Save The Queen." 5½"d. 2"h. Aynsley BC. $43.—$48.

E2-002 - Album, Coronation. Fold-out photo album on key ring. Black and white photos. Gold tone. 1"x1". $28.—$33.

E2-005 - Ashtray, Coronation. Pressed glass. Crown and "Elizabeth R 1953". 4¼"d. ¼" deep. $17.—$21.

E2-008 - Beaker, Coronation. Wide blue band. 3½"h. Poole Pottery. $32.—$38.

E2-011 - Beaker, Coronation. Color decoration. Cypher and crown on reverse. 4"h. Official design. Pottery. $17.—$22.

E2-014 - Beaker, 25th Anniversary of Coronation. Color decoration. Gold lion head handles. 4½"h. Caverswall. $100.—$110.

E2-017 - Bell, Silver Jubilee. Color decoration. Gold handle and trim. 4"h. Aynsley BC. $38.—$46.

E2-020 - Bell, Silver Jubilee. Color and gold decoration. Crown and cypher on reverse. 6"h. Hammersley BC. $38.—$47.

E2-023 - Bowl, Coronation. Color portrait. Gold and cobalt blue decoration. 9¼"d. 3" deep. Aynsley BC. $895.—$995.

E2-026 - Bowl, St. Lawrence Seaway Opening 1959. Sepia portrait. Gold decoration. 3"d at top. Aynsley BC. $83.—$92.

E2-029 - Bowl, Silver Jubilee. Gold and ruby decoration. LE 500. 9¼"d. 3¼"h. Wedgwood BC. $385.—$425.

E2-032 - Bowl, 25th Wedding Anniversary. Westminster Abbey. 4½"d. 1½" deep. Aynsley bone china. $45.—$53.

E2-003 - Album, Coronation. Spiral bound. Color portraits. Gold on blue background. 6½"x5". Metal Box Co. $16.—$21.

E2-006 - Automobile, 40th Wedding Anniversary. Rolls Royce model. Ruby red. 3¼" long. Lledo. $42.—$49.

E2-009 - Beaker, Coronation. Sepia portrait. Color decoration. 4"h. Royal Doulton. $62.—$73.

E2-012 - Beaker, 40th Wedding Anniversary. Gold and ruby red on white background. Caverswall BC. $88.—$100.

E2-015 - Bell, Silver Jubilee. Cast metal. Silver tone finish. 4¼"h. 2½"d. at base. $48.—$55.

E2-018 - Bell, Silver Jubilee. Brown on beige. Pottery. 4½"h. 3¼"d. at base. $32.—$37.

E2-021 - Bowl, Canada Visit 1959. Color portrait and decoration. Gold trim. 8"x7". Royal Albert bone china. $47.—$55.

E2-024 - Bowl, Coronation. Footed. Color portrait with gold decoration on blue background. 5½"d. Aynsley BC. $145.—$165.

E2-027 - Bowl, Silver Jubilee. Color and gold decoration. 7¾"x6¾"x1¼". Coalport BC. $37.—$46.

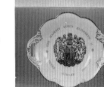

E2-030 - Bowl, Silver Wedding Anniversary. Black and gold decoration. LE 500. 10"d. Royal Worcester. $440.—$490.

E2-033 - Box, Coronation. Glass. Color portrait on lid. 3¼"d. 1½" deep. $32.—$38.

E2-034 - Box, Coronation. Plastic. Gold arms on red background. 3"d. 1½"deep. Wilmot Breeden Ltd. $19.—$24.

E2-035 - Box, Coronation. Sepia portrait. Color decoration. Gold trim. Pottery. 1¼"h. 3¼"d. Made in England. $34.—$39.

E2-036 - Box, Coronation. Color and gold decoration. Cream background. Pottery. 1½"h.x4"x3¼". Made in England. $27.—$31.

E2-037 - Box, Coronation. Purple and gold decoration. 3¾"h. 3¾"d. Wedgwood & Co. Ltd. $85.—$95.

E2-038 - Box, Coronation. Sepia portrait. Gold trim. Marbelized finish. 1"h. 5"d. No mark. $45.—$51.

E2-039 - Box, Coronation. Orb shape. Heavy embossed gold decoration. LE 600. 6"h. 4¼"d. Minton. $475.—$525.

E2-040 - Box, Coronation. Embossed gold on red, blue or aqua background. Orb shape. LE 50. 6"h. 4¼"d. Minton BC. $875.—$975.

E2-041 - Box, Coronation. Orb shape. Color and gold decoration. Pottery. 4¼"h. 4"d. Wedgwood & Co. Ltd. $90.—$100.

E2-042 - Box, Coronation. Raised design. Brass clad wood. 3½"h.x6"x3¼". $56.—$62.

E2-043 - Box, Coronation. White on light blue jasperware. 1½"h.x3½"x3". Wedgwood. $94.—$102. pair.

E2-044 - Box, St. Lawrence Seaway Opening 1959. Color and gold decoration on light blue. 5"d. 1½"deep. Paragon BC. $84.—$93.

E2-045 - Box, 60th Birthday. Color portrait of Queen on horseback. Commemoration around sides. 1¼"x4¼"x3". Aynsley. $55.—$63.

E2-046 - Box, 60th Birthday. Color portrait and decoration. Gold trim. 1¾"h. 3"d. Coalport bone china. $28.—$34.

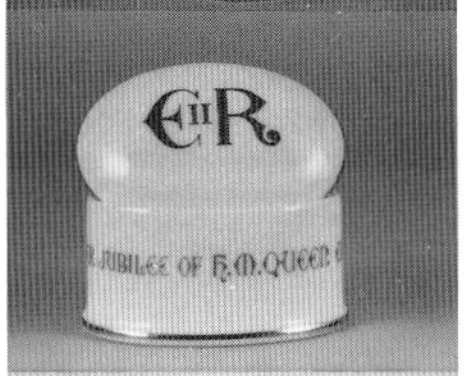

E2-047 - Box, Silver Jubilee. Silver cypher. Silver and color decoration. 2¼"x1¼". Crown Staffordshire bone china. $23.—$27.

E2-048 - Box, Silver Jubilee. Raised flowers. Silver and color decoration. 1½"h. 2"d. Crown Staffordshire BC. $24.—$28.

E2-049 - Box, Silver Jubilee. White on royal blue jasperware. 2"h.x2¾"x2¾". Wedgwood. $48.—$55.

E2-050 - Box, Silver Jubilee. White on royal blue jasperware. 1½"h. 4"d. Wedgwood. $67.—$73.

E2-051 - Box, Silver Jubilee. White on royal blue jasperware. Sterling Silver. LE 1000. 1½"d. 1"deep. Wedgwood. $205.—$225.

E2-052 - Box, Silver Jubilee. Color portrait on black background. 1¼"h. 2"d. Crown Staffordshire BC. $28.—$34.

E2-053 - Box, Silver Jubilee. Color and gold arms on lid. Commemoration around sides. 1¼"h. 4"d. Coalport BC. $42.—$48.

E2-054 - Box, Silver Jubilee. Pink and gold decoration. 1¾"h. 4"d. Coalport bone china. $64.—$70.

E2-055 - Box , Silver Jubilee. Color portrait on black. Silver trim. Color decoration. 5"x4"x2"deep. Crown Staffordshire BC. $41.—$48.

E2-056 - Box, Silver Jubilee. White on royal blue jasperware. 2"h.x5"x3¼". Wedgwood. $115.—$125. Pair.

E2-057 - Box, 25th Anniversary of Coronation. Red, beige and gold trim. 4¼"d. 1¼"deep. Coalport bone china. $48.—$52.

E2-058 - Box, 25th Anniversary of Coronation. Color decoration. 1¼"h. 4¼"d. Coalport bone china. $42.—$46.

E2-059 - Box, 25th Wedding Anniversary. Color decoration. Gold trim. Commemoration on base. 4"x3¾" x1½". Aynsley BC. $48.—$56.

E2-060 - Brooch, Coronation. Sepia portrait. Red, blue and gold decoration on white. 2"d. Coalport BC. $39.—$46.

E2-061 - Brooch, Coronation. Black and white portrait. Commemoration reverse. 2"x1½". Royal Worcester BC. $55.—$65.

E2-062 - Brooch, Coronation. Black and white portrait. Color decoration. Silver tone. 2½"x1¼". $27.—$31.

E2-063 - Brooch, Coronation. White cameo profiles. Gold tone. 1¼"x1". $31.—$36.

E2-064 - Brooch. Coronation . Color portrait with "jewels". Silver tone. 1½"x1". $20.—$25.

E2-065 - Brooch, Coronation. Color portrait. Gold tone frame. 2"x1¼". $24.—$28.

E2-066 - Brooch, Coronation. Red, blue and white "jewels" in gold tone setting. 1½"x1¾". $31.—$36.

E2-067 - Brooch, Coronation. Color portrait partially hand painted. Bone china in metal holder. 1½"d. $39.—$43.

E2-068 - Brooch, Wedding 1947. Raised framed portraits. Lions to sides. Date below. Silver tone. 2"x1½". On card. $60.—$66.

E2-069 - Bust, Coronation. Color. Silver "glitter" jewels in crown and necklace. 6½"h. "GL" on reverse. Felt base. $53.—$59.

E2-070 - Bust, Coronation and 1953 Bermuda Visit. White bisque head. Glazed light blue below. 5½"h. Foley BC. $94.—$102.

E2-071 - Bust, Coronation. White pottery. 7½"h. $37.—$42.

E2-072 - Bust, Coronation. Glazed white bone china. 5"h. 2¾" across at shoulders. $45.—$52.

E2-073 - Bust, Coronation. Light blue bone china. No mark. 6½"h. $47.—$55.

E2-074 - Bust, Coronation. White composition. 6¼"h. 3¾" across at shoulders. $48.—$55.

E2-075 - Bust, Coronation. White composition. 7"h. Marked GHQ, S. Guiterman & Co. $63.—$69. Pair.

E2-076 - Bust, 25th Wedding Anniversary. Black basalt. Each 11"h. Limited Edition of 750. Wedgwood. $485.—$535. Pair.

E2-077 - Calendar, Coronation. Days, date, months change. Color decoration. Plastic frame. 6¾"x4¾". $27.—$31.

E2-078 - Calendar, Silver Jubilee. Color portrait and flag. Shows month, day of week and date. Metal. 3"h. 2½"d. Felt base. $28.—$34.

E2-079 - Clock, Coronation. Color flags, cypher and crown. White metal case. Black wooden feet. 4¼"h.x6". Smiths. $85.—$95.

E2-080 - Clock, Coronation. Color portrait. "Elizabeth" and "EIIR" form numerals. 2¼"x2¼". Ingersoll Ltd. $87.—$98.

E2-081 - Coach, Coronation. Cardboard stand-up model with crowd in background. 7½"x15" $27.—$35.

E2-082 - Coach, Silver Jubilee. Modeled on State Coach built in 1762. 3"long 1½"h. Sterling Silver. Toye, Kenning & Spencer. $235.—$265.

E2-083 - Coach, Silver Jubilee. Gold tone coach. Red and white decoration. 12" long. Crescent Toy Co. $74.—$80.

E2-084 - Coach, Silver Jubilee. Gold tone metal. 4" long. Crescent Toy Co. $19.—$24.

E2-085 - Compact, Coronation. Color portrait and decoration. Gold tone background. 3½"d. $39.—$46.

E2-086 - Compact, Coronation. Color portrait. Gold tone finish. 3"x3¼". $45.—$52.

E2-087 - Compact, Coronation. Assorted decorations. $39.—$52. Each.

E2-088 - Compact, Wedding, 1947. Black and white portrait. Gold tone. 3"x3". $55.—$65.

E2-089 - Condiment Set, Coronation. Milk glass with metal stand. Color decoration. 6"h. 3¾" at base. $130.—$145.

E2-090 - Creamer and Sugar, Coronation. Sepia portrait. Color decoration. $56.—$61.

E2-091 - Creamer and Sugar, Coronation. Light blue on white queensware. Wedgwood. $95.—$105.

E2-092 - Creamer and Sugar, Coronation. Color portrait and decoration. Royal Stafford BC. $85.—$95.

E2-093 - Creamer and Sugar, Coronation. Sepia portrait. Color decoration. Gold bands. Pottery. $92.—$100.

E2-094 - Cup and Saucer, Coronation. Color portrait and decoration. Royal Stafford BC. Also made by Gladstone. $37.—$44.

E2-095 - Cup and Saucer, Coronation. Sepia portrait. Color decoration. Gold trim. Pottery. Alfred Meakin. $23.—$29.

E2-096 - Cup and Saucer, Coronation. Gold and color decoration. Phoenix bone china. $30.—$35.

E2-097 - Cup and Saucer, Coronation. Color decoration in Art Deco style. Gold trim. Foley BC. $58.—$66.

E2-098 - Cup and Saucer, Coronation. Sepia portrait. Color decoration. Gold handle and trim. Rosina bone china. $78.—$87.

E2-099 - Cup and Saucer, Coronation. Color decoration. Gold trim. Victoria bone china. $35.—$40.

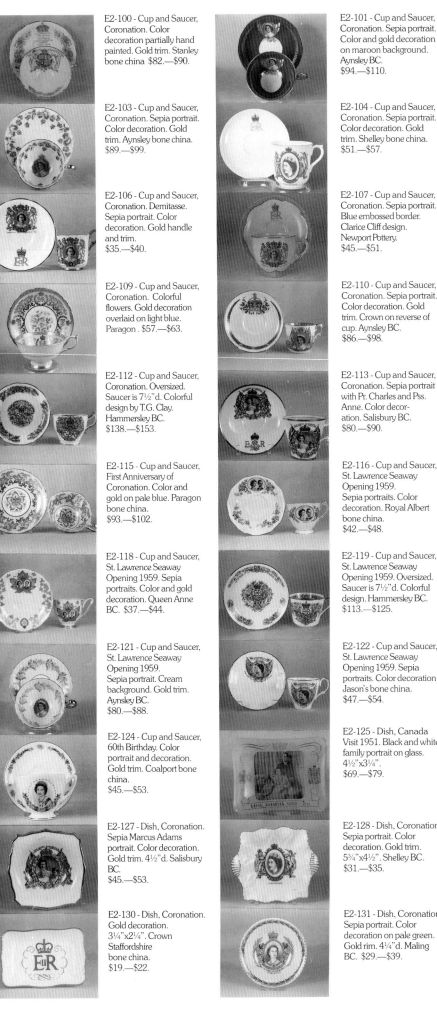

E2-100 - Cup and Saucer, Coronation. Color decoration partially hand painted. Gold trim. Stanley bone china $82.—$90.

E2-101 - Cup and Saucer, Coronation. Sepia portrait. Color and gold decoration on maroon background. Aynsley BC. $94.—$110.

E2-102 - Cup and Saucer, Coronation. Sepia portrait. Gold decoration on light green background. Aynsley bone china. $90.—$101.

E2-103 - Cup and Saucer, Coronation. Sepia portrait. Color decoration. Gold trim. Aynsley bone china. $89.—$99.

E2-104 - Cup and Saucer, Coronation. Sepia portrait. Color decoration. Gold trim. Shelley bone china. $51.—$57.

E2-105 - Cup and Saucer, Coronation. Sepia portraits. Color decoration. Gold trim. Hughes bone china. $30.—$37.

E2-106 - Cup and Saucer, Coronation. Demitasse. Sepia portrait. Color decoration. Gold handle and trim. $35.—$40.

E2-107 - Cup and Saucer, Coronation. Sepia portrait. Blue embossed border. Clarice Cliff design. Newport Pottery. $45.—$51.

E2-108 - Cup and Saucer, Coronation. Color decoration with gold trim. Paragon bone china. $50.—$55.

E2-109 - Cup and Saucer, Coronation. Colorful flowers. Gold decoration overlaid on light blue. Paragon . $57.—$63.

E2-110 - Cup and Saucer, Coronation. Sepia portrait. Color decoration. Gold trim. Crown on reverse of cup. Aynsley BC. $86.—$98.

E2-111 - Cup and Saucer, Coronation. Sepia portrait. Color decoration. Gold trim. Royal Stafford bone china. $48.—$54.

E2-112 - Cup and Saucer, Coronation. Oversized. Saucer is 7½"d. Colorful design by T.G. Clay. Hammersley BC. $138.—$153.

E2-113 - Cup and Saucer, Coronation. Sepia portrait with Pr. Charles and Pss. Anne. Color decoration. Salisbury BC. $80.—$90.

E2-114 - Cup and Saucer, Coronation. Sepia portrait. Color decoration. Gold Trim. Tuscan bone china. $61.—$69.

E2-115 - Cup and Saucer, First Anniversary of Coronation. Color and gold on pale blue. Paragon bone china. $93.—$102.

E2-116 - Cup and Saucer, St. Lawrence Seaway Opening 1959. Sepia portraits. Color decoration. Royal Albert bone china. $42.—$48.

E2-117 - Cup and Saucer, St. Lawrence Seaway Opening 1959. Color decoration. Gold overlay on pale blue border. Paragon bone china. $56.—$62.

E2-118 - Cup and Saucer, St. Lawrence Seaway Opening 1959. Sepia portraits. Color and gold decoration. Queen Anne BC. $37.—$44.

E2-119 - Cup and Saucer, St. Lawrence Seaway Opening 1959. Oversized. Saucer is 7½"d. Colorful design. Hammersley BC. $113.—$125.

E2-120 - Cup and Saucer, St. Lawrence Seaway Opening 1959. Sepia portrait. Color decoration. Gold trim. Tuscan bone china. $58.—$66.

E2-121 - Cup and Saucer, St. Lawrence Seaway Opening 1959. Sepia portrait. Cream background. Gold trim. Aynsley BC. $80.—$88.

E2-122 - Cup and Saucer, St. Lawrence Seaway Opening 1959. Sepia portraits. Color decoration. Jason's bone china. $47.—$54.

E2-123 - Cup and Saucer, Silver Jubilee. Black and white portrait. Color decoration. Gold trim. Liverpool Road BC. $36.—$40.

E2-124 - Cup and Saucer, 60th Birthday. Color portrait and decoration. Gold trim. Coalport bone china. $45.—$53.

E2-125 - Dish, Canada Visit 1951. Black and white family portrait on glass. 4½"x3¼". $69.—$79.

E2-126 - Dish, Canada Visit 1951. Color decoration. Gold trim. 4"d. Paragon BC. $46.—$52

E2-127 - Dish, Coronation. Sepia Marcus Adams portrait. Color decoration. Gold trim. 4½"d. Salisbury BC. $45.—$53.

E2-128 - Dish, Coronation. Sepia portrait. Color decoration. Gold trim. 5¾"x4½". Shelley BC. $31.—$35.

E2-129 - Dish, Coronation. Colorful decoration. Gold rim. 4¼"d. Hammersley bone china. $30.—$34.

E2-130 - Dish, Coronation. Gold decoration. 3¼"x2¼". Crown Staffordshire bone china. $19.—$22.

E2-131 - Dish, Coronation. Sepia portrait. Color decoration on pale green. Gold rim. 4¼"d. Maling BC. $29.—$39.

E2-132 - Dish, Coronation. Hand decorated in color. 4"d. 1"deep. Poole Pottery. $28.—$34.

E2-133 - Dish, Coronation. Sepia portrait and commemoration. Gold trim. 4"d. Tuscan BC. $32.—$36.

E2-134 - Dish, Coronation. Sepia portrait. Color decoration. 4"d. Royal Grafton bone china. $25.—$29.

E2-135 - Dish, Coronation. Sepia portrait. Color decoration. Gold rim. 4½"d. Shelley bone china. $29.—$34.

E2-136 - Dish, Coronation. Sepia portrait. Color decoration. Gold rim. 3¼"d. Coalport bone china. $29.—$34.

E2-137 - Dish, Coronation. Glass. Black and white portrait royal family in Clarence House garden. 4¾"x3½". $57.—$64.

E2-138 - Dish, Coronation. Color decoration on milk glass. Sterling silver rim. 4¼"d. $27.—$31.

E2-139 - Dish, Coronation. Sepia portrait. Color decoration. Gold rim. 5½"x5". Aynsley BC. $30.—$35.

E2-140 - Dish, Coronation. Gold and color decoration. Gold rim. 5"d. 1"deep. Adderley BC. $23.—$29.

E2-141 - Dish, Coronation. Color and gold decoration. Pale blue on border with gold rim. 4¼"d. Paragon bone china. $29.—$34.

E2-142 - Dish, Coronation. Sepia portrait on cream. Gold border. 4½"d. James Kent. $28.—$33.

E2-143 - Dish, Coronation. Sepia portrait and decoration. Gold trim. 5"x3". ¾" deep. Fotostile BC. $30.—$35.

E2-144 - Dish, Coronation. Glass. Black and white portrait. "Royal Souvenir" below. $40.—$46. 9¾"d. $19.—$23. 4½"d.

E2-145 - Dish, Coronation. Embossed gold on white. John Wadsworth design. 4½"d. Minton BC. $79.—$89.

E2-146 - Dish, Coronation. Sepia portrait on yellow background. Color decoration. Gold rim. 4"d. Rosina BC. $19.—$22.

E2-147 - Dish, Coronation. Cypher with crown above surrounded by animals. Wade pottery. 4½"d. $25.—$30.

E2-148 - Dish, Coronation. Sepia portrait. Color decoration. Gold trim. 5"d. Aynsley BC. $35.—$40.

E2-149 - Dish, Coronation. Commemorative coin in center. Sterling silver. 4½"d. $165.—$180.

E2-150 - Dish, Coronation. Color portrait and decoration on ivory ground. Gold trim. 4"x3". Royal Cr. Derby BC. $50.—$55.

E2-151 - Dish, Coronation. Color decoration partially hand painted. Gold rim. 4¾"d. Paragon bone china. $28.—$34.

E2-152 - Dish, Coronation. Black and white royal family portrait. Gold rim. 4½"d. Royal Standard bone china. $70.—$77.

E2-153 - Dish, Coronation. Milk glass. Color portrait or color coat of arms. 4"d. $12.—$15. Each.

E2-154 - Dish, Coronation. Glass. Black and white portrait of Queen on horseback. "A Royal Souvenir". 4½"d. $36.—$41.

E2-155 - Dish, 40th Wedding Anniversary. Color portrait and decoration. Gold rim. 4¼"d. Coalport BC. $25.—$28.

E2-156 - Dish, 40th Wedding Anniversary. Color flowers. Gold decoration. 4½"d. LE 1250. Royal Crown Derby bone china. $58.—$64.

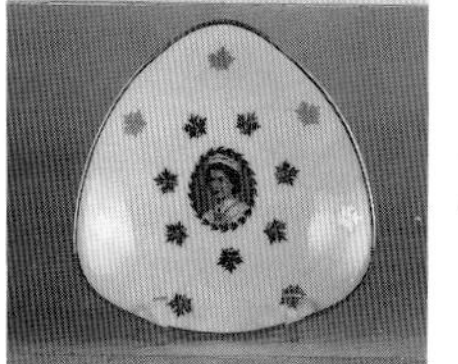

E2-157 - Dish, St. Lawrence Seaway Opening 1959. Sepia portrait. Gold decoration. 5½"x5¼". Aynsley bone china. $65.—$70.

E2-158 - Dish, St. Lawrence Seaway Opening 1959. Sepia portraits.. 4½"d. Shelley BC. $35.—$39.

E2-159 - Dish, St. Lawrence Seaway Opening 1959. Sepia portraits. Gold rim. 3½"d. Delphine BC. $26.—$30.

E2-160 - Dish, St. Lawrence Seaway Opening 1959. Sepia portrait. Color decoration. Gold rim. 4"d. Tuscan BC. $22.—$26.

E2-161 - Dish, St. Lawrence Seaway Opening 1959. Color decoration. 4½"d. Paragon BC. $29.—$33.

E2-162 - Dish, St. Lawrence Seaway Opening 1959. Sepia portrait. Color decoration. 5¼"d. Sandland Ware. $44.—$50.

E2-163 - Dish, Silver Jubilee. Color decoration. Brown glazed rim and back. 6¼"d. Hornsea Pottery. $12.—$16.

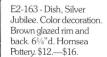

E2-164 - Dish, Silver Jubilee. Deep red decoration. 8¼"x1½"x½"deep. Hammersley BC. $22.—$26.

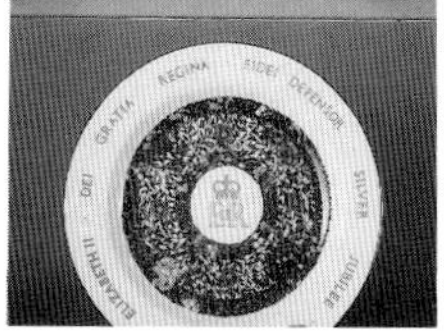

E2-165 - Dish, Silver Jubilee. Color decoration. Gold trim. 5¼"d. Crown Staffordshire bone china. $16.—$19.

E2-166 - Dish, Silver Jubilee. Black and white portrait. Color decoration. 4½"d. No mark. $10.—$13.

E2-167 - Dish, Silver Jubilee. White on royal blue jasperware. 4¼"d. Wedgwood $33.—$38.

E2-168 - Dish, Silver Jubilee. Color portrait . Color decoration. Silver rim. 4"d. Crown Staffordshire BC. $22.—$27.

E2-169 - Dish, Silver Jubilee. Gold decoration in center. Royal blue border. 4¼"d. Wedgwood bone china. $17.—$22.

E2-170 - Dish, Silver Jubilee. Black and white portrait. Color decoration. 8¼"x2¼"x1"deep. $22.—$28.

E2-171 - Dish, 60th Birthday. Color portrait and decoration. Gold rim. 4¼"d. Coalport BC. $16.—$20.

E2-172 - Dish, 30th Anniversary of Coronation. Color portrait and decoration. 4"d. Caverswall BC. $19.—$24.

E2-173 - Dish, 25th Anniversary of Coronation. Colorful decoration. Gold rim. 4"d. Coalport BC. $23.—$28.

E2-174 - Dish, 25th Wedding Anniversary. White on pale blue jasperware. 4½"d. Wedgwood. $36.—$41.

E2-175 - Egg Cup, Coronation. Color design on milk glass. 2"h. $22.—$26.

E2-176 - Egg Cup, "EIIR". Blue on white. "1958" on base. 1¾"h. Crown Staffordshire. $26.—$32.

E2-177 - Egg Cup, Silver Jubilee. Black and white portrait. Gold Jubilee emblem on reverse. 1¾"h. Panorama. $25.—$29.

E2-178 - Egg Cup, 60th Birthday. Color portrait. Gold trim. 2"h. Coronet BC. $15.—$19.

E2-179 - Fabric, Coronation. Hand embroidered linen. Colorful decoration. 16¼"x11". $54.—$60.

E 2-180 - Fabric, Coronation. Color decoration on beige background. 12"x19". $47.—$55.

E2-181 - Figurine, Coronation. Hand painted metal. 3"h. $39.—$46.

E2-182 - Figurine, No commemoration. Hand painted metal. 3¼"h. Britains. $43.—$50.

E2-183 - Figurine, No commemoration. Queen in white gown. Duke in black formal suit. 3½"x3" base, 4"h. Plastic. Dapol. $35.—$40.

E2-184 - Film Strip, "Coronation of Queen Elizabeth II." Two black and white strips with viewer. Boxed. $47.—$55.

E2-185 - Film Strip, Wedding 1947. Black and white. Contains over 55 positive images. Photo-Union Ltd. $51.—$59.

E2-186 - Goblet, Silver Jubilee. White on lilac jasperware medallion. Amethyst glass. 5"h. 4"d. Wedgwood. $225.—$240.

E2-187 - Goblet, Silver Jubilee. Blue on white. Silver trim. 4½"h. 4"d. at top. Coalport BC. $84.—$90.

E2-188 - Goblet, Silver Jubilee. Shades of blue, cream and gold. LE 2000. 4½"h. Coalport bone china. $94.—$103.

E2-189 - Goblet, 25th Anniversary of Coronation. Gold on cobalt blue. LE 2000 each numbered. Coalport bone china. $110.—$120.

E2-190 - Goblet, 25th Wedding Anniversary 1972. White on light blue medallion. Blue glass. White stem. 5¼"h. Wedgwood. $185.—$205.

E2-191 - Handkerchief, Coronation. Color decoration. Red band around border. 12"square. Rayon. $20.—$25.

E2-192 - Handkerchief, Coronation. Colorful Commonwealth flags. Red border. 9½"square. Cotton. $15.—$20.

E2-193 - Handkerchief, Coronation. Color decoration. Pale green border. 11"square. Rayon. $20.—$25.

E2-194 - Handkerchief, Coronation. Black and white portrait. Color decoration. 13" square. Rayon. $22.—$28.

E2-195 - Handkerchief, Coronation. Color decoration. Flags and London scenes. 11"square. Rayon. $16.—$20.

E2-196 - Handkerchief, Coronation. Color decoration. Flags and royal residences. 12"square. Rayon. $15.—$19.

E2-197 - Handkerchief, Coronation. Colorful design. Flags and royal residences. 12"square. Rayon. $16.—$20.

E2-198 - Humidor, Coronation. Raised profile portrait. Brass clad wood. 5¼"h. 3½"d. $51.—$57.

E2-199 - Humidor, Coronation. Profile on front with quote from Coronation address. Chrome. 6¼"h. 4"d.
$47.—$55.

E2-200 - Humidor, Coronation. Crown with commemoration below. Thistle finial. Copper. 5¼"h.
$47.—$54.

E2-201 - Ingot, Silver Jubilee. Sterling silver. 1½"x3½". Weighs approximately 3½ ounces. Danbury Mint London.
$140.—$155.

E2-202 - Ingot, 25th Anniversary of Coronation. Sterling silver replica of 9p stamp. 2½"x1¼". Danbury Mint, London.
$115.—$125.

E2-203 - Jar, Coronation. Color decoration from original drawing by Cutts c. 1840. 6½"h. Royal Doulton.
$58.—$66.

E2-204 - Jar, Coronation. Raised design. Aqua/green color. Cypher, crown on reverse. 5"h. 3¼"d. Pottery.
$61.—$68.

E2-205 - Jar, Coronation. Purple and gold crown. Gold decoration. 3¾"h. Pottery. Wedgwood & Co. Ltd.
$62.—$70.

E2-206 - Jar, Coronation. White on royal blue jasperware. Duke of Edinburgh on reverse. 4"h. Wedgwood.
$143.—$152.

E2-207 - Jar, No commemoration. Glass. Blue and white decoration. 4¾"h. 3"d. at base.
$21.—$26.

E2-208 - Jar, Silver Jubilee. White on royal blue jasperware. Duke of Edinburgh on reverse. Arms on lid. 4"h. 3¼"d. Wedgwood. $118.—$129.

E2-209 - Jar, Silver Jubilee. Portland blue on light blue jasperware. Duke of Edinburgh on reverse. 4"h. 3¼"d. Wedgwood.
$190.—$205.

E2-210 - Jar, Silver Jubilee. White profile portraits on red background. Colorful national flowers. 4½"h. Mason's. $38.—$47.

E2-211 - Jigsaw Puzzle, Coronation. Color portraits. Over 200 pieces. 13"x9½". Tower Press.
$53.—$60.

E2-212 - Jigsaw Puzzle, Coronation. Color portraits in coronation robes. Wooden pieces. 14"x9½".
$94.—$103.

E2-213 - Jigsaw Puzzle, Coronation. Color Dorothy Wilding portrait. 250 plywood pieces. 14½"x11¾". Academy.
$90.—$100.

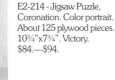

E2-214 - Jigsaw Puzzle, Coronation. Color portrait. About 125 plywood pieces. 10¾"x7¾". Victory.
$84.—$94.

E2-215 - Jigsaw Puzzle, Coronation. Color portrait. About 160 wooden pieces. 12"x9¼". Kolorbax.
$80.—$90.

E2-216 - Jigsaw Puzzle, Coronation. Scenes from Queen's life around border. Over 500 pieces. 20"d. Waddington's.
$92.—$100.

E2-217 - Jigsaw Puzzle, No commemoration. 125 color pieces. 11¾"x9". Waddington's.
$29.—$33.

E2-218 - Jigsaw Puzzle, No commemoration. 250 cardboard pieces. Color. Waddington's.
$32.—$36.

E2-219 - Jigsaw Puzzle, No commemoration. Color portrait. Over 250 cardboard pieces. 14"x9½". Tower Press.
$39.—$45.

E2-220 - Jigsaw Puzzle, No commemoration. About 75 plywood pieces. 7¾"x5¾". Victory.
$50.—$60.

E2-221 - Jigsaw Puzzle, Silver Jubilee. Double sided. 500 cardboard pieces. 20"x15". Philmar.
$32.—$39.

E2-222 - Jigsaw Puzzle, Silver Jubilee. Color royal family portrait. 500 cardboard pieces. 14"x19" Hestair.
$30.—$35.

E2-223 - Jigsaw Puzzle, 60th Birthday. Color portrait by Karsh. 500 cardboard pieces. 20"x13¼".
$32.—$38.

E2-224 - Jug, Coronation. Sepia portrait. Gold trim. Miniature. 2¼"h. 3¼" across.
$26.—$30.

E2-225 - Jug, Coronation. Sepia portrait. Color decoration. Gold on blue stripes. 4¾"h. 6" across. Ringtons.
$71.—$77.

E2-226 - Jug, Coronation. Sepia portrait. Color decoration. Cypher and crown on reverse. 3½"h. 4¼" across.
$37.—$42.

E2-227 - Jug, Coronation. Raised portrait in wreath with crown above. Green. 7½"h. 5¾" across. Delcroft Pottery.
$55.—$62.

E2-228 - Jug, Coronation. Color embossed decoration. Westminster Abbey on reverse. 8¼"h. 7½" across. Burleigh Ware. $235.—$260.

E2-229 - Jug, Coronation. Black on white. Mask spout. Royal Worcester BC.
$100.—$110. 4½"h.
$90.—$100. 4"h.

E2-230 - Jug, Coronation. Raised beige design on brown. 4"h. Dartmouth Pottery, Devon.
$35.—$39.

E2-231 - Jug, Coronation. Color decoration. Story of Great Gothic Chair on bottom. $6¼"h. Burleighware.
$178.—$205.

E2-232 - Jug, Coronation. Brown tone portrait. Color flags. 6¼"h. 6½"across. Royal Doulton. $160.—$175.

E2-233 - Jug, Coronation. Flower and crown atop handle. Hand painted. 7¼"h. Burleighware. $760.—$790.

E2-234 - Jug, Coronation. Raised portraits. Prince Philip on reverse. Beige. 2¼"h. 3¼"across. Pottery. $30.—$35.

E2-235 - Jug, Silver Jubilee. White and light blue coronation scene. Silver trim. 8½"h. 7½"across. Burleighware. $190.—$220.

E2-236 - Letter Opener, Silver Jubilee. Royal arms and commemoration on reverse. Sterling silver. 6¼"long. $88.—$99.

E2-237 - Lighter, Coronation. White on light blue jasperware. 2½"h. 2"d. Wedgwood. $61.—$69.

E2-238 - Lighter, Coronation. White on light blue jasperware. 3"h. 2"d. Wedgwood. $81.—$89.

E2-239 - Lighter, Silver Jubilee. White on light blue jasperware. 2½"h. 3½"d. Wedgwood (Ronson lighter). $60.—$67.

E2-240 - Lighter, Silver Jubilee. White on royal blue jasperware. 3¼"h. Wedgwood. $119.—$127.

E2-241 - Loving Cup, Coronation. Black and white decoration. Puce trim. 5½"h. Made for Courage & Co. by Royal Doulton. $180.—$200.

E2-242 - Loving Cup, Coronation. Color decoration. Gold trim. 3¾"h. Brentleigh. $30.—$37.

E2-243 - Loving Cup, Coronation. Color decoration with gold highlights. 4"h. 6½"across. Foley BC. $102.—$119.

E2-244 - Loving Cup, Coronation. Gold decoration on pale green. Embossed gold commemorative band. 4"h. LE 250. Minton. $305.—$335.

E2-245 - Loving Cup, Silver Jubilee. Color and gold decoration. Drury Lane Theater on reverse. 4"h. LE 1000. Coalport BC. $90.—$100.

E2-246 - Loving Cup, Silver Jubilee. Black and white portrait. Color decoration. 3½"h. 5½"across. Crown Mark. $41.—$48.

E2-247 - Loving Cup, Silver Jubilee. White on royal blue jasperware. Gold inscription. LE 500. 5"h. 8"across. Wedgwood. $180.—$205.

E2-248 - Loving Cup, Silver Jubilee. British Kings and Queens on reverse. Gold decoration. 3¼"h. 5½"across. Aynsley BC. $55.—$60.

E2-249 - Loving Cup, Silver Wedding Anniversary. Color decoration. Silver lions and trim. 3"h. 5¼"across. Paragon BC. $152.—$168.

E2-250 - Loving Cup, 60th Birthday. Color portrait. Gold trim. 3"h. 4¼"across. Fenton bone china. $40.—$46.

E2-251 - Loving Cup, 60th Birthday. Color portraits. Gold trim. Commemoration reverse. 3"h. 4½"across. Coronet BC. $41.—$47.

E2-252 - Loving Cup, 30th Anniversary of Coronation. Color coronation scene. 3½"h. 5½"across. Caverswall BC. $47.—$55.

E2-253 - Loving Cup, 25th Anniversary of Coronation. Color decoration. Gold lions and trim. 3¼"h. 5"across. Paragon BC. $82.—$89.

E2-254 - Luncheon Cloth, Coronation. Red and blue on white. Princes Charles and Philip above. 33" square. Cotton. $52.—$59.

E2-255 - Luncheon Cloth, Coronation. Hand embroidered color decoration. Hemstitched border. Linen. 34"x34". $70.—$80.

E2-256 - Magazine, The Illustrated London News. Coronation Number, 1953. 15 color plates. 14½"x10¼". $47.—$58.

E2-257 - Matchbook Cover, Coronation. Red and blue enamel on white metal. 2¼"x1½". Chrome finish. $19.—$25.

E2-258 - Match Holder, Coronation. Crystal. Etched "EIIR" and "1953" below crown. 3"h. Webb England. $87.—$98.

E2-259 - Money Box, Coronation. Printed design on gold background. 5"d. 1¼"deep. Puck. $30.—$35.

E2-260 - Money Box, Coronation. Red and gold. Commemoration in raised letters around base. 3¼"h. 2¾"across base. $52.—$59.

E2-261 - Money Box, Silver Jubilee. Color portraits and decoration. Gold trim. Color crown and "1977 Jubilee". 3"x3"x3". $35.—$40.

E2-262 - Money Box, Silver Jubilee. Color decoration on red background. Metal. 4½"h. 2½"d. $13.—$17.

E2-263 - Money Box, Silver Jubilee. Red and blue decoration. 3"h.x3½". Adams. $35.—$44.

E2-264 - Mug, Canada Visit 1959. Sepia portraits. Color decoration. Gold trim. 3"h. Shelley BC. $42.—$48.

E2-265 - Mug, Canada Visit 1957. Color decoration. Gold trim. Partially hand painted. Color flowers inside. 3"h. Hammersley BC. $157.—$170.

E2-266 - Mug, China Visit 1986. Color portraits and decoration. Gold trim. 3½"h. LE 250. Dorin-court BC. $43.—$49.

E2-267 - Mug, Coronation. Sepia portrait. Color decoration. Pottery. 3½"h. Wacol. $15.—$19.

E2-268 - Mug, Coronation. Sepia M. Adams portrait. Color decoration. 3"h. Salisbury BC. $72.—$80. $57.—$62. in pottery.

E2-269 - Mug, Coronation. Brown portrait. Color and gold decoration. Pottery. 4"h. $29.—$34.

E2-270 - Mug, Coronation. Color decoration. Eric Ravilious design. 4¼"h. 4¼"d. Wedgwood. $164.—$173.

E2-271 - Mug, Coronation. Color decoration. Gold trim. Floral band inside rim. 3¼"h. Hammersley BC. $68.—$73.

E2-272 - Mug, Coronation. Color portrait and decoration. Gold trim. 3"h. Royal Winton. $25.—$30.

E2-273 - Mug, Coronation. Sepia Portrait. Color decoration. Cypher and crown reverse. 3"h. Shelley BC. $39.—$48.

E2-274 - Mug, Coronation. Pewter. Profile and commemorative medallion. Handle opposite. 2½"h. Spelman. $36.—$41.

E2-275 - Mug, Coronation. Pewter. Glass bottom has Queen's profile, commemoration. 4"h. $50.—$56.

E2-276 - Mug, Coronation. Sepia portrait. Color decoration. Black handle and rim. Enamel on tin. 3"h. $54.—$60.

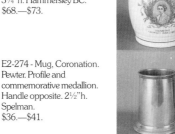

E2-277 - Mug, Coronation. Raised profile portrait. Cypher and wreathed crown on reverse. 3"h. Melba Ware by Wain. $41.—$47.

E2-278 - Mug, Coronation. Color decoration partially hand painted. Gold trim. 3"h. Hammersley BC. $50.—$56.

E2-279 - Mug, Coronation. Musical. Raised design. Plays "Here's a Health Unto Her Majesty". 5¾"h. Royal Winton. $130.—$145.

E2-280 - Mug, Coronation. Color decoration. Gold trim and handle. 4"h. Stanley BC. $87.—$96.

E2-281 - Mug, Coronation. Brown, pink and gold decoration by Richard Guyatt. 4"h. 4"d. Wedgwood. $175.—$190.

E2-282 - Mug, Coronation. Color and gold decoration. Gold trim. 4"h. Minton BC. $70.—$78.

E2-283 - Mug, Coronation. Sepia portrait. Color and gold decoration. Lion handle. 4"h. 3¼"d. $38.—$43.

E2-284 - Mug, Coronation. Sepia portrait. Color decoration. Gold trim. 4¼"h. 3"d. at top. Royal Albert BC. $36.—$41.

E2-285 - Mug, Coronation. Musical. Color and gold. Plays "Here's a Health Unto Her Majesty." 5¼"h. Crown Devon. $140.—$155.

E2-286 - Mug, Coronation. Color decoration. Gold trim. 3¼"h. 3"d. Foley bone china. $65.—$72.

E2-287 - Mug, Coronation. Embossed gold on pale green. John Wadsworth design. 4"h. Minton bone china. $235.—$255.

E2-288 - Mug, Coronation. Sepia portrait. Color decoration. 3¼"h. 3"d. Copeland Spode. $44.—$49.

E2-289 - Mug, Coronation. Sepia portrait. Color and gold decoration. Pottery. 4¾"h. Arthur Wood. $48.—$55.

E2-290 - Mug, Coronation. Sepia Portrait. Color decoration. 3¼"h. Royal Doulton. $60.—$67.

E2-291 - Mug, Coronation. Sepia portrait. Color decoration. Gold "E" handle. 3½"h. Royal Doulton BC. $86.—$93.

E2-292 - Mug, Coronation. Gold and color decoration. Gold lion handle. 3"h. 2¾"d. at top. Paragon BC. $82.—$88.

E2-293 - Mug, Coronation. Gold and color decoration. Also for Bermuda Visit 1953. 2¾"h. Crown Staffordshire BC. $59.—$66.

E2-294 - Mug, Coronation. Sepia portrait. Color decoration. Gold trim. 3½"h. Tuscan BC. $59.—$67.

E2-295 - Mug, Coronation. Color portrait and decoration. Gold trim. 4"h. Gladstone BC. $57.—$63.

E2-296 - Mug, Coronation. Color and gold decoration. Gold trim. 3½"h. Crown Staffordshire BC. $44.—$50.

E2-297 - Mug, Coronation. Brown tone portrait. Color decoration on pale green. Gold trim. 3¼"h. Aynsley BC. $90.—$99.

E2-298 - Mug, 40th Wedding Anniversary. Gold silhouettes. Colorful decoration includes ruby red. 3½"h. Caverswall BC. $42.—$48.

E2-299 - Mug, 40th Wedding Anniversary. Color portrait and flowers. 3"h. Coalport bone china. $45.—$50.

E2-300 - Mug. No commemoration. Miniature. Sepia Portraits. Gold trim. 2"h. Coronet BC. $27.—$33. Pair.

E2-301 - Mug, Silver Jubilee. Buckingham Palace in black on white. Handle opposite. 4½"h. Chiswick Ceramics. $41.—$46.

E2-302 - Mug, Silver Jubilee. Color portrait and decoration. Silver trim. 4½"h. Crown Staffordshire bone china. $37.—$42.

E2-303 - Mug, Silver Jubilee. Sepia Portrait. Color decoration. 4¼"h. Ovaltine Pottery, Devon. $30.—$34.

E2-304 - Mug, Silver Jubilee. Gold cypher on deep red. Gold and deep red crown. 3½"h. Royal Grafton bone china. $19.—$23.

E2-305 - Mug, Silver Jubilee. Army Review at Sennelager, Germany 7.7.77. Color portrait. 4¾"h. LE 15,000. Wedgwood. $62.—$67.

E2-306 - Mug, Silver Jubilee. Color and gold decoration. Cypher, crown and "Silver Jubilee" on reverse. 4"h. Spode. $72.—$79.

E2-307 - Mug, Silver Jubilee. Black on ivory. Snowdon portrait and design. 4¾"h. 3½"d. Wedgwood. $50.—56

E2-308 - Mug, Silver Jubilee. Silver on white. Duke of Edinburgh on reverse. 3¾"h. Kiln Craft pottery. $17.—$20.

E2-309 - Mug, Silver Jubilee. Color decoration. Silver trim. 3"h. 3"d. Burleigh pottery. $26.—$30.

E2-310 - Mug, Silver Jubilee. Gold and black on white queensware. Richard Guyatt design. 4"h. 4"d. Wedgwood. $60.—$67.

E2-311 - Mug, Silver Jubilee. Gold on white. Commemoration on reverse. 4"h. Royal Doulton BC. $54.—$59.

E2-312 - Mug, Silver Jubilee. Miniature. Gold and color decoration on glass. 2½"h. 2"d. $10.—$13.

E2-313 - Mug, Silver Jubilee. Queen on horseback on reverse. Red and blue on white. 3½"h. $34.—$38.

E2-314 - Mug, Silver Jubilee. Color decoration. 4"h. J&J May. Bone china. $54.—$59.

E2-315 - Mug, Silver Jubilee. Design etched on purple glass. Clear handle. 4¼"h. 3¾"d. Wedgwood. $57.—$63.

E2-316 - Mug, Silver Jubilee. White on royal blue medallion. Amethyst glass body. Clear handle. 4"h. 4"d. Wedgwood. $130.—$145.

E2-317 - Mug, Silver Jubilee. Color decoration. Silver trim. Floral band around mug. 3¼"h. 3¼"d. Crown Staffordshire. $25.—$30.

E2-318 - Mug, Silver Jubilee. Gold and color decoration. 4¼"h. 3"d. at top. $55.—$65.

E2-319 - Mug, Silver Jubilee. Color decoration. Gold trim. British Kings and Queens reverse. 3¼"h. Aynsley bone china. $36.—$41.

E2-320 - Mug, Silver Jubilee. Red and blue decoration on white background. Handle opposite. 3½"h. Adams Ironstone. $23.—$27.

E2-321 - Mug, Silver Jubilee. Blue silhouette. Color decoration. Duke of Edinburgh on reverse. 4¾"h. Wedgwood. $25.—$32.

E2-322 - Mug, Silver Wedding Anniversary 1972. Purple on white decoration. 3¼"h. 3"d. Pottery. $48.—$52.

E2-323 - Mug, Silver Wedding Anniversary. Color decoration. Gold trim. 3½"h. Aynsley bone china. $53.—$58.

E2-324 - Mug, Silver Wedding Anniversary. Gold and white on black design by Richard Guyatt. 4¼"h. 4¼"d. Wedgwood. $68.—$75.

E2-325 - Mug, Silver Wedding Anniversary. Gold silhouette portraits. Gold decoration. 4¼"h. 3¼"d. Crown Staffordshire. $46.—$51.

E2-326 - Mug, Silver Wedding Anniversary. Black, gold, silver and white on drabware. Richard Guyatt design. 4¼"h. Wedgwood. $59.—$65.

E2-327 - Mug, 60th Birthday. Color portrait and decoration. Gold trim. 3½"h. Coronet BC. $20.—$24.

E2-328 - Mug, 60th Birthday. Color and gold decoration. Gold trim. Richard Guyatt design. LE 500. 4¼"h. 4¼"d. Wedgwood. $235.—$250.

E2-329 - Mug, 60th Birthday. Color portrait and decoration. Gold trim. 3"h. 3¼"d. at base. Coalport bone china. $39.—$43.

E2-330 - Mug, 60th Birthday. Color decoration. Gold trim. 3½"h. Aynsley bone china. $49.—$53.

E2-331 - Mug, Tonga Visit 1977. Sepia portraits. Color decoration. Gold trim. 4"h. Mercian BC. $67.—$72.

E2-332 - Mug, 25th Anniversary of Coronation. Color decoration. Silver trim. 4¾"h. Crown Staffordshire bone china. $25.—$30.

E2-333 - Mug, 25th Anniversary of Coronation. Color decoration. Gold trim. 3"h. Coalport bone china. $47.—$53.

E2-334 - Mug, 25th Anniversary of Coronation. Blue and gold design by R. Guyatt. LE 5000. 4¼"h. 4¼"d. Wedgwood. $94.—$100.

E2-335 - Mug, 25th Anniversary of Coronation. Orange and blue decoration. 3½"h. Adams Ironstone. $25.—$29.

E2-336 - Mug, 25th Anniversary of Coronation. Color decoration. Gold trim. 3"h. LE 2500. Coalport bone china. $48.—$53.

E2-337 - Needles, Coronation. Six cloth pages of needles in book. Color portrait. 5"x3". A. Shrimpton & Sons. $17.—$20.

E2-338 - Needles, Coronation. Color portraits. Purple and gold decoration. 25 needles. 5¾"x4½". Milward & Sons. $17.—$20.

E2-339 - Paperweight, Coronation. Color decoration. Gold felt backing. 3½"d. $29.—$34.

E2-340 - Paperweight, Silver Jubilee. Color canes on purple background. 1¾"h. 3"d. Whitefriars. $410.—$440.

E2-341 - Paperweight, Silver Jubilee. "1952 - EIIR - 1977" seen in side windows. Deep blue background. LE 1500. Whitefriars. $420.—$445.

E2-342 - Paperweight, Silver Jubilee. White profile on royal blue jasperware. Etched "1977" and stars. 2½"h. 3"d. Wedgwood. $110.—$117.

E2-343 - Paperweight, Silver Jubilee. White profile. Color canes on lavender background. LE 500. 2¼"h. 3¼"d. Baccarat. $505.—$540.

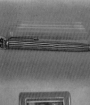

E2-344 - Pencil, Coronation. Red, white and blue stripes. Color crown with "jewels". 4¼"long. $27.—$32.

E2-345 - Pendant, No commemoration. Gold tone pendant and chain. One penny coin 2"d. $22.—$25.

E2-346 - Picture, Coronation. Color portrait in wooden ship's wheel. Inner frame and spokes are brass. 3¼"d. $19.—$23.

E2-347 - Picture, Coronation. Color pictures on paper tape roll past viewer. Green plastic case. 3½"x2½"x1". Logga. $20.—$25.

E2-348 - Picture, Coronation. Color portraits in butterfly design brass frames. Portraits 3½"d. Frames 6"d. $22.—$26.

E2-349 - Picture, Coronation. Color portraits 4¼"d. 6¼"d. Wooden backs with hangers. $25.—$29.

E2-350 - Pin Cushion, Silver Jubilee. Red velvet with silver tone crown. 3½"h. 3"d. $71.—$76.

E2-351 - Plaque, Coronation. Stand alone. Sepia portrait. Gold rim. Commemoration on reverse. 3½"x2¾". Tuscan BC. $40.—$45.

E2-352 - Plaque, Coronation. Brass. Raised design. "Elizabeth Regina June 1953" beneath profile. 8"d. $26.—$30.

E2-353 - Plaque, Coronation. White on basalt. Gold commemoration on reverse. 4¼"x3¼". Wedgwood. $185.—$200.

E2-354 - Plaque, No commemoration. White profile on dark blue velvet. Profile is 4"x2". Background is 6½"x4¼". $55.—$60.

E2-355 - Plaque, Silver Jubilee. Silver tone. 8½"d. Commemoration on front. Hand made by Marcus Designs. $110.—$120.

E2-356 - Plaque, Silver Jubilee. Black, grey and gold decoration. S.A. Arnold design. 5¾"x4¾". Coalport bone china. $41.—$46.

E2-357 - Plaque, Silver Jubilee. Black and white portrait on framed ceramic plaque. 4¼"x3½". Staffordshire Ceramics. $30.—$35.

E2-358 - Plaque, Silver Jubilee. Sterling silver plaque with Wedgwood medallions on each side. Frame is 4¼"x7¼". $170.—$185.

E2-359 - Plaque, Silver Jubilee. Black and white portrait. Silver plate on copper holder. 5"d. overall. $36.—$40.

E2-360 - Plaque, Silver Jubilee. White on light blue framed in portland blue jasperware. Each 4½"x4". In case. Wedgwood. $235.—$250. Pair.

E2-361 - Plaque, Silver Wedding Anniversary. Black basalt. 4¼"x3¼". Wedgwood. $125.—$140.

E2-362 - Plaque, Silver Wedding Anniversary. White on pale blue jasperware. 4¼"x3". In presentation box. Wedgwood. $115.—$125.

E2-363 - Plate, Canada Confederation. Sepia Portrait and decoration. Clarice Cliff design. 10½"d. Royal Staffordshire. $45.—$51.

E2-364 - Plate, Canada Visit 1951. Deep red on white. Gold trim. 9"d. Cassidian. $50.—$55.

E2-365 - Plate, Coronation. Color portrait. Lavish gold overlaid on deep red border. 10¼"d. Aynsley bone china. $340.—$355.

E2-366 - Plate, Coronation. Color portrait. Gold on cobalt blue border. 10¼"d. Aynsley bonechina. $280.—$310.

E2-367 - Plate, Coronation. Sepia portrait. Gold overlaid on cobalt blue border. 10"d. Crown Ducal. $51.—$55.

E2-368 - Plate, Coronation. Metal. Color portraits and decoration. 10"d. Portland Ware by Metal Box Co. $38.—$44. Pair.

E2-369 - Plate, Coronation. Sepia portrait. Color decoration. Gold rim. 8"d. Tuscan bone china. $69.—$75.

E2-370 - Plate, Coronation. Color decoration partially hand painted. Gold trim. 10½"d. Paragon bone china. $245.—$260.

E2-371 - Plate, Coronation. Sepia portrait. Color decoration. Clarice Cliff design. 6½"d. Newport Pottery. $26.—$31.

E2-372 - Plate, Coronation. Sepia portrait. Color decoration. Gold rim. 8½"d. Alfred Meakin. $23.—$28.

E2-373 - Plate, Coronation. Sepia portrait. Color decoration. Gold trim. Embossed rim. 9"d. Weatherby. $43.—$50.

E2-374 - Plate, Coronation. Black and white portrait. Color decoration. Gold overlay design around border. 7"d. Victoria. $28.—$33.

E2-375 - Plate, Coronation. Sepia portrait Queen with Pr. Charles and Pss. Anne. 6½" d. Salisbury BC. $51.—$58.

E2-376 - Plate, Coronation. Metal. Color portrait and decoration. Gold trim. 10"d. Metal Box Co. $21.—$26.

E2-377 - Plate, Coronation. Sepia portrait. Color decoration. Gold trim. 10¼"x9". Aynsley bone china. $92.—$98.

E2-378 - Plate, Coronation. Sepia portrait. Color decoration. Gold rim. 6"d. Aynsley BC. $37.—$42.

E2-379 - Plate, Coronation. Sepia portrait. Color and gold decoration. Gold on deep red border. 8¼"d. Coalport BC. $120.—$130.

E2-380 - Plate, Coronation. Sepia portrait. Official design. Color decoration. Gold rim. 7½"d. Johnson Bros. $23.—$27.

E2-381 - Plate, Coronation. Color decoration. Gold rim. 6¼"d. Foley bone china. $37.—$41.

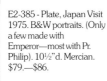

E2-382 - Plate, Coronation. Color portrait and decoration. Gold trim. 11"x 9¾". Royal Winton. $27.—$31.

E2-383 - Plate, Coronation. Sepia portrait. Color decoration. Blue bands around portrait. 9¾"d. Burleigh. $23.—$27.

E2-384 - Plate, 40th Wedding Anniversary. Gold silhouettes and rim. Color decoration includes ruby red. 8½"d. Caverswall BC. $49.—$55.

E2-385 - Plate, Japan Visit 1975. B&W portraits. (Only a few made with Emperor—most with Pr. Philip). 10½"d. Mercian. $79.—$86.

E2-386 - Plate, No commemoration. Color portrait. Gold rim. 8½"d. Alfred Meakin. $30.—$34.

E2-387 - Plate, St. Lawrence Seaway Opening 1959. Sepia portraits. President Eisenhower below. 10"d. Alfred Meakin. $46.—$51.

E2-388 - Plate, Silver Jubilee. Queen's Beasts in color and gold around border. LE 1000 numbered. 10¼"d. Minton BC. $295.—$310.

E2-389 - Plate, Silver Jubilee. Blue on white jasperware. 8"d. Wedgwood. $56.—$61.

E2-390 - Plate, Silver Jubilee. Color and gold decoration. Blue bands. Silver rim. 8"d. Elizabethan BC. $37.—$41.

E2-391 - Plate, Silver Jubilee. Color portrait on black. Gold rim. J.A. Bailey design. 7¼" d. Crown Staffordshire BC. $51.—$57.

E2-392 - Plate, Silver Jubilee. Color decoration with silver trim. 9¾" d. Wood & Sons. $23.—$26.

E2-393 - Plate, Silver Jubilee. White on light blue jasperware. 8"d. Wedgwood. $50.—$55.

E2-394 - Plate, Silver Jubilee. Black, grey and gold silhouette. Color and gold decoration. LE 1000. 10½"d. Coalport BC. $115.—$125.

E2-395 - Plate, Silver Jubilee. Color and gold decoration. Embossed gold border. 8"d. LE 2000. Coalport bone china. $68.—$75.

E2-396 - Plate, Silver Jubilee. Silver, gold and color decoration. LE 1500. 10¼"d. Paragon bone china. $100.—$108.

E2-397 - Plate, Silver Jubilee. Color decor-ation. Gold overlaid on light blue border. 10½"d. Aynsley BC.
$68.—$73.

E2-398 - Plate, Silver Jubilee. Black and white portrait on blue. Color flowers and decoration. 6½"d. Bone china.
$20.—$25.

E2-399 - Plate, Silver Jubilee. Color and gold decoration. Gold on white border. LE 2000. 8"d. Coalport bone china.
$68.—$73.

E2-400 - Plate, Silver Jubilee. Arms in center. Blue on blue design. LE 2000. 10½"d. Royal Worcester BC.
$140.—$150.

E2-401 - Plate, Silver Jubilee. Color decoration mainly beige, blue and maroon. 10½"d. Royal Tuscan BC.
$48.—$52.

E2-402 - Plate, Silver Jubilee. Gold on white center. Gold on cobalt blue border. LE 1000 numbered. 10¾"d. Wedgwood BC.
$195.—$205.

E2-403 - Plate, Silver Wedding Anniversary. Blue on ivory decoration. 6½"d. Rye Pottery.
$51.—$56.

E2-404 - Plate, 60th Birthday. White on light blue jasperware. 6½"d. Wedgwood.
$30.—$35.

E2-405 - Plate, 60th Birthday. Color portrait and decoration. Gold rim. 10½"d. Coalport BC.
$82.—$88.

E2-406 - Plate, 60th Birthday. Sepia portrait and decoration. Gold rim. 7½"d. Johnson Ceramics BC.
$25.—$29.

E2-407 - Plate, 60th Birthday. Gold on cobalt blue and white. Embossed commemoration. LE 600. 10¾"d. Caverswall BC.
$285.—$300.

E2-408 Plate, "The Royal Year" 1983. Color portraits and decoration. 11"d. Caverswall BC.
$58.—$63.

E2-409 - Plate, 25th Anniversary of Coro-nation. Color and gold decoration. 10¾"d. LE 1000. Coalport BC.
$130.—$137.

E2-410 - Plate, 25th Anniversary of Coro-nation. Colorful Windsor Castle scene by J.A. Bailey. 7¾"d. Crown Staffordshire.
$46.—$50.

E2-411 - Plate, 30th Anniversary of Coro-nation. Color portrait and decoration. Gold trim. 10¾"d. Caverswall BC.
$62.—$67.

E2-412 - Plate, USA Visit 1957. Color portrait and decoration. "Welcome to Our Friendly Land…". 10¼"d.
$27.—$31.

E2-413 Playing Cards, Coronation. Black and white portrait. Single deck. Boxed.
$31.—$36.

E2-414 - Playing Cards, Coronation. Color portraits. Maroon and gold box. Double deck.
$70.—$75.

E2-415 - Playing Cards, Denmark Visit 1957. Color decoration with blue and maroon borders. Double deck in clear plastic box.
$70.—$75.

E2-416 - Playing Cards, Silver Jubilee. Color portrait. Single deck.
$14.—$16.

E2-417 - Playing Cards, Silver Jubilee. Sepia portrait. Single deck.
$17.—$19.

E2-418 - Playing Cards, 25th Anniversary of Coronation. Color decoration. Double deck in clear plastic. Worshipful.
$46.—$51.

E2-419 - Pocket Knife, Coronation. Color portrait. Mother-of-pearl back. 2"long.
$51.—$56.

E2-420 - Pocket Knife, Coronation. Color portrait. Mother-of-pearl back. 3¼"long.
$59.—$63. 3¼"long.
$53.—$56. 2"long.

E2-421 - Pomander, Silver Jubilee. Black and white portrait. Color decoration. 2¼"h. 3"d. Aidees, Torquay Pottery.
$19.—$23.

E2-422 - Postcard, 60th Birthday. Set of four showing 17p and 34p commemorative stamps.
$7.—$9. set of four.

E2-423 - Potty, Silver Jubilee. Color portraits and decoration. 3¾" h. 7"d. Portmeirion Pottery.
$50.—$55.

E2-424 - Ribbon, Silver Jubilee. Color decoration repeats every 1¾". 1 yard x 1½"wide.
$13.—$15.

E2-425 - Scarf, Coronation. Color decoration. 24"x24". Rayon.
$37.—$42.

E2-426 - Scarf, Coronation. London scenes in color on yellow background. 31"x31". Rayon.
$45.—$49.

E2-427 - Scarf, Wedding 1947. Color decoration. 34"x34". Sally Gee Silk.
$51.—$59.

E2-428 - Shot Glass, Coronation. Color decoration. Gold rim. 2½"h. 2"d. at top.
$14.—$17.

E2-429 - Spoon, Silver Jubilee. Sterling silver. Profile and commemora-tion in bowl. Color enamel national flowers. Each 3¾"long.
$90.—$100. Set of 4.

E2-430 - Tape Measure, Coronation. Bronze color medallion on ivorine case. "Dean 60 Inch Measure". 2¼"d. $37.—$42.

E2-431 - Teapot, Coronation. Metal. 3¼"h. 7"across. Swan Cromalin. $38.—$43.

E2-432 - Teapot, Coronation. Sepia portrait. Color decoration. Gold trim. Metal spout whistles. 4"h. 7½"across. $53.—$59.

E2-433 - Teapot, Coronation. Sepia portrait. Color decoration. Gold on blue. 5"h. 8½"across. Ringtons. $82.—$89.

E2-434 - Teapot, Coronation. Sepia Portrait. Color decoration on gold background. 5"h. 8¾" across. Sadler. $82.—$89.

E2-435 - Teapot, Coronation. Sepia Portrait. Color decoration. Gold trim. 3¼"h. 6¼"across. Corona. $47.—$52.

E2-436 - Teapot, Coronation. Aluminum with black handle and finial. Embossed commemoration. 3½"h. 6½"across. $37.—$41.

E2-437 - Teapot, Coronation. Sepia Portrait. Color decoration. Gold bands and trim. 6"h. 8½"across. Rita. $97.—$105.

E2-438 - Teapot, Coronation. White on royal blue jasperware. Prince Philip on reverse. 5"h. 8½"across. Wedgwood. $235.—$245.

E2-439 - Teapot, Coronation. Raised beige profile portrait on medium brown. Crown finial. 5"h. 8½" across. Dartmouth. $98.—$108.

E2-440 - Teapot, Silver Jubilee. Black and white portrait on blue ground. Color decoration. Silver trim. 6"h. 8¾"across. Sadler. $61.—$67.

E2-441 - Teapot, Silver Jubilee. Black and white portrait. Color decoration. 5¼"h. 7"across. Price Kensington. $76.—$84.

E2-442 - Teapot Stand, Coronation. Glass. 6"d. $19.—$23.

E2-443 - Tea Set, Coronation. Light blue on white queensware. Teapot 5"h. 8½"across. 3 pieces. Wedgwood. $265.—$295.

E2-444 - Tea Set, Coronation. White on light blue jasperware. Teapot 5"h. 8½"across. 3 pieces. Wedgwood. $350.—$400.

E2-445 - Tea Strainer, Coronation. Sterling silver. 5½"long. $100.—$110.

E2-446 - Tea Towel, Silver Jubilee. Color decoration. 30"x18". Cotton. $16.—$20.

E2-447 - Tea Towel, Silver Jubilee. Color decoration. 31"x18". Cotton. $16.—$20.

E2-448 - Thermos Bottle, Coronation. Black and white portrait. Red, white and blue on gold. 9¾"h. 3"d. Thermos. $45.—$59.

E2-449 - Tile, Coronation. "E" and "R" on side tiles. Crown and date on center tile. Frame is 19"x6¼". $52.—$58.

E2-450 - Tile, Coronation. Color cypher, crown and date. 6"d. Pilkington. $31.—$37.

E2-451 - Tile, Silver Jubilee. Color and gold decoration. 6"x6". H&R Johnson Ltd. $27.—$31.

E2-452 - Tin, Coronation. Color portrait. Red and gold decoration. 10"x7"x2". E. Sharp & Sons. $31.—$37.

E2-453 - Tin, Coronation. Color portraits. Gold on red sides. 8¼"x6¼"x1¼". G.F. Lovell & Co. $31.—$37.

E2-454 - Tin, Coronation. Color portrait. Color and gold decoration on blue. 4¾"x4¼"x¾". Boy Blue Toffee. $20.—$25.

E2-455 - Tin, Coronation. Color portraits and decoration. Gold trim. 7¼"x5"x2¼". $21.—$26.

E2-456 Tin, Coronation. Color portraits. Color national flowers on sides. 2½"h.x7"x5". A.S. Wilkin Ltd. $36.—$40.

E2-457 - Tin, Coronation. Color portraits. Blue background. 3"h.x7½"x3¼". Meredith & Drews. $30.—$35.

E2-458 - Tin, Coronation. Color portrait and decoration. Windsor and Buckingham Palace. 5¾"x3¾"x2¾". Daintee. $25.—$30.

E2-459 - Tin, Coronation. Color portrait repeated on reverse. Windsor and Buckingham Palace. 4"h.x4"x3". $26.—$31.

E2-460 - Tin, Coronation. Color portraits. Color and gold decoration. 5½"x 4"x1½". Waller & Hartley. $27.—$31.

E2-461 - Tin, Coronation. Color portraits. Gold and white decoration on pale blue. 6½"x4½"x 1½"deep. $28.—$33.

E2-462 - Tin, Coronation. Color portrait. 6½"x5½"x 1½"deep. Edward Sharp & Sons Ltd. $29.—$33.

E2-463 - Tin, Coronation. Color portrait and decoration. Gold trim on light blue. 5½"h.x 4¾"x4". $28.—$32.

E2-464 - Tin, Coronation. Color portraits. Prince Philip on reverse. Eight sides. Color arms on lid. 5½"h. 4"d. $25.—$29.

E2-465 - Tin, Coronation. Color portraits. Prince Philip on reverse. Blue background. 5"h.x5¼"x4". Gray Dunn. $32.—$37.

E2-466 - Tin, Coronation. Color portrait. Cream background. Hinged lid. 6"h.x3"x3". $28.—$32.

E2-467 - Tin, Coronation. Color portraits. Prince Philip on reverse. 5½"h.x 4½"x3". $23.—$27. $18.—$22. 4"h.x3¾".

E2-468 - Tin, Coronation. Color portrait and decoration. Red and beige background. 3½"h. 3½"d. $19.—$24.

E2-469 - Tin, Coronation. Color portraits. Prince Philip on reverse. 5½"h.x 4"x4". $27.—$32.

E2-470 - Tin, Coronation. Color portrait. Gold background. Hinged lid. 5½"h.x4½"x3". Fox's Mints. $23.—$26.

E2-471 - Tin, Coronation. Color portrait. Blue and gold decoration. 9½"h.x6¾"x1¼". W&M Duncan Ltd. $32.—$37.

E2-472 - Tin, Coronation. Black and white portrait. Color decoration. Different portrait on reverse. 4¼"h. 3¼"d. $28.—$32.

E2-473 - Tin, Coronation. Color portraits. Prince Philip on reverse. Purple background. 4¾"h.x 4"x3". $23.—$27.

E2-474 - Tin, Coronation. Color portrait and decoration. 5½"h.x 4½"x3". Hinged lid. $25.—$30.

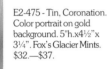

E2-475 - Tin, Coronation. Color portrait on gold background. 5"h.x4½"x 3¼". Fox's Glacier Mints. $32.—$37.

E2-476 - Tin, Coronation. Color portraits. Prince Philip on reverse. Buckingham Palace. 5"h.x 5¾"x3¾". Thorne's. $31.—$36.

E2-477 - Tin, Coronation. Color portraits. Prince Philip on reverse. Blue background. 4¼"h.x5¼"x4". Lyons Tea. $22.—$26.

E2-478 - Tin, Coronation. Color portrait. Color and gold decoration on blue base. 5½"x 4"x1½". E. Sharp. $24.—$28.

E2-479 - Tin, Coronation. Color portrait. 1¼"h. 5"d. Henry Thorne & Co. $20.—$23.

2-480 - Tin, Coronation. Color portraits. Same portrait on reverse. 6¼"h.x4¼"x4¼". Rington's Tea. $28.—$32.

E2-481 - Tin, Coronation. Color portraits. Gold decoration on red ground. 5½"h.x4½". Edward Sharp & Sons. $22.—$26.

E2-482 - Tin, Coronation. Color portraits. Westminster and royal residences on sides. 3½"h. 7"d. Wright's. $30.—$35.

E2-483 - Tin, Coronation. Color portrait. Gold lettering on deep maroon. City of Manchester. 2½"d. ¾"deep. $15.—$18.

E2-484 - Tin, Coronation. Color portrait. Gold and red background. 3"h. 5"d. Mackintosh. $21.—$25.

E2-485 - Tin, Coronation. Color portrait and decoration. 3¼"h. 7"d. Huntley & Palmers. $27.—$31.

E2-486 - Tin, Coronation. Color portrait amd decoration. Gold trim. 11¼"x 7¼"x1½". Carr & Co. Ltd. Biscuits. $27.—$31.

E2-487 - Tin, Coronation. Color portrait. 8"d. 1"deep. Huntley & Palmers Biscuits. $20.—$24.

E2-488 - Tin, Coronation. Color portrait and decoration on red. 9"x6"x 1½"deep. W&R Jacob. $31.—$34.

E2-489 - Tin, Coronation. Color portrait. Light blue and beige background. Gold trim. 5¾"h.x 3½"x3½". $26.—$30.

E2-490 - Tin, Coronation. Color portraits. Prince Philip on reverse. Gold trim. 5½"h.x4¼"x3¼". Rowntree. $26.—$31.

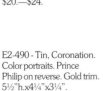

E2-491 - Tin, Coronation. Color portraits. Prince Philip on reverse. Gold trim. 6¼"h.x5"x3¾". Bilsland Brothers, Glasgow. $42.—$47.

E2-492 - Tin, Coronation. Color portrait. Lavender border. 10"x7"x1½" deep. Edward Sharp. $32.—$37.

E2-493 - Tin, Coronation. Color portrait. Windsor and Buckingham Palace. Pale blue background. 6"h.x4"x4". $28.—$32.

E2-494 - Tin, Coronation. Color decoration on deep blue background. 9"x 6½"x2¼"deep. Scribbans-Kemp Ltd. $29.—$33.

E2-495 - Tin, Coronation. Color coronation procession scene with Queen in carriage on lid. 6¾"d. 3"deep. $25.—$29.

E2-496 - Tin, Coronation. Color decoration. Red on sides. Hinged lid. 6"x4"x1". W&R Jacob & Co. $29.—$34.

E2-497 - Tin, Coronation. Color decoration. Cypher, crown, royal standards on sides. 8"d. 3¾" deep. Peek, Frean. $23.—$26.

E2-498 - Tin, Coronation. Black and white portrait. Color flag. Gold background. 6"x4¼"x½". MacDonald's Canada. $41.—$46.

E2-499 - Tin, Coronation. Color portrait. Gold background. 9¼"x7¾"x1¾". Macfarlane Lang. $39.—$44.

E2-500 - Tin, Coronation. Color portrait and decoration. Blue background. 8"x5"x2¼". C.W.S. Biscuit Works. $25.—$29.

E2-501 - Tin, Coronation. Color portrait. Gold or blue background. 6"x4¼"x 1¼". Hinged Lid. Wills Cigarettes. $19.—$22.

E2-502 - Tin, Coronation. Color portrait on gold background. 2¼"h.x 7"x6¼". McVitie. $28.—$32.

E2-503 - Tin, Coronation. Color portrait on deep red background. Commemoration on ivory sides. 6"x3¾"x2". $25.—$29.

E2-504 - Tin, Coronation. Color portrait in gold frame. Red and gold trim on beige. 1¼"h.x5¾"x3¾". Vincent. $22.—$26.

E2-505 - Tin, Coronation. Color portrait. Coronation coach and horses on sides. 10"x7"x2". $32.—$36.

E2-506 - Tin, Coronation. Color portrait. Commemoration on sides. 9"x 4¼"x2¼". Meredith & Drew Ltd. Biscuits. $29.—$34.

E2-507 - Tin, Coronation. Color portrait. Gold and color decoration on aqua. 1½"h.x5¼"x3". Wills Cigarettes. $19.—$22.

E2-508 - Tin, Coronation. Color portrait. Raised frame, cypher and crown. Gold decoration. 6¼"x2"x½". Rowntree. $28.—$32.

E2-509 - Tin, Coronation. Color portrait and decoration. 9"x 4¼"x2¼". Meredith & Drew Ltd. Biscuits. $29.—$33.

E2-510 - Tin, Coronation. Color portrait. Blue background. Gold and beige trim. 5½"x 3½"x1¼". $19.—$22.

E2-511 - Tin, Coronation. Color portrait. Light blue sides. 7"x5¼"x1½". George W. Horner. $30.—$34.

E2-512 - Tin, Coronation. Color portrait. Beige background. 5¼"x4"x 1¼". George W. Horner. $26.—$30.

E2-513 - Tin, Coronation. Color portrait and decoration on silver grey background. 7"d. 4"deep. $25.—$28.

E2-514 - Tin, Coronation. Black and white portrait. Color and gold decoration on red background. 3¾"x2½"x¾"deep. Oxo. $15.—$18.

E2-515 - Tin, Coronation. Color portrait. Gold and red trim on ivory background. 7½"x5¼"x2¼". $28.—$31.

E2-516 - Tin, Coronation. Color portrait. Deep blue background. Cadbury. $26.—$30. 6¼"x4½". $22.—$25. 4"x2"x½".

E2-517 - Tin, Coronation. Raised profile. Gold tone finish. 3½"d. ¾"deep. Mackintosh's Toffee. $25.—$28.

E2-518 - Tin, Coronation. Color portrait on lid. Coronation scene and procession on sides. 4"h. 9"d. $44.—$49.

E2-519 - Tin, Coronation. Color portrait. Dark red background. 5"d. 3"deep. Caley Cranford Chocolates. $21.—$25.

E2-520 - Tin, No commemoration. Gold profile and decoration on purple background. 7¾"d. 3½"deep. Guildcraft. $21.—$25.

E2-521 - Tin, St. Lawrence Seaway Opening 1959. Black and white portrait. Color flag. 5¼"x4¼"x ½". W.C. Macdonald. $32.—$37.

E2-522 - Tin, St. Lawrence Seaway Opening 1959. Color portraits. Color map on bottom. 5¼"x3½"x 1½". George Horner. $29.—$33.

E2-523 - Tin, Silver Jubilee. Color portrait and decoration. 10"d. 3"deep. $31.—$35.

E2-524 - Tin, Silver Jubilee. Color portrait. Blue and gold decoration. 2¼"h. 5"d. Meltis Newberry Fruits. $17.—$20.

E2-525 - Tin, Silver Jubilee. Color portraits and arms. Contains safety matches. 2"h. 2½"d. $21.—$24.

E-526 - Tin, Silver Jubilee. Color portrait repeated on reverse. Crown and commemoration on sides. 5¾"h. 4½"d. $25.—$29.

E2-527 - Tin, Silver Jubilee. Color portraits. Red background. 6½"x4¼"x4¼". $20.—$24.

E2-528 - Tin, Silver Jubilee. Color portraits. Silver trim on purple background. 9"x6½"x¾"deep. Milk Tray Chocolates. $25.—$28.

E2-529 - Tin, Silver Jubilee. Color portrait. Crowns on purple around sides. 5½"d. 2½"deep. Mackintosh's. $20.—$23.

E2-530 - Tin, Silver Jubilee. Drum shape. Color portraits. Silver on blue background. 3½"h. 4½"d. $21.—$24.

E2-531 - Tin, Silver Jubilee. Color portrait on deep red background. 1½"h. 3¼"d. Smith Kendon's Travel Sweets. $19.—$22.

E2-532 - Tin, Silver Jubilee. Sepia portrait. Color decoration on dark blue background. 4½"h.x3½"x3½". Robert Jackson & Co. $21.—$24.

E2-533 - Tin, Silver Jubilee. Color portrait and decoration. 10"d. 3"deep. $23.—$26.

E2-534 - Tin - Silver Jubilee. Color portrait. Gold trim. 2½"h.x 8½"x8½". $22.—$25.

E2-535 - Tin, Silver Jubilee. Color portrait and decoration. Color decoration on sides. 2¼"h. 9¼"d. $31.—$35.

E2-536 - Tin, Silver Jubilee. Black and white profile portrait. Color decoration on white. 2¼"h.x9"x6¼". Spicers Ltd. $23.—$26.

E2-537 - Tin, State Visit 1957. Color portrait and decoration. 1¾"h.x10¼"x7½". Huntley & Palmers. $30.—$34.

E2-538 - Tray, Silver Jubilee. Metal. Color portraits. Gold on cream design. 16¾"x12½". $22.—$25.

E2-539 - Tray, Silver Jubilee. Color family portraits and decoration. Wood grain tray on reverse. 19½"x15½". Melamine. $47.—$52.

E2-540 - Tray, Silver Jubilee. Metal. Color portrait on white background. 4"x4"x4½"deep. $15.—$18.

E2-541 - Tray, Silver Jubilee. Metal. Color portrait on red background. 12"d. 1½"deep. $28.—$31.

E2-542 - Trivet, King's Arms (George I's Arms). "Copyright 1953" impressed on reverse. Brass. 6"x5½". $44.—$48.

E2-543 - Tumbler, 1951 Canada Visit. Glass. Blue transfer. 5"h. 2½"d. $28.—$32.

E2-544 - Tumbler, Coronation. Glass. Blue and gold decoration. 5¼"h. $18.—$21.

E2-545 - Tumbler, Coronation. Crystal. Etched "EIIR", crown and date. 4"h. 4"d. Stuart. $60.—$66.

2-546 - Vase, Coronation. Brown tone and color portrait framed in gold. 9¼"h. 4½"d. at center. Aynsley BC. $445.—$470.

Queen Elizabeth II and Prince Philip, Duke of Edinburgh — Family

E2-547 - Pss. Anne Dish, c. 1953. Glass. Black and white portrait from a Marcus Adams photograph. 4½"d. $38.—$42.

E2-548 - Pss. Anne Jigsaw Puzzle. Color portrait of Prince Charles kissing her. 200 pieces. 14"x9½". Cecil Beaton photo. $48.—$53.

E2-549 - Pss. Anne Jigsaw Puzzle. Color christening portrait. Over 400 pieces. Cardboard. 14½"x19½". $62.—$67.

E2-550 - Prince Charles Bust. White composition. 4½"h. $48.—$52.

E2-551 - Prince Charles Dish, c. 1953. Glass. Black and white portrait from a Marcus Adams photograph. 4½"d. $38.—$42.

E2-552 - Prince Charles Mug. Sepia portrait. "A Souvenir of Prince Charles". Gold trim. c. 1953. 2¾"h. Paragon BC. $145.—$160.

E2-553 - Prince Charles Plate. Sepia portrait. "A Souvenir of Prince Charles". (Age about five). Gold rim. 6¼"d. Paragon BC. $175.—$190.

E2-554 - Prince Philip 60th Birthday Loving Cup. Gold profile on dark blue. LE 500. 3"h. 4¾"across. Royal Crown Derby BC. $195.—$215.

E2-555 - Royal Family Thimbles. Set of 8. Color portraits. Gold trim. St. George's BC. $42.—$46.

G5-001 - Album, Silver Jubilee. B&W foldout photos. Raised profile portraits. Silver tone lid. Plastic base. 1¼"x1"x¼"deep. $37.—$42.

G5-002 - Ashtray, Silver Jubilee. Color portraits and decoration. Silver trim. 4¼"d. 1"deep. $41.—$44.

G5-003 - Bank, Coronation. Profiles. "Coronation Bank" and date. Cast iron. 6¼"h. 4"d. 1"deep. $215.—$235.

G5-004 - Beaker, Coronation. Color portraits and decoration. Gold rim. Ribbed. 3½"h. 2½"d. Late Foley Shelley. $70.—$80.

G5-005 - Beaker, Coronation. Color decoration partially hand painted. Fluted. 3"h. 2½"d. Late Foley Shelley bone china. $54.—$59.

G5-006 - Beaker, Coronation. Color portraits and decoration. Gold rim. 4¼"h. Royal Wintonia. $65.—$70.

G5-007 - Beaker, Coronation. Color portraits and decoration. Gold rim. Enamel on tin. 3¾"h. 3¼"d. $59.—$64.

G5-008 - Beaker, Coronation. Sepia portraits. Color decoration. 4"h. Pottery. $58.—$63.

G5-009 - Beaker, Coronation. Green tone portraits and decoration. Gold rim. 3¾"h. Wm. Whiteley bone china. $59.—$64.

G5-010 - Beaker, Coronation. B&W portraits. Color decoration. 3¾"h. Hammersley BC. $83.—$90.

G5-011 - Beaker, Coronation. B&W portraits. Color decoration. Gold rim. 4"h. 3"d. Devon Ware. $58.—$64.

G5-012 - Beaker, Coronation. B&W portraits. Small portrait Pr. Edward. Color decoration. 3½"h. Bone china. $70.—$77.

G5-013 - Beaker, Coronation. Sepia portraits. Color decoration. Crown and cypher reverse. 4"h. Royal Doulton. $80.—$90.

G5-014 - Beaker, Coronation. Brown tone portraits. Queen Mary reverse. Facsimile signatures. 5"h. Royal Doulton. $64.—$70.

G5-015 - Beaker, Coronation. Blue on white decoration. 4"h. Wedgwood. $80.—$90.

G5-016 - Beaker, Coronation. B&W portraits with Pr. Edward between. Enamel on tin. 4"h. $96.—$106.

G5-017 - Beaker, Coronation. Color portraits with arms between. Gold rim. Enamel on tin. $66.—$75.

G5-018 - Beaker, Coronation. Color portraits and decoration. Gold rim. 3½"h. Bishop & Stonier. $85.—$95.

G5-019 - Beaker, Coronation. Lithophane. King's portrait seen in bottom when held to light. Arms of Bradford. 3"h. BC. $140.—$155.

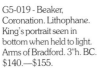

G5-020 - Beaker, Silver Jubilee. Sepia portraits. Color decoration. Silver rim. Empire shields. 4"h. 2¾"d. Aynsley BC. $76.—$84.

G5-021 - Bell, Silver Jubilee. Profiles on top of handle and "1910—1935". 4½"h. 2½"d. at base. Brass. $53.—$58.

G5-022 - Bowl, Coronation. B&W portraits. Color decoration. Gold trim. 8"x5"x1½"deep. $59.—$64.

G5-023 - Bowl, Coronation. Covered. Color decoration. 2¾"h. Lid is 4"d. Bowl is 6"d. Late Foley Shelley bone china. $100.—$110.

G5-024 - Bowl. Color portrait King George V in blue uniform. Gold rim. 5"d. 2¾"deep. Bone china. $48.—$53.

G5-025 - Box, Coronation. Color decoration partially hand painted. Gold trim. 3½"x¾"x 1½"deep. Aynsley BC. $79.—$89.

G5-026 - Box, Silver Jubilee. Crown shape, covered. Hand painted on deep red. Hers 4"h. His 3¾"h. Crown Staffordshire BC. $305.—$340. Pair.

G5-027 - Box, Silver Jubilee. Coach shape covered box. Orange and silver. "1910" and "1935" on sides. 5¼"h.x6"x2½". Pottery. $150.—$165.

G5-028 - Brooch, Coronation. Sepia portrait on gold tone mount. 1¼"d. $43.—$48.

G5-029 - Brooch, Coronation. Arms with "George V" below. Enamel on gold tone metal. 1"x1¼". $32.—$37.

G5-030 - Buckle. Color portrait on porcelain in bronze tone mount. 2¼"x2". $80.—$90.

G5-031 - Bust, Accession. Parian busts on glazed bases which show names, birth and accession dates. 4¾"h. Arcadian. $205.—$230. Pair.

G5-032 - Bust, Accession. Parian bust on glazed base. Name, birth and accession dates on base. 5"h. Arcadian. $105.—$115.

G5-033 - Bust. Parian busts. Each 4½"h. 2¼"d. at shoulders. $160.—$175. Pair.

G5-034 - Bust. Hand painted pair of busts on black plinths. Each 7"h. 2¾"across at shoulders. $180.—$195.

G5-035 - Bust. Parian. "King George V" incised in base. 5½"h. 4½"across at shoulders. $100.—$110.

G5-036 - Cigar Pouch, Coronation. Color portraits and decoration on beige. 5"x3¼"x¾". I. Bottomley. $45.—$50.

G5-037 - Cigarette Cards, Silver Jubilee. Book of 50 color cards. 5"x7¼". W.D. and H.O. Wills. $45.—$50.

G5-038 - Cigarette Cards. Framed color portraits. King, Queen, Prince Edward. Clear glass reverse. 6½" x 8¼". Wills. $46.—$52.

G5-039 - Cigarette Cards. Framed color cards of Proclamation, Coronation, and Delhi Durbar, 6½"x8¼". W.D. & H.O. Wills. $41.—$46.

G5-040 - Compact, Silver Jubilee. Color enamel emblem on silver tone finish. 3¼"x2½". $45.—$50.

G5-041 - Creamer and Sugar. Color portraits. King in blue uniform. Creamer 4½"h. Sugar 4"d. Bone china. $85.—$95.

G5-042 - Creamer and Sugar, Wedding 1893. Color decoration partially hand painted. Creamer 3¼"h. Sugar 4"d. Foley BC. $305.—$335.

G5-043 - Cup and Saucer, Coronation. B&W portraits with Prince Edward between. Color decoration. BC. $85.—$95.

G5-044 - Cup and Saucer, Coronation. Color portraits. (King in blue uniform). Color decoration. Gold trim. BC. $85.—$95.

G5-045 - Cup and Saucer, Coronation. Color portraits and decoration. Bugle, banner in cup. Late Foley Shelley BC. $95.—$105.

G5-046 - Cup and Saucer, Coronation. Demitasse size. Sepia and color portraits. Color decoration. Late Foley Shelley BC. $74.—$80.

G5-047 - Cup and Saucer, Coronation. Green tone portraits and decoration. Dreadnought and ships. Aynsley BC. $84.—$94.

G5-048 - Cup and Saucer, Coronation. Color portraits and decoration partially hand painted. Gold trim. Aynsley BC. $90.—$100.

G5-049 - Cup and Saucer, Coronation. Color portraits (King in blue uniform). Color decoration. Royal Doulton BC. $155.—$170.

G5-050 - Cup and Saucer, Coronation. Lithophane of King seen in cup when held to light. Gold trim. Bone china. $150.—$165.

G5-051 - Cup and Saucer, Coronation. B&W portraits. Color decoration. Gold trim. Birth and wedding dates. Bone china. $95.—$105.

G5-052 - Cup and Saucer, Coronation. Color portraits Queen Mary on reverse. Color decoration. Bishop & Stonier BC. $130.—$145.

G5-053 - Cup and Saucer, Coronation. Color portraits. Gold trim. Royal Doulton bone china. $95.—$105.

G5-054 - Cup and Saucer, Silver Jubilee. Sepia portraits. Color decoration. Silver trim. Arms on reverse. $48.—$53.

G5-055 - Cup and Saucer, Silver Jubilee. Sepia portraits. Color decoration. Silver trim. Aynsley bone china. $85.—$95.

G5-056 - Cup and Saucer, Silver Jubilee. Color portraits and decoration. Silver trim. Royal Albert BC. $80.—$90.

G5-057 - Cup and Saucer, Silver Jubilee. Sepia portraits. Color decoration. Gold trim. Wellington BC. $48.—$53.

G5-058 - Cup and Saucer, Silver Jubilee. With 5" tea plate. Color portraits and decoration. Silver trim. Empire. $80.—$90.

G5-059 - Cup and Saucer, Wedding 1893. Color decoration. Crown, bugle and "Happiness" in cup. Foley bone china. $200.—$225.

G5-060 - Dish, Coronation. Color portraits and decoration. Gold rim. Victoria BC. $72.—$79.

G5-061 - Dish, Coronation. Color portrait (in red uniform). Gold trim. 4¼"d. Royal Doulton bone china. $74.—$81

G5-062 - Dish, Coronation. Colorful design. Gold rim. 6¼"x3". W.H. Goss bone china. $69.—$76.

G5-063 - Dish, Coronation. Color portraits and decoration. Gold rim. 6"x5"x1"deep. Late Foley Shelley BC. $79.—$89.

G5-064 - Dish, Coronation. Color decoration. Gold rim. 3½"x3½"x¾"deep. Shelley BC. $49.—$54.

G5-065 - Dish, Silver Jubilee. Sepia portraits. Color decoration. Silver rim. 4"d. Aynsley BC. $43.—$48.

G5-066 - Dish, Silver Jubilee. Sepia portraits. Color decoration. 4½"d. 1"deep. $37.—$42.

G5-067 - Dish - Silver Jubilee. Sepia portraits. Color decoration. Silver trim. 4½"d. ¾" deep. Aynsley bone china. $58.—$63.

G5-068 - Egg Cup, Coronation. Color portraits. Germany. Bone china. $75.—$82. Pair.

G5-069 - Egg Cup, Silver Jubilee. Color portraits and decoration. Silver rim. 2½"h. $27.—$32.

G5-070 - Handkerchief, Coronation. "Rule Britannia". Blue on white. 17"x17". $68.—$75.

G5-071 - Handkerchief, Coronation. Prince Edward below. Blue on white. 19½"x 19½". $74.—$81.

G5-072 - Handkerchief. "The Heart of Empire". B&W and color portrait. 17"x16". Linen. $53.—$58.

G5-073 - Handkerchief, Manchester Library Opening 1934. Blue on white. 12½"x12½". $42.—$47.

G5-074 - Handkerchief, Silver Jubilee. B&W portraits in green wreath. Windsor Castle, Buckingham Palace. 11½"x11½". $42.—$47.

G5-075 - Handkerchief, Silver Jubilee. Blue on white. 19"x19". $48.—$53.

G5-076 - Jug, Character. Hand painted with gold highlights. Each 6"h. 4"across. Handles on reverse. Bone china. $280.—$310. Pair.

G5-077 - Jug, Coronation. Color decoration partially hand painted. Gold trim. 3"h. 4½"across. Foley bone china. $74.—$81.

G5-078 - Jug, Coronation. B&W portraits. Color decoration. 2¾"h. Bone china. $52.—$57.

G5-079 - Jug, Coronation. Color portraits. Gold trim. Embossing. 5¾"h. 5"across. Made in Austria. $130.—$145.

G5-080 - Jug, Coronation. Color portraits and decoration. Gold trim. 3½"h. 3½"across. Arcadian bone china. $85.—$95.

G5-081 - Jug, Coronation. B&W portraits. Color decoration. Birth, wedding and coro-nation dates. 3"h. BC. $95.—$105.

G5-082 - Jug. "HRH Duke of York". B&W portrait in gold frame. Puce background. 5"h. 4¾"across. Germany. Bone china. $154.—$169.

G5-083 - Jug. Color portrait King in blue uniform. 3½"h. 3"across. Bone china. $47.—$52.

G5-084 - Jug. Color portrait King in blue uniform. Gold trim. Embossing. 3½"h. 4¼"across. Bone china. $47.—$52.

G5-085 - Jug. Color portrait King in blue uniform. Gold medallion on reverse. Gold trim. 2"h. 2¼"across. BC. $47.—$52.

G5-086 - Jug. "HM Queen Mary". Color portrait. Puce and white background. Gold trim. 5½"h. 3¾"across. BC. $79.—$85.

G5-087 - Jug. "Prince and Princess of Wales". Color portraits. Gold highlights. 5½"h. 5"across. Austria. Bone china. $160.—$175.

G5-088 - Jug, Silver Jubilee. Raised profile. Silver trim. Cream background. 5"h. 6¼"across. Mason's Ironstone. $58.—$65.

G5-089 - Jug, Wedding 1893. "George - May". Color decoration partially hand painted. Gold trim. 3¼"h. Wileman. $180.—$200.

G5-090 - Loving Cup, Coronation. Color portraits and decoration. Gold trim. 4"h. 6"across. Royal Winton. $140.—$155.

G5-091 - Loving Cup, Coronation. Three handles. Color portraits. Gold on cobalt blue decoration. 2¾"h. 2½"d. BC. $285.—$320.

G5-092 - Loving Cup, Silver Jubilee. Sepia portraits. Color decoration. Silver trim. Color flower handles. 3½"h. Paragon BC. $185.—$205.

G5-093 - Match Holder. Raised crown and cypher. Brass. 2¼"h.x1½"x¾" deep. $47.—$52.

G5-094 - Mirror. Black and white photograph. Ivory color frame. 2"d. $10.—$12.

G5-095 - Mug, Coronation. Raised portraits. Color decoration. Devon slipware. 3"h. 3"d. Pottery. $110.—$120.

G5-096 - Mug, Coronation. Color portraits and decoration. Brown rim. Enamel on tin. 3"h. 3"d. at top. $78.—$88.

G5-097 - Mug, Coronation. Color portraits. King in red uniform. Gold trim. 2¾"h. Royal Doulton bone china. $99.—$109.

G5-098 - Mug, Coronation. Color portraits and decoration. Gold trim. 2¾"h. Bone china. $88.—$91.

G5-099 - Mug, Coronation. Brown tone portraits and decoration. 3"h. Royal Doulton pottery. $88.—$98.

G5-100 - Mug, Coronation. Color portraits. Color decoration. Gold trim. 3"h. 3"d. $62.—$68.

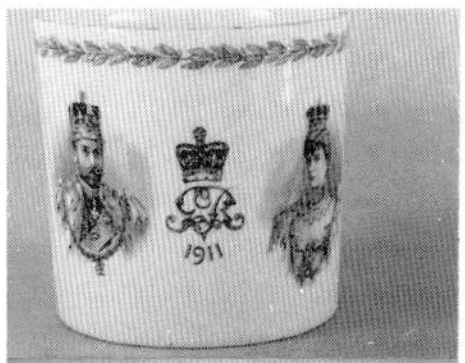

G5-101 - Mug, Coronation. Color portraits and decoration. Gold trim. 3"h. 3¼"d. Bishop and Stonier. $92.—$105.

G5-102 - Mug, Coronation. Color portraits and decoration. Gold trim. 3"h. Harrod's exclusive design. $85.—$95.

G5-103 - Mug, Coronation. Color portraits and decoration. Gold trim. 3¼"h. Royal Wintonia bone china. $75.—$85.

G5-104 - Mug, Coronation. B&W portraits. Color decoration. Gold trim. 3"h. 3"d. Paragon bone china. $73.—$78.

G5-105 - Mug, Coronation. Color portraits and decoration. Ships on sides. 3"h. 2½"d. at top. Aynsley BC. $95.—$105.

G5-106 - Mug, Coronation. Color portraits and decoration. 3¼"h. 3¼"d. C.W.S. Pottery. $58.—$63.

G5-107 - Mug, Coronation. Sepia portraits. St. George slaying dragon reverse. Color decoration. 3½"h. Bone china. $85.—$95.

G5-108 - Mug, Coronation. Blue tone portraits, decoration. Gold trim. Handle opposite portraits. 3"h. Royal Albert BC. $64.—$70.

G5-109 - Mug, Coronation. Color portraits. Pastel floral decoration. Gold trim. Military scenes sides. 3"h. 3"d. Aynsley BC. $150.—$165.

G5-110 - Mug, Coronation. Color portraits and decoration. Gold trim. 3¼"h. Bone china. $68.—$75.

G5-111 - Mug, Coronation. B&W portraits. Color decoration. Birth, marriage, coronation dates. 3"h. Paragon. $80.—$90.

G5-112 - Mug, Coronation. Sepia portraits. Color decoration. Gold trim. 2¾"h. 3"d. Grimwade's. $63.—$69.

G5-113 - Mug, Coronation. Color portraits and decoration. Bugle, crown, date inside. 3"h. Late Foley Shelley. $63.—$75.

G5-114 - Mug, Coronation. Color portraits. Queen Mary on reverse. Gold trim. 2¼"h. 2¼"d. Bone china. $70.—$77.

G5-115 - Mug, Coronation. Sepia portraits. Queen Mary on reverse. Treacle brown. Gold rim bands. 4"h. Ridgway's. $100.—$110.

G5-116 - Mug, Coronation. B&W portraits. Purple slip decoration. "Ripley Celebration". 4"h. $125.—$138.

G5-117 - Mug, Coronation. Color decoration. Gold rim. 2½"h. 2¾"d. W.H. Goss bone china. $75.—$82.

G5-118 - Mug, Coronation. Green decoration on white. 3"h. 3"d. $65.—$71.

G5-119 - Mug, Coronation. Color portraits. Pr. Edward between. Color decoration. Handle opposite. 2¾"h. $75.—$82.

G5-120 - Mug, Coronation. Color decoration partially hand painted. Gold trim. Commemoration inside. 3"h. Foley BC. $79.—$89.

G5-121 - Mug, Coronation. Color decoration on ivory. 3½"h. Moorcroft Pottery. $495.—$585.

G5-122 - Mug, Coronation. Color decoration. Gold trim. 3"h. 2¼"d. at top. Williamson's BC. $70.—$77.

G5-123 - Mug, "HM King George V". Color portrait. 3¾"h. 2½"d. at top. Bone china. $54.—$59.

G5-124 - Mug. Lithophane. King George V's likeness seen in bottom when held to light. Color decoration. 2¾"h. $130.—$145.

G5-125 - Mug, Silver Jubilee. Color portraits. Queen Mary on reverse. Silver trim. 2½"h. Empire. $51.—$56.

G5-126 - Mug, Silver Jubilee. Sepia portraits. Color decoration. Color floral handle. Silver trim. 3"h. Paragon BC. $100.—$110.

G5-127 - Mug, Silver Jubilee. Color decoration. Silver trim. 3¾"h. 2¾"d. Shelley bone china. $54.—$59.

G5-128 - Mug, Silver Jubilee. Sepia portrait. Gold trim. 4¼"h. Tuscan BC. $95.—$105.

G5-129 - Mug, Silver Jubilee. Blue tone portrait. Blue decoration. 3½"h. Pottery. $60.—$66.

G5-130 - Mug, Silver Jubilee. Brown tone portraits and decoration. Gold trim. 2¾"h. Royal Doulton BC. $75.—$82.

G5-131 - Mug, Silver Jubilee. Color portraits and decoration. Color portrait of the King on reverse. Gold trim. 4¼"h. $59.—$64.

G5-132 - Mug, Silver Jubilee. Sepia portraits. Color decoration. Silver trim. Flags, crown, flowers. 3"h. Morley, Fox Co. $55.—$65.

G5-133 - Mug, Silver Jubilee. Color portraits and decoration. Silver trim. 2½"h. 2½"d. Empire. $42.—$47.

G5-134 - Mug, Silver Jubilee. B&W portraits. Color decoration. Silver trim. 4"h. 3"d. at top. Falcon Ware. $37.—$42.

G5-135 - Mug, Silver Jubilee. Sepia portraits. Color decoration. Gold Rim. 4"h. 4"d. Alfred Meakin. $42.—$47.

G5-136 - Mug, Silver Jubilee. Color portraits and decoration. Silver trim. 2¾"h. 2¾"d. $42.—$47.

G5-137 - Mug, Wedding 1893. Sepia portraits. Sepia and color decoration. 3"h. Made by Doulton's for William Whiteley. $200.—$230.

G5-138 - Mug, Wedding 1893. "George - May". Color decoration. Gold trim. Foley BC. $180.—$205.

G5-139 - Napkin Ring, Silver Jubilee. Gold tone with red and blue profiles on silver tone mount. 1¼"h. 1¾"d. Hexagonal. $33.—$36.

G5-140 - Pendant, Wedding 1893. Enamel and silver tone on gold tone mount. 1¼"d. $58.—$63.

G5-141 - Pendant, Wedding 1893. Their names and wedding date on reverse. 2"d. Brass. $52.—$57.

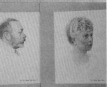

G5-142 - Picture. Prints from pencil drawings in grey matting. Prints 10"x7½". Mats 14"x11½". $40.—$45. Pair.

G5-143 - Picture, Silver Jubilee. Print from The Queen, May 1, 1935. Facsimile signatures. By Hudson & Kearns. 12"x9". $25.—$28.

G5-144 - Picture. Color portraits on plastic. Glass reverse permits light to pass through for lithophane effect. 14"x12½". $125.—$138.

G5-145 - Picture. Color print of Queen Mary from Illustrated London News. 14"x10". $20.—$23.

G5-146 - Picture. Framed color print of Queen Mary. 7"x5". Gold color frame is 12"x10". $70.—$77.

G5-147 - Pin Holder, Silver Jubilee. Pin heads can be seen protruding around edge. Arms reverse. 1¼"d. Brass. $78.—$85.

G5-148 - Pine Cone, Coronation. Colorful design on white background. 3¾"h. 1½"d. W.H. Goss BC. $65.—$71.

G5-149 - Plaque. King George V in profile wearing crown. Sterling silver. 3½"x2½". Hallmarked 1936-37. $75.—$82.

G5-150 - Plaque. King George V (then Pr. of Wales) profile bronze plaque (7"d.) in 11¼" wood frame. Signed "F. Bowcher 1906." $150.—$165.

G5-151 - Plate, Canada Visit 1901. Black and white portraits on white. Gold trim. 8½"d. Bone china. $225.—$250.

G5-152 - Plate, Coronation. Color portraits. Gold trim. 7"d. Bone china. $58.—$65.

G5-153 - Plate, Coronation. Color portraits. Gold rim. 6"d. Royal Doulton bone china. $65.—$72.

G5-154 - Plate, Coronation. Color portraits and decoration. Gold rim. 6"d. Aynsley BC. $58.—$65.

G5-155 - Plate, Coronation. Color portraits and decoration. Wide gold and red banded border. 6¾"d. BC. $74.—$81.

G5-156 - Plate, Coronation. Color portraits. Prince Edward in center. Embossed border. Gold rim. BC. $95.—$105.

G5-157 - Plate, Coronation. Color portraits. Prince Edward between. Color decoration. Gold rim. 7½"d. BC. $95.—$105.

G5-158 - Plate, Coronation. Flow blue. Gold rim. 10½"d. Royal Doulton. $135.—$150.

G5-159 - Plate, Coronation. Blue on white. "George V - King and Emperor". 10"d. K&T Longton. $115.—$130.

G5-160 - Plate, Coronation. Color portraits and decoration. Gold trim. 7"d. Victoria, Austria. Bone china. $59.—$64.

G5-161 - Plate, Coronation. Color portraits and decoration. Gold trim. 7½"d. Bone china. $69.—$79.

G5-162 - Plate, Coronation. Color portraits and decoration. Green garlands. Gold rim. 9"d. Royal Winton. $64.—$70.

G5-163 - Plate, Coronation. Color portraits and decoration. Gold trim. 8½"d. Bone china. $64.—$70.

G5-164 - Plate, Coronation. Color portraits and decoration. Gold rim. 7"d. Royal Doulton bone china. $120.—$135.

G5-165 - Plate, Coronation. Color portraits and decoration. Color flowers. Gold trim. 8½"d. Bone china. $85.—$93.

G5-166 - Plate, Coronation. Color portraits and decoration. 8½"d. C.T. Maling & Sons. $66.—$72.

G5-167 - Plate, Coronation. B&W portraits. Color decoration. Gold rim. 8¾"d. Cauldon BC. $62.—$68.

G5-168 - Plate, Coronation. Color portraits. Prince Edward in center. Color decoration. Gold rim. 7½"d. BC. $90.—$100.

G5-169 - Plate, Coronation. Color portraits and decoration. Gold rim. 7"d. Bone china. $68.—$75.

G5-170 - Plate, Coronation. Color portrait King in red uniform. Gold rim. Embossing. 7"d. Royal Doulton bone china. $75.—$83.

G5-171 - Plate, Coronation. Sepia portrait of Queen Mary on treacle brown. 9"d. Ridgway's. $67.—$73.

G5-172 - Plate, Coronation. Color decoration. Gold rim. 6"d. Late Foley Shelley bone china. $42.—$47.

G5-173 - Plate, Coronation. Color decoration partially hand painted. Gold rim. 7"d. Hammersley bone china. $60.—$65.

G5-174 - Plate, Coronation. Color decoration partially hand painted. Gold trim. 10"d. Late Foley Shelley bone china. $130.—$145.

G5-175 - Plate, Coronation. Blue decoration on white. 7"d. Royal Copenhagen bone china. $165.—$180.

G5-176 - Plate. Color portraits with their names below. Gold decoration. 6¾"d. Bone china. $125.—$140. Pair.

G5-177 - Plate, Silver Jubilee. Sepia portraits. Color decoration. Silver band around rim. 6"d. Paragon bone china. $64.—$70.

G5-178 - Plate, Silver Jubilee. Color portraits and decoration. Silver rim. 5"d. Empire. $32.—$37.

G5-179 - Plate, Silver Jubilee. Sepia portraits. Color decoration. Silver trim. Art Deco design. 8¾"d. Pottery. $42.—$47.

G5-180 - Plate, Silver Jubilee. Color portraits and decoration. Silver rim. 6"d. Shelley BC. $58.—$63.

G5-181 - Plate, Wedding 1893. Sepia portraits. Puce background. Gold trim. 6¾"d. Germany. $160.—$175.

G5-182 - Plate, Wedding 1893. Color decoration partially hand painted. 7½"d. Foley bone china. $160.—$175.

G5-183 - Plate, Wedding 1893. Sepia portraits and decoration. 7¼"d. Made by Doulton's for William Whiteley. Bone china. $185.—$205.

G5-184 - Playing Cards, Coronation. Color portrait of King in blue uniform on red background. Single deck. Goodall & Son. $67.—$83.

G5-185 - Playing Cards, Silver Jubilee. Color portraits and decoration. Double deck. $65.—$70.

G5-186 - Pocket Knife. Raised portraits of King George V and Queen Mary with crowns and arms. Silver tone. 2¾"long. $58.—$65.

G5-187 - Postcard, Coronation. Color portraits and decoration. Birth, wedding, coronation dates. Tuck's. $12.—$14.

G5-188 - Postcard, Proclamation. Black and white portraits. $11.—$13.

G5-189 - Postcard. Three-dimensional color portrait cards. Deep red background. By Bas-Relief. $20.—$22. Pair.

G5-190 - Purse, Coronation. Color portraits and pastel color decoration. Cloth. Reverse is plain. 3¼"x2¾". $59.—$66.

G5-191 - Silent Butler, Silver Jubilee. Brass. 11½"long. 3"wide at base. $52.—$57.

G5-192 - Sugar, Silver Jubilee. Sepia portrait. Gold handles and finial. Art Deco design. 3"h. 3½"across. Royal Doulton. $110.—$122.

G5-193 - Teapot, Coronation. Sepia portraits. Color decoration. Same design reverse. Gold trim. 6½"h. 9"across. $135.—$150.

G5-194 - Teapot, Coronation. Color portraits and decoration. Gold trim. 4½"h. 7¼"across. Bone china. $105.—$115.

G5-195 - Teapot, Coronation. Color portraits. Prince Edward in center. Gold trim. 6"h. 9¼" across. Bone china. $235.—$260.

G5-196 - Teapot. Color portrait King George V in blue uniform. Gold trim. 3½"h. 5½"across. Bone china. $120.—$135.

G5-197 - Teapot, Silver Jubilee. Raised profiles. Queen Mary on reverse. Aluminum. 5"h. 10"across. $70.—$77.

G5-198 - Teapot, Silver Jubilee. Sepia portraits. Color decoration and trim. 5½"h. 8½"across. $80.—$90.

G5-199 - Teapot Stand, Silver Jubilee. Color portraits and decoration. Silver band around rim. 5½"d. Shelley. $65.—$71.

G5-200 - Tea Set, Silver Jubilee. Play. Color portrait on teapot. Arms on other pieces. Teapot 2"h. 4 cups and saucers. $100.—$110.

G5-201 - Tea Strainer, Silver Jubilee. "G - 1935 - M" formed by holes in bowl. Sterling silver. 5¾"long. $170.—$190.

G5-202 - Tea Strainer, Silver Jubilee. Dates, initials, commemoration in red and blue enamel. 5"long. Bowl 2¼"d. Silver plate. $33.—$38.

G5-203 - Tin, Bolton Visit 1913. Color portraits and decoration. 4½"x2"x ½"deep. Rowntree & Company. $40.—$44.

G5-204 - Tin, Christmas 1914. Color portrait. Gold decoration. Card to wounded servicemen from Cad-bury in lid. 3¼"x1½". $45.—$50.

G5-205 - Tin, Christmas Broadcast 1935. Their profiles on lid. Silver tone finish. 6¾"x4"x2¾"h. $38.—$43.

G5-206 - Tin, Coronation. Color portraits. Prince Edward and Princess Mary on ends. 7"h.x9"x6". $100.—$110.

G5-207 - Tin, Coronation. Color portraits. Queen Mary on reverse. 8"h.x 6"x2¾". $56.—$61.

G5-208 - Tin, Coronation. Color portrait Queen Mary. Gold on red sides. Red base. 1½"d. ½"deep. $44.—$49.

G5-209 - Tin, Coronation. Blue and white portrait on blue. Gold trim. 2¼"d. 1"deep. $44.—$49.

G5-210 - Tin, Coronation. Color portrait and decoration. Blue background. 4¾"x3¼"x 1"deep. Hartley's. $50.—$55.

G5-211 - Tin, Coronation. Color portraits. Sepia family portraits on sides. 6½"x4¼"x1½"deep. Rowntree & Co. $70.—$77.

G5-212 - Tin, Coronation. Color portraits and decoration. 5¼"x2¾"x ½"deep. Rowntree & Company. $37.—$41.

G5-213 - Tin, Coronation. Color portraits and decoration. 5¼"x2¼"x ½"deep. Rowntree & Company. $37.—$41.

G5-214 - Tin, Coronation. Color portraits and decoration. 4"x3"x½"deep. Rowntree & Co. $42.—$46.

G5-215 - Tin, Coronation. Blue tone portraits. Color and gold decoration. 7"x6"x 2¼"deep. Mazawattee. $63.—$69.

G5-216 - Tin, Coronation. Color portraits. Color and gold decoration. 8"x5"x 1¾"deep. Callard & Bowser Nougat. $45.—$50.

G5-217 - Tin, Coronation. Color portraits and decoration. Newcastle-Upon-Tyne. 4"x3"x ¾"deep. J. Phillips. $49.—$54.

G5-218 - Tin, Coronation. Color portraits and decoration. Bristol. 6"x3½"x¾"deep. J.S. Fry & Sons. $49.—$54.

G5-219 - Tin, Coronation. Color portraits. Color and gold decoration. 6"x4¼"x¾"deep. J.S. Fry & Sons. $49.—$54.

G5-220 - Tin, Coronation. Color portraits and decoration on purple. 4"x3"x1½"deep. City of Manchester. $44.—$49.

G5-221 - Tin, Coronation. Color portraits and decoration on red. 3¼"x2"x½"deep. Cadbury. $44.—$49.

G5-222 - Tin, Color portraits. Queen Mary on reverse. 4"x4"x3¾"h. Mazawattee Tea. $55.—$60.

G5-223 - Tin, Coronation. Color portraits and decoration on dark blue. 4"x3"x1"deep. Clarke, Nichols & Coombs. $45.—$50.

G5-224 - Tin, Silver Jubilee. Color portraits. Queen Mary reverse. Other family members on lid and sides. 6"h.x4½"x3½". $85.—$95.

G5-225 - Tin. King George V. Red, blue, silver and black decoration. 6"d. 1½"deep. $59.—$64.

G5-226 - Tin. King George V color portrait. Prince Edward on reverse. 5½"h.x5"x3½". $54.—$59.

G5-227 - Tin. King George V color portrait. Probably made when he was Prince of Wales. 4½"x3¼"x1½"deep. $70.—$77.

G5-228 - Tin. King George V color portrait on color Union Jack background. 4½"h.x3¼"x1¼". $43.—$48.

G5-229 - Tin. King George V color portrait. Match striker on base. 6"x3"x1"deep. $55.—$60.

G5-230 - Tin. Color portraits with names below. Gold tone background. Each 1½"d.x½"deep. $50.—$55. Pair.

G5-231 - Tin. King George V color portrait. 1½"x1¼"x ½"deep. $49.—$54.

G5-232 - Tin. Queen Mary color portrait. Blue base. 1¾"x1½"x ½"deep. $44.—$49.

G5-233 - Tin. "Our Sailor King." Color portrait and decoration. 5½"x3¼"x1"deep. Pascall's Confection. $75.—$83.

G5-234 - Tin. "Our Sailor King." Color portrait and decoration. 5¼"x3½"x 1"deep. Pascall's. $75.—$83.

G5-235 - Tin, Glasgow Visit 1914. Color portraits and decoration. Gold trim. 3"x2"x¾"deep. J.S. Fry. $44.—$49.

G5-236 - Tin, In Memoriam. Color portraits on blue background. 6½"h.x 3½"x3½". $100.—$110.

G5-237 - Tin, Manchester Visit 1913. Sepia portraits. Color decoration. 4½"x2¾"x ¾"deep. Cadbury. $49.—$54.

G5-238 - Tin, Silver Jubilee. Sepia portraits. Gold on red background. 5¾"h. 4"d. $49.—$54.

G5-239 - Tin, Silver Jubilee. B&W portraits. Gold trim on red background. 4¼"h.x3½"x3". $44.—$49.

G5-240 - Tin, Silver Jubilee. B&W portraits. Gold on red background. 6"h.x4¾"x3¼". $44.—$49.

G5-241 - Tin, Silver Jubilee. Color portraits. Queen Mary on reverse. Silver and blue decoration. 6"h.x 4¾"x3½". $52.—$56.

G5-242 - Tin, Silver Jubilee. B&W portraits. Blue on ivory decoration. 5¾"h.x4"x4". $42.—$47.

G5-243 - Tin, Silver Jubilee. Sepia portraits. Blue and gold decoration. 7¼"h.x4"x3". $65.—$75.

G5-244 - Tin, Silver Jubilee. Color portraits on green. Silver frames. 5"d. 1"deep. Huntley and Palmers. $44.—$49.

G5-245 - Tin, Silver Jubilee. Sepia portraits. Blue and silver decoration. 3"x 2¼"x½"deep. Grips by Lightbrowns. $34.—$39.

G5-246 - Tin, Silver Jubilee. Sepia portraits. Color decoration. Gold background. 6"x3½"x 2¼"deep. Ringtons. $39.—$44.

G5-247 - Tin, Silver Jubilee. Color portraits. Silver and blue decoration. 5½"x 3¼"x1½"deep. Mackintosh's. $44.—$49.

G5-248 - Tin, Silver Jubilee. Color portraits. Color and silver decoration on red. 10"x7½" x3"deep. $50.—$55.

G5-249 - Tin, Silver Jubilee. Color portraits and decoration. Blue background. 5¾"x3¾"x 2½"deep. $44.—$49.

G5-250 - Tin, Silver Jubilee. Color portraits. Silver and blue decoration on light blue background. 6¾"x4¾"x3½"deep. $50.—$55.

G5-251 - Tin, Silver Jubilee. Color portraits and decoration. Coin slot. City of Kingston Upon Hull. 4¼"x2½"x2¼"deep. $49.—$54.

G5-252 - Tin, Silver Jubilee. Color portraits and decoration. Silver background. 6½"x3"x 1¼"deep. $39.—$44.

G5-253 - Tin, Silver Jubilee. Color portraits. Royal residences on sides. Blue on silver. 9½"x3¼"x3½"deep. $50.—$55.

G5-254 - Tin, Silver Jubilee. Color portraits and decoration. Silver background. 7½"x4"x ½"deep. J.S. Fry. $44.—$49.

G5-255 - Tin, Silver Jubilee. Color portraits. Embossed frames, crowns. Silver background. 6"x2½"x ½"deep. Rowntree. $39.—$44.

G5-256 - Tin, Silver Jubilee. Sepia portraits. Silver background. Borough of Shoreditch. 7¼"x 2"x¾"deep. Wilkin's. $39.—$44.

G5-257 - Tin, Silver Jubilee. Color portraits and decoration. Silver background. 6¼"x5"x 3"deep. $50.—$55.

G5-258 - Tin, Silver Jubilee. Raised portraits and decoration. Purple and silver decoration. 6½"x 5"x2"deep. $39.—$44.

G5-259 - Tin, Silver Jubilee. Color portraits. Silver on blue decoration. 5½"x 4¼"x¾"deep. McVitie & Price Biscuits. $39.—$44.

G5-260 - Tin, Silver Jubilee. Sepia portraits. Mustard background. 4¼"x3"x 1¾"deep. $40.—$45.

G5-261 - Tin, Silver Jubilee. B&W portrait. Color and gold decoration. Family members on ends. 10"x7½"x3"deep. $55.—$60.

G5-262 - Tin, Silver Jubilee. Color portraits. Silver and light blue decoration. 5¾"x3¾"x1¾"deep. Cremona Toffee. $39.—$44.

G5-263 - Tin, Wedding 1893. Qn. Victoria on lid. Their parents, Pss. Victoria and Pss. Maud on sides. 7"h. 6½"d. $225.—$250.

G5-264 - Tin, Wedding 1893. Color portraits. Qn. Victoria on lid. Their parents on sides. 6¾"h.x7"x5". $250.—$275.

King George V and Queen Mary

G5-265 - Tray. King George V in blue uniform. Color portrait. Metal. 4½"x3½". $37.—$42.

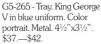

G5-266 - Vase, Coronation. Color decoration. Gold rim. 2"h. 2"d. at center. W.H. Goss BC. $40.—$50.

G5-267 - Vase, Coronation. Color decoration. Gold rim. 4½"h. 1"d. at top. W.H. Goss BC. $40.—$50.

G5-268 - Vase, Coronation. Sepia portraits. Gold trim. 2¼"h. 1¼"d. Bone china. $45.—$50.

G5-269 - Vase, Coronation. B&W portraits. Color decoration. Birth, wedding, coronation dates. 6¼"h. Devon. $65.—$72.

G5-270 - Vase, Coronation. Color portraits. Embossed flower on reverse. Gold trim. 3½"h. 2½"across. BC. $45.—$50.

G5-271 - Vase, Coronation. Color decoration. Gold trim. 2¾"h. W.H. Goss BC. $55.—$65.

G5-272 - Vase, Coronation. Sepia portraits. Color decoration. St. George slaying dragon reverse. 4"h. 4½"across. $55.—$60.

G5-273 - Vase, Coronation. Color portrait Queen Mary. Gold trim. 6¼"h. 4"d. 2"deep. Russell & Sons. BC. $75.—$85.

G5-274 - Vase, Coronation. Sepia portraits. Color decoration. Gold trim. 3¼"h. 2¼"wide. 3¼" front to back. BC. $55.—$62.

G5-275 - Vase, Coronation. Thistle shape. Color decoration. 3"h. W.H. Goss bone china. $55.—$65.

G5-276 - Vase, Coronation. Color decoration. Gold trim. 3"h. 2"d. at top. W.H. Goss bone china. $55.—$65.

King George V and Queen Mary — Family

G5-277 - Beaker, Prince Edward's Investiture 1911. Color portrait and decoration. Gold rim. 4"h. 3"d. Pottery. $200.—$220.

G5-278 - Loving Cup, Prince Edward's Birth 1894. Name and date. Color decorated slipware. 7¾"h. 4¼"d. Unmarked Aller Vale. $975.—$1075.

G5-279 - Mug, Prince Edward's Investiture 1911. Color portraits and decoration. 3"h. 3"d. Crown Pottery. $210.—$225.

G5-280 - Plaque. Sepia portrait Prince Edward c. 1911. 7½"x6". Ridgways. $200.—$220.

G5-281 - Plate, Prince Edward's Investiture 1911. Blue tone portraits (also King and Queen). 7¾"d. Burleigh Ware. $190.—$210.

G5-282 - Plate. "Prince Edward of Wales—Our Future King". Color portrait. Gold trim. 7"d. Bone china. $90.—$100.

G5-283 - Tin, Prince Edward's Investiture 1911. Color portrait and decoration. 8¼"x 5"x2"deep. Squirrel Confections. $105.—$115.

G5-284 - Tin. Prince of Wales sepia portrait. Lid is stand alone or hanging frame. 5½"x4½". $55.—$62.

G5-285 - Tin. Princess Mary Christmas 1914 gift to men and women in service. Embossed design. 4¾"x3"x1"deep. Brass. $60.—$70.

King George VI and Queen Elizabeth

G6-001 - Ashtray, Coronation. Raised gold cypher and crown. Gold rim. 4"d. Foley BC. $33.—$37.

G6-002 - Ashtray, Coronation. Metal. Raised portraits and commemoration. 4¼"d. $33.—$38.

G6-003 - Ashtray, Coronation. Sepia portraits. Color decoration. Gold trim. 3¼"x2¼"x½"deep. $30.—$34.

G6-004 - Ashtray, Coronation. Beige silhouette portraits. Color decoration. 4"d. Alfred Meakin. $27.—$32.

G6-005 - Bank, Coronation. Post Office Savings Bank. Raised profile portraits. Gold tone metal. 4½"x3"x1". $45.—$50.

G6-006 - Basket, Coronation. Pressed glass. 5½"h. 7½"d. $45.—$50.

G6-007 - Beaker, Coronation. Color decoration partially hand painted. Gold trim. 3"h. 2¾"d. Hammersley BC. $79.—$89.

G6-008 - Beaker, Coronation. Puce crown on white. (Also made in green on blue). 4"h. 3"d. Moorcroft. Pottery. $465.—$525.

G6-009 - Beaker, Coronation. Beige tone profile portraits. Color decoration. Gold rim. 4"h. 3"d. at top. Crown Ducal. $57.—$63.

G6-010 - Beaker, Coronation. Brown tone Marcus Adams portrait. Color decoration. 4½"h. Copeland Spode. $79.—$89.

G6-011 - Beaker, Coronation. B&W portraits (Princesses below) on blue background. 4½"h. 2¾"d. Wedgwood & Co. Ltd. $65.—$75.

G6-012 - Beaker, Coronation. Sepia Marcus Adams portrait. Color decoration. Blue rim band. 3½"h. 2¾"d. at top. Pottery. $70.—$78.

G6-013 - Beaker, Coronation. Brown tone portraits. Color decoration. 4½"h. Wedgwood. $70.—$78.

G6-014 - Beaker, Coronation. Color portraits. Gold decoration. LE 2000. Minton BC. $295.—$325.

G6-015 - Beaker, Coronation. Raised profile portraits. Red, blue, gold bands. 4"h. 3"d. Crown Devon Pottery. $50.—$55.

G6-016 - Beaker, USA Visit 1939. Color and gold decoration. LE 3000 numbered. Made for W.H. Plummer by Minton. 4¼"h. 3¼"d. $525.—$595.

G6-017 - Bowl, Coronation. Sepia Marcus Adams portrait. Color decoration. Gold rim. 6¼"d. 1¼" deep. J&G Meakin. $50.—$56.

G6-018 - Bowl, Coronation. Sepia portraits. Gold decoration. 8½"d. 3¾" deep. Copeland Spode bone china. $225.—$250.

G6-019 - Bowl, Coronation. Amber pressed glass. Gold backing. 8½"d. 1¼" deep. $63.—$69.

G6-020 - Bowl, Coronation. Color arms, cypher and date. 5½"d. 1¼" deep. Paragon BC. $50.—$55.

G6-021 - Bowl, Coronation. Sepia portraits. Color decoration. Gold rim. 3¼"d. 1"deep. Bone china. $29.—$33.

G6-022 - Bowl, Coronation. Pale green pressed glass. Profiles and commemoration in well. 8½"x7"x1¼" deep. $59.—$65.

G6-023 - Box, Coronation. Crown shape. Gold on deep red. Pearlized jewels. 4"h. 2½"d. at base. Crown Staffordshire. $160.—$180.

G6-024 - Box, Coronation. Red with gold decoration. White and color jewels. 3¾"h. 3¼"d. Made for Plummers—Coalport. $445.—$470.

G6-025 - Box, Coronation. Crown shape. Red, gold and white. LE 500 made for Plummers by Coalport. 3¼"h. 3½"d. $375.—$410.

G6-026 - Bucket, Coronation. Miniature. Raised silhouette. Name and date. Brass. 2¼"h. 2"d. $37.—$41.

G6-027 - Cigarette Card, Coronation. Album contains 50 colorful cards. Album is 10"x8". Soft cover. $30.—$35.

G6-028 - Cigarette Card, Coronation. Three framed cards: King, Queen, Princesses. See-thru Frame 8½"x6½". $43.—$47.

G6-029 - Clock, Coronation. In metal crown mount. 4½"h. 4"wide. 1¾"deep. $85.—$95.

G6-030 - Compact, Coronation. Color portrait. Silver tone finish. 1¾"d. Lylax brand hard powder. $39.—$44.

G6-031 - Creamer and Sugar, Coronation. Brown tone portraits. Princesses on reverse both pieces. Shelley bone china. $150.—$165.

G6-032 - Cuff Links, Coronation. Profile portraits, names and "1937" on each link. Links are ¾"x½". Bronze. $49.—$54.

G6-033 - Cup and Saucer, Canada 1939 Visit. Sepia portraits. Princesses below. Alfred Meakin. $73.—$78.

G6-034 - Cup and Saucer, Canada/USA 1939 Visit. Sepia portraits. Color decoration. Gold trim. Chelsea bone china. $44.—$49.

G6-035 - Cup and Saucer, Canada/USA 1939 Visit. Sepia portraits. Color decoration. Gold trim. Royal Albert BC. $53.—$58.

G6-036 - Cup and Saucer, Coronation. Sepia portraits. Color decoration. Gold trim. Delphine BC. $43.—$47.

G6-037 - Cup and Saucer, Coronation. Beige portraits. Color decoration. Blue trim. Pottery. $42.—$46.

G6-038 - Cup and Saucer, Coronation. Black and white portraits. Color decoration. Aynsley bone china. $90.—$100.

G6-039 - Cup and Saucer, Coronation. Sepia Marcus Adams portrait on both pieces. Royal Albert bone china. $100.—$110.

G6-040 - Cup and Saucer, Coronation. Sepia portraits. Princesses on both pieces. Color decoration. Welworth BC. $49.—$55.

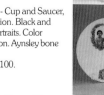

G6-041 - Cup and Saucer, Coronation. Sepia portraits. Pss. Elizabeth on saucer. Pss. Margaret on cup. Bone china. $46.—$50.

G6-042 - Cup and Saucer, Pudsey 1928 Visit. Sepia Vandyk portraits. Color decoration. Gold trim. Wellington BC. $110.—$120.

G6-043 - Cup and Saucer, "The King of Great Britain". Black and white portrait. Gold trim. Demitasse size. Made in Japan. $37.—$41.

G6-044 - Cup and Saucer, "The Queen is Still in London". Sepia portrait. World War II Paragon Patriotic Series. Bone china. $305.—$330.

G6-045 - Cup and Saucer, "There'll Always Be An England." Color decoration. Roslyn bone china. $100.—$110.

G6-046 - Dish, Coronation. Color decoration. Gold rim. 4¾"x3¾"x1½"deep. Hammersley bone china. $62.—$67.

G6-047 - Dish, Coronation. Yellow crown on blue/green background. 3"d. 1¼"deep. Moorcroft. Pottery. $200.—$225.

G6-048 - Dish, Coronation. Gold on cobalt blue. Profiles, names, flags. 5"x4"x1". Coalport bone china. $60.—$68.

G6-049 - Dish, Coronation. Sepia portraits. Gold decoration on deep red. 3¾"x3¾"x1"deep. Crown Staffordshire. $60.—$68.

G6-050 - Dish, Coronation. Color decoration on cream background. Gold trim. 4"d. 1¼"deep. Paragon BC. $48.—$53.

G6-051 - Dish, Coronation. Brown tone portraits. Color decoration. Gold rim. Marked "Canada". 3¾"d. 1½"deep. $38.—$42.

G6-052 - Dish, Coronation. Covered Butter. Beige tone portraits. Color decoration. Gold trim. 3½"h. Base 6"x5". $85.—$95.

G6-053 - Dish, Coronation. Sepia portraits with Pss. Elizabeth above. Color and gold. 5½"x4¾"x ¾"deep. Phoenix. $36.—$41.

G6-054 - Dish, USA Visit 1939. Black and white portraits on blue. 4"d. Royal Doulton BC. $49.—$55.

G6-055 - Dish, Coronation. Sterling silver card receiver. Cypher and "1937". Crown handles. 1¾"h.x7¼"x4". $150.—$160.

G6-056 - Dish, Australia Visit 1949. Raised decoration. Visit canceled because of King's illness. 5½"x5¼". Sylvac. $75.—$83.

G6-057 - Dish, Canada/ USA Visit 1939. Sepia portraits. Color decoration. Gold rim. 4½"d. ¾"deep. Chelsea BC. $30—$34.

G6-058 - Dish, Canada/ USA Visit 1939. Footed. Sepia portrait. Color decoration. 1¾"h. 5"d. Aynsley BC. $39.—$43.

G6-059 - Egg Cup, Coronation. Sepia portraits. Color decoration. Gold rim. Pottery. 2½"h. $32.—$35.

G6-060 - Egg Cup, Coronation. Sepia portraits. Color decoration. Gold rim. Pottery. 2½"h. $32.—$35.

G6-061 - Figurine, Coronation. Hand painted. 8¼"h. Base is 6½"x5". Carlton Ware. $1005.—$1065.

G6-062 - Flag, Coronation. Black and white portraits above world maps. Red, white and blue. Cotton. 33"x22". $43.—$48.

G6-063 - Flag, Coronation. Black and white portraits. Red, white and blue. 5"x3". Metal staff with wire ties. $17.—$21.

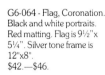

G6-064 - Flag, Coronation. Black and white portraits. Red matting. Flag is 9½"x 5¼". Silver tone frame is 12"x8". $42.—$46.

G6-065 - Goblet, Coronation. Crystal. Etched crown, cypher and date. 5"h. 3¼"d. at top. Stuart Glass. $78.—$83.

G6-066 - Goblet, Coronation. Red and blue enamel medallion. Silver plate. 2¾"h. 3¼"d. at top. $36.—$40.

G6-067 - Goblet, Coronation. Crystal. Etched crown, cypher and date in wreath. 4¼"h. 2¾"d. at top. $35.—$40.

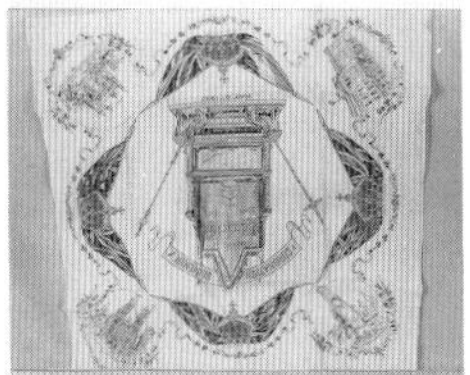

G6-068 - Handkerchief, Coronation. Color decoration. Names in gold. 16"x16". Rayon. $33.—$36.

G6-069 - Handkerchief, Coronation. Blue on white linen. Birth, accession dates. 18½"x18½". $35.—$40.

G6-070 - Handkerchief, Coronation. Blue and white portraits. Color decoration. 11"x11". $35.—$40.

G6-071 Handkerchief, "Duchess of York". Black and white Bertram Park portrait. Color flowers. Red border. 8"x8". $39.—$43.

G6-072 - Jar, Coronation. Color decoration mainly blues and greens. 5½"h. 4½"d. Moorcroft Pottery. $795.—$845.

G6-073 - Jar, Coronation. Color decoration. Gold lion finial. Gold trim. 3½"h. 3"d. Paragon bone china. $165.—$180.

G6-074 - Jar, Coronation. Sepia portraits. Queen Elizabeth on reverse. Color decoration. 7½"h.x6"x4". Rington's. $195.—$210.

G6-075 - Jigsaw Puzzle, Coronation. King and Queen inside coronation coach. 250 cardboard pieces. 15"x11". Lumar. $63.—$68.

G6-076 - Jigsaw Puzzle, c. 1940's. 250 plywood pieces in each 16"x12" puzzle. Color decoration. By Saga. $135.—$150. Pair.

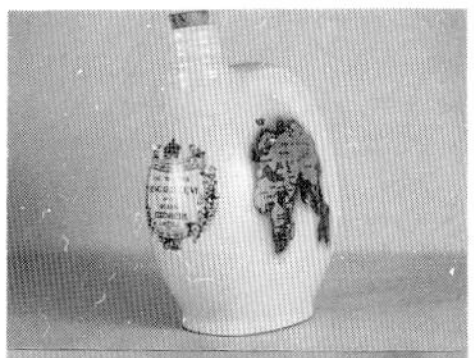

G6-077 - Jug, Coronation. Color world map on beige. 7½"h.x6"x2¼". Made by Crown Ducal for Emu Wines. $48.—$53.

G6-078 - Jug, Coronation. Sepia portraits. Red and blue decoration. 7½"h. 7"across. Lancaster and Sons Pottery. $65.—$72.

G6-079 - Jug, Coronation. Sepia portraits. Color decoration. Gold trim. 5¼"h. 6¼"across. Aynsley bone china. $75.—$82.

G6-080 - Jug, Coronation. Musical. Brown tone portraits. Princesses on reverse. 7¼"h. 8"across. Shelley. $245.—$265.

G6-081 - Jug, Coronation. Musical. Color decoration on cream. Plays "God Save The King". 7¾"h. 7½"across. Pottery. $340.—$375.

G6-082 - Jug, King George VI. Miniature. Hand painted. 2½"h. 3"across. Royal Winton. $79.—$85.

G6-083 - Loving Cup, Coronation. Sepia portraits. Color decoration. Gold trim. 3¼"h. 5"across. Old Royal China BC. $90.—$100.

G6-084 - Loving Cup, Coronation. Brown tone Marcus Adams portrait. Color and gold decoration. 3¼"h. 5"across. Sampson BC. $130.—$145.

G6-085 - Loving Cup, Coronation. Sepia portraits. Color decoration. Gold handles and trim. 3¼"h. 5"across. $80.—$90.

G6-086 - Loving Cup, Coronation. Color and gold decoration on cobalt blue. Color flower handles. 3¼"h. 3¼"d. Adderly BC. $180.—$195.

G6-087 - Loving Cup, Coronation. Sepia portraits. Color decoration. Gold trim. 3"h. 5"across. Radfords Crown BC. $75.—$83.

G6-088 - Loving Cup, Coronation. Color decoration. Gold trim. Brown lion handles. 3½"h. 6"across. Paragon BC. $100.—$115.

G6-089 - Match Safe. Qn. Eliz. II coin on reverse. Strike around sides. Silver tone. 1¼"d.x½". $38.—$42.

G6-090 - Mirror, Coronation. Color portraits and decoration. Black rim. 2¾"d. $20.—$23.

G6-091 - Mug, Australia Visit 1949. Visit canceled because of King's illness. Pss. Margaret on reverse. 3"h. 3"d. Royal Art. $95.—$105.

G6-092 - Mug, Australia Visit 1949. Visit canceled because of King's illness. Sepia decoration. 3"h. Brentleigh Ware. $100.—$110.

G6-093 - Mug, Canada/ USA Visit 1939. Sepia portrait. Color decoration. Gold trim. 3"h. 3"d. Aynsley BC. $55.—$62.

G6-094 - Mug, Coronation. Color decoration partially hand painted. Gold trim. 3"h. 3"d. Hammersley BC. $100.—$110.

G6-095 - Mug, Coronation. Sepia portraits. Color decoration. Gold trim. 3"h. 3"d. Pottery. $28.—$32.

G6-096 - Mug, Coronation. Sepia portraits. Color decoration. Gold trim. Crown, sceptre, orb. 4"h. J. Kent Ltd. BC. $68.—$75.

G6-097 - Mug, Coronation. Sepia portraits. Color decoration. Gold trim. 3½"h. By Copeland for Thos. Goode. $85.—$95.

G6-098 - Mug, Coronation. Sepia portraits. Color decoration. Gold trim. 3¾"h. 3¼"d. at top. Marked C.W.S. $45.—$50.

G6-099 - Mug, Coronation. "GVIR", crown and "1937". Green slipware with blue in crown. 4¾"h. 3¼"d. at top. $55.—$61.

G6-100 - Mug, Coronation. Colorful Dame Laura Knight circus design. Gold trim. 3½"h. 3"d. at top. Grafton BC. $125.—$140.

G6-101 - Mug, Coronation. Musical. Color decoration. "Here's a Health Unto His Majesty". 4¾"h. 4½"d. Crown Devon. $225.—$275.

G6-102 - Mug, Coronation. Sepia Marcus Adams portrait. Color decoration 3¼"h. Copeland Spode. $77.—$85.

G6-103 - Mug, Coronation. Amber glass. Raised profile portraits. "Long live the King." Flags. 4"h. 3"d. at top. $48.—$53.

G6-104 - Mug, Coronation. Sepia portraits. Princess Elizabeth on reverse. Color decoration. Blue trim. 2¾"h. 2¾"d. BC. $50.—$55.

G6-105 - Mug, Coronation. Brown on beige unglazed background. Gold trim. 3½"h. Gray's Pottery. $52.—$57.

G6-106 - Mug, Coronation. Sepia portraits. Psses. Elizabeth and Margaret on reverse. 2¾"h. Shelley BC. $80.—$90.

G6-107 - Mug, Coronation. Black and white portrait on blue. Color decoration. 3"h. Royal Doulton. $70.—$77. in BC. $53.—$57. in Pottery.

G6-108 - Mug, Coronation. Color decoration partially hand painted. Gold trim. 3"h. 3"d. Hammersley BC. $100.—$110.

G6-109 - Mug, Coronation. Sepia Marcus Adams portrait. Color decoration. Gold trim. 3¼"h. Albert Crown China. $80.—$90.

G6-110 - Mug, Coronation and 1939 Canada/USA Visit. Color decoration. Gold lion handle. 3"h. 3¼"d. Paragon BC. $125.—$135.

G6-111 - Mug, Coronation. Amber glass. Raised profiles and commemoration. Marked "Half Pint". 4"h. 3¼"d. at top. $48.—$53.

G6-112 - Mug, Coronation. Color decoration mostly blue and green. 4½"h. 4"d. at top. Moorcroft. Pottery. $475.—$535.

G6-113 - Mug, Coronation. Shaving. Sepia portraits. Color decoration. Pottery. 4"h. 6"across. $75.—$84.

G6-114 - Picture, Coronation. Color portraits in metal frame. Dates upper corner. 6½"x4¾". $21.—$24.

G6-115 - Picture, Coronation. Color. Stand alone, self framed. 15"x11". $110.—$120. Pair.

G6-116 - Picture. Black and white prints from pencil drawings. Light grey mats. Prints 10½"x7¾". Mats are 14¼"x11¾". $38.—$43. Pair.

G6-117 - Picture. Black and white Marcus Adams portrait on metal. Stand alone. 7¼"x5¾". $35.—$40.

G6-118 - Paperweight, Coronation. Black and white Marcus Adams portrait. Heavy rounded glass. Felt base. 1¼"h. 2½"d. $31.—$35.

G6-119 - Pin, Coronation. On original card. ¾"d. In silver or gold tone. $25.—$28.

G6-120 - Pin, Coronation. 1"h. 2" across. Silver tone. $23.—$25.

G6-121 - Plaque, Coronation. Stand alone. Sepia Marcus Adams portrait. Gold trim. 3½"h. 3"d. BC. $80.—$88.

G6-122 - Plaque, Coronation. Brass mounted on wood. Plaque is 4¾"d. Mount is 5¼"d. Hanger on reverse. $49.—$54.

G6-123 - Plaque, Coronation. Sterling silver on black wooden mount. Mount is 7¼"x6¼". C. Hutton. $145.—$160.

G6-124 - Plaque. "King George VI Memorial". Bronze. Marked "Master Model" on reverse. 11"x8". $160.—$175.

G6-125 - Plate, Canada/USA Visit 1939. Sepia portraits. Color decoration. Gold trim. 8½"d. Colclough BC. $40.—$45.

G6-126 - Plate, Canada/USA Visit 1939. Sepia portraits. Color decoration. Maple leaf border. 8"d. Royal Albert BC. $41.—$46.

G6-127 - Plate, Canada/USA Visit 1939. Sepia portraits. Princesses on four corners. 6½"d. Alfred Meakin. $44.—$49.

G6-128 - Plate, Canada Visit 1939. Color portraits and decoration. 10½"d. Royal Winton. $89.—$99.

G6-129 - Plate, Canada/USA Visit 1939. Sepia portraits. Color decoration. Gold rim. 6¾" d. Aynsley BC. $55.—$62.

G6-130 - Plate, Canada/USA Visit 1939. B&W portraits on blue. Princesses below. 8¼"d. Wedgwood & Co. Ltd. $70.—$80.

G6-131 - Plate, Coronation. Sepia portraits. Princess Elizabeth above. 8"d. $43.—$48.

G6-132 - Plate, Coronation. Sepia portraits. Princess Elizabeth below. Color decoration. 6½"d. Falcon Ware. $42.—$46.

G6-133 - Plate, Coronation. Sepia Marcus Adams portrait. Blue highlights on embossed border. 8½"d. Fryer. $85.—$95.

G6-134 - Plate, Coronation. Colorful decoration partially hand painted. Gold trim. 10½"d. Paragon bone china. $195.—$215.

G6-135 - Plate, Coronation. Color decoration partially hand painted. Gold rim. 7"d. Hammersley bone china. $78.—$88.

G6-136 - Plate, Coronation. Color decoration includes national flowers. Gold rim. 5¾"d. Hammersley BC. $78.—$88.

G6-137 - Plate, Coronation. Color decoration partially hand painted. Gold rim. 7"d. Hammersley bone china. $78.—$88.

G6-138 - Plate, Coronation. Mostly hand painted decoration. Westminster Abbey and Windsor. 7"d. Hammersley BC. $78.—$88.

G6-139 - Plate, Coronation. Commemorative bands on border. Color decoration in center. Gold rim. 6"d. Paragon BC. $49.—$55.

G6-140 - Plate, Coronation. Color flowers. Gold cypher and trim. 9¼"x9". Commemoration on reverse. Paragon BC. $72.—$79.

G6-141 - Plate, Coronation. Orange and black design by Charlotte Rhead. Gold highlights. 9¼"d. Crown Ducal. $80.—$90.

G6-142 - Plate, Coronation. Sepia portraits. Gold on blue border. 8¾"d. Marked H&K. $50.—$55.

G6-143 - Plate, Coronation. Sepia portraits. Color decoration. Gold trim. Embossed border. 9"d. Solian Ware. $36.—$40.

G6-144 - Plate, Coronation. Sepia portraits. Color decoration. Gold rim. 6¼"d. Tuscan BC. $43.—$47.

G6-145 - Plate, Coronation. B&W portraits on blue. Color decoration. Crown, orb, sceptre. 6"d. Royal Doulton. $53.—$59.

G6-146 - Plate, Coronation. Sepia Marcus Adams portrait. Gold rim. 6"d. Stanley BC. $55.—$60.

G6-147 - Plate, Coronation. Sepia portraits. Color decoration. Pudsey commemoration. 6½"d. Wellington BC. $68.—$75.

G6-148 - Plate, Coronation. Sepia Vandyk portraits. Color flags and decoration. Beige handles. 9¾"x8¼". Shelley BC. $69.—$75.

G6-149 - Plate, Coronation. Pressed glass. Gold backed profiles. Commemoration and national flowers. 9½"d. $59.—$64.

G6-150 - Plate, Coronation. Baby's plate. Sepia Vandyk portraits. Color decoration. 6¼"d. 1½"deep. Shelley. $62.—$68.

G6-151 - Plate, USA Visit 1939. Etched glass. 11¾"d. $88.—$98.

G6-152 - Playing Cards, Coronation. Color Vandyk portraits. Double deck in box. $75.—$83.

G6-153 - Playing Cards, Coronation. Color portraits. Double deck in box. Canadian Playing Card Co. $79.—$85.

G6-154 - Post Card, Wedding 1923. Sepia portraits include wedding attendants. Marlborough Printing Company. $22.—$27.

G6-155 - Spoon, Coronation. Sterling silver anointing spoon. Profiles atop handle. 5¼"long. Birks. $41.—$46.

G6-156 - Spoon, Coronation. Commemoration and date inside bowl. Brass. 2¾"long. Bowl 1½"d. $25.—$29.

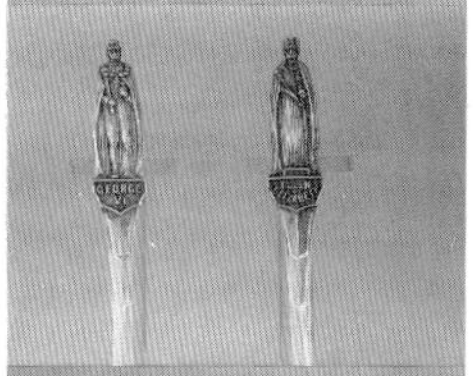

G6-157 - Spoon. Coronation. King and Queen in coronation robes. Their names below. 4¼"long. Sterling silver. $72.—$79. Pair.

G6-158 - Stamps, Coronation. Plastic spiral book contains over 200 stamps. 7"x5¼". Kenmore Stamp Co. $79.—$85.

G6-159 - Tape Measure, Coronation. Color portraits. 2"d. Silver tone. $70.—$77.

G6-160 - Teapot, Coronation. Sepia portraits. Color decoration. Blue trim. 5"h. 8"across. Norbury Pottery. $93.—$102.

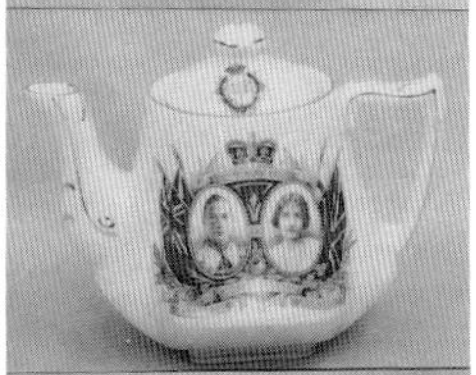

G6-161 - Teapot, Coronation. Sepia portraits. Color decoration. Gold trim. 4½"h. 6¼"across. J. Kent Ltd. $80.—$88.

G6-162 - Teapot, Coronation. Sepia portraits. Color decoration. Gold trim. 5"h. 8"across. Marked England. $80.—$88.

G6-163 - Teapot, Coronation. Sepia portraits. Gold trim. Embossing. Cream background. 5"h. 8½" across. $310.—$360.

G6-164 - Tile, Coronation. Color decoration. 6"x6". Minton Tiles. $67.—$72.

G6-165 - Tin, Canada/ USA Visit 1939. Sepia Marcus Adams portrait. Color decoration on blue. 4"h. 5"d. $60.—$66.

G6-166 - Tin, Canada/ USA Visit 1939. Color portraits on red background. 7"x5¾"x1¾"deep. $36.—$40.

G6-167 - Tin, Coronation. B&W portrait. Gold, red and silver decoration. 1¼"h.x7"x5¾". A. S. Wilkin Ltd. $32.—$36.

G6-168 - Tin, Coronation. B&W portraits. Red and blue decoration on gold background. 5¾"x 3¾"x2½". $32.—$35.

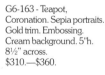

G6-169 - Tin, Coronation. Color portrait. Gold decoration on red. Blue border. 5¼"x3½"x1" deep. Glasgow. $35.—$40.

G6-170 - Tin, Coronation. Sepia portrait on beige. Red sides. 1¼"h.x4½"x4½". $39.—$43.

G6-171 - Tin, Coronation. Raised gold profiles on blue background. 4½"x 4½"x1¼"deep. Glasgow. $48.—$53.

G6-172 - Tin, Coronation. Sepia portraits. Color decoration. King in naval uniform on lid. 5¾"h.x5"x3½". Price. $52.—$57.

G6-173 - Tin, Coronation. Color portraits. Red on gold decoration. 6"h.x 4½"x3¼". $45.—$50.

G6-174 - Tin, Coronation. Beige tone Vandyk portrait. Red, blue and gold. 5¾"h.x4½"x3". $50.—$55.

G6-175 - Tin, Coronation. Beige Vandyk portraits. Qn. Elizabeth on reverse. 5"h.x 5½"x3½". $38.—$43.

G6-176 - Tin, Coronation. Slot for coins. Gold and black medallion profiles on red background. 3"h.x2½"x1¼". Oxo. $20.—$23.

G6-177 - Tin, Coronation. Brown tone portraits on each side—King, Queen and Princesses. 5¾"h.x4" x4". E.I. & Co. Ltd. $47.—$52.

G6-178 - Tin, Coronation. Sepia portraits. Red, gold and brown decoration on beige background. 2"h.x4"x3". $20.—$24.

G6-179 - Tin, Coronation. Color portraits in gold frames. Accession and coronation dates. 6½"x4½"x2". $49.—$53.

G6-180 - Tin, Coronation. Color and gold decoration on beige background. 7½"x4"x¾". J. S. Fry. $25.—$29.

G6-181 - Tin, Coronation. Color portraits and decoration. Beige background. 8"x4½"x 2¼". Carr's Biscuits. $27.—$31.

G6-182 - Tin, Coronation. Color portraits. Red and gold decoration. 2½"h.x5½"x3½". Hinged lid. $36.—$41.

G6-183 - Tin, Coronation. Color portraits and decoration. 3½"h.x 11¼"x3¼". $32.—$35.

G6-184 - Tin, Coronation. Color portraits. Gold on blue decoration. 9¾"x 3½"x3¼"deep. William Crawford. $36.—$40.

G6-185 - Tin, Coronation. Black and white portraits on blue background. 6¼"x 1¾"x1½"deep. $21.—$24.

G6-186 - Tin, Coronation. Color portraits and decoration. Gold background. 7¼"x 2"x¾"deep. Cremona. $39.—$43.

G6-187 - Tin, Coronation. Color portraits. Embossed frames and design. Gold background. $39.—$43. 6¾"x3½"x1". $36.—$40. 6"x2½"x½".

G6-188 - Tin, Coronation. Color portraits in gold frames on red background. Gold base. 5¼"x3½"x1". $35.—$40.

G6-189 - Tin, Coronation. Color portraits. Buckingham Palace in background. 6"x3¼"x1¼". Walter's Palm Toffee. $48.—$53.

G6-190 - Tin, Coronation. Gold medallion portraits. Coin slot. Color flag. Black base. 4¾"x2¾"x 2"deep. $39.—$43.

G6-191 - Tin, Coronation. Color decoration. 9"d. 4½"deep. Waller & Hartley. $42.—$46.

G6-192 - Tin, Coronation. Sepia portrait and background. 1¾"h.x7"d. Albert Talbot. $37.—$41.

G6-193 - Tin, Coronation. Raised portraits. Gold tone background. 4"d. 1"deep. $21.—$24.

G6-194 - Tin, Coronation. Color portrait and background. 1¾"h.x5½"d. Mackintosh's. $41.—$45.

G6-195 - Tin, Coronation. Color portrait. Princesses and royal residences on side. 4"h. 5"d. $55.—$60.

G6-196 - Tin, Coronation. Color portrait and decoration. Color background. 10"d. 5"deep. $42.—$47.

G6-197 - Tin, Coronation. Color portraits and decoration. Gold on red. 1½"h. 6"d. $40.—$45.

G6-198 - Tin, Coronation. Sepia portrait on removable medallion. Color and gold decoration. 1½"h. 4¾"d. $35.—$39.

G6-199 - Tin, Coronation. Color Marcus Adams portrait. Color decoration. 5"h. 10"d. $46.—$51.

G6-200 - Tin, Coronation. Color Marcus Adams portrait. Gold background. 9¼"x7½"x 2"deep. Macfarlane. $53.—$58.

G6-201 - Tin, Coronation. Sepia Marcus Adams portrait. Gold on red background. 5¼"x4"x 1¼"deep. Riley's. $42.—$46.

G6-202 - Tin, Coronation. Sepia Marcus Adams portrait. Brown background. 1¾"h. 7"d. E.I. & Co. $39.—$44.

G6-203 - Tin, Wedding 1923. Color portraits and decoration. 4½"x2"x½" deep. Rowntree & Co. $85.—$95.

G6-204 - Tin, Wedding 1923. Sepia portraits. York Minster and Glamis Castle on sides. 4¼"h.x3½"x3". $130.—$140.

G6-205 - Tray, Canada Visit 1939. Silver plate on copper. Impressed portraits and decoration. 12"d. ½"deep. Wm. A. Rogers. $95.—$105.

G6-206 - Trivet, Coronation. Silver plate. ½"h. 4½"d. $34.—$38.

G6-207 - Tumbler, Coronation. White portraits, decoration and commemoration. 4¼"h. 2¼"d. at top. $32.—$36.

King George VI and Queen Elizabeth

G6-208 - Tumbler, Canada Visit 1939. Blue decoration. 4¾"h. 2½"d. $19.—$22.

G6-209 - Vase, Coronation. Sepia portraits. Color decoration. 3½"h. 2¾"d. Pottery. $29.—$33.

G6-210 - Vase, Coronation. Brown tone portraits. Color decoration. 4¼"h. 3"d. Pottery. $29.—$33.

Queen Elizabeth, The Queen Mother

G6-211 - Automobile, 90th Birthday. Rolls Royce model. Die cast metal. Purple with lavender top. 1½"h. 3¾"long. Lledo. $30.—$33.

G6-212 - Bell, 80th Birthday. Color portrait and decoration. Gold trim. 5½"h. 3"d. Crown Staffordshire BC. $65.—$70.

G6-213 - Bowl, 80th Birthday. Color portrait. Gold trim. 8½"d.x7¾"x1¼"deep. Crown Staffordshire bone china. $79.—$85.

G6-214 - Box, 80th Birthday. Sepia portrait framed in gold. Color and gold decoration. LE 2000. 3¾"d. 1½"deep. Spode. $73.—$79.

G6-215 - Box, 80th Birthday. Color portrait and decoration. Gold trim. 1¾"h. 3¾"d. Crown Staffordshire BC. $65.—$71.

G6-216 - Box, 80th Birthday. Black profile surrounded by gold commemoration and flowers. Gold trim. 2"h. 4¾"d. Prinknash. $18.—$22.

G6-217 - Crown, 80th Birthday. Purple, gold and white decoration. 2"h. 1½"d. Caverswall bone china. $59.—$65.

G6-218 - Dish, 80th Birthday. Color portrait and decoration. Gold rim. 4"d. Crown Staffordshire bone china. $25.—$28.

G6-219 - Dish, 80th Birthday. Maroon tone portrait and decoration. Gold rim. 4½"d. Coronet BC. $19.—$22.

G6-220 - Dish, 80th Birthday. Brown tone portrait and decoration. Gold rim. 4¾"d. Royal Albert bone china. $22.—$25.

G6-221 - Egg Cup, 90th Birthday. Color portrait and flowers. 2¼"h. Coronet BC. $17.—$20.

G6-222 - Figurine, 80th Birthday. Color decorated stoneware. Light blue dress. 9"h. 4¾"d. at base. Naturecraft Ltd. $150.—$160.

G6-223 - First Day Cover, 80th Birthday. Color portrait on stamp. Canceled Crawley W. Sussex 4 Aug 1980. 4½"x8½". $25.—$28.

G6-224 - Goblet, 80th Birthday. Etched portrait. Commemoration on reverse. 8"h. 4"d. at top. $95.—$105.

G6-225 - Jigsaw Puzzle. Color Portrait. 500 cardboard pieces. 20"x15". Philmar. $35.—$39.

G6-226 - Loving Cup, 80th Birthday. Gold profile and decoration on cobalt blue. LE 500. 3"h. 5"across. Royal Crown Derby. $230.—$245.

G6-227 - Loving Cup, 80th Birthday. Brown tone portrait. Color and gold decoration. Gold trim. 3¾"h. 6" across. Royal Doulton. $68.—$73.

G6-228 - Loving Cup, 80th Birthday. Color portraits and decoration. Gold trim. 3¼"h. 5"across. Crown Staffordshire BC. $92.—$99.

G6-229 - Loving Cup, 80th Birthday. Color and gold decoration. Gold lion handles. 3¼"h. 5½"across. Paragon bone china. $72.—$79.

G6-230 - Loving Cup, 80th Birthday. Color and gold decoration. Gold lion handles. LE 750 numbered. 5¼"h. 8¾"across. Paragon. $515.—$535.

G6-231 - Loving Cup, 80th Birthday. Pss. Margaret's 50th Birthday on reverse. Sepia portrait. 3½"h. 5¼" across. Caverswall BC. $119.—$129.

G6-232 - Loving Cup, 85th Birthday. Color and gold decoration. LE 500. 3"h. 5"across. Royal Crown Derby bone china. $215.—$229.

G6-233 - Mug, 80th Birthday. Color portrait and decoration. Gold trim. 3¾"h. Crown Staffordshire bone china. $70.—$77.

G6-234 - Mug, 80th Birthday. Color portrait and decoration. Gold trim. Stephen Barnsley design. 3½"h. 3"d. Caverswall BC. $69.—$75.

G6-235 - Mug, 80th Birthday. Gold on black decoration. 4"h. Portmeirion Pottery. $25.—$29.

G6-236 - Mug, 80th Birthday. Miniature. Sepia portrait. Gold trim. 2"h. 1¾"d. at top. Coronet BC. $14.—$18.

G6-237 - Mug, 80th Birthday. Maroon tone portrait and decoration. Gold trim. 3½"h. Coronet bone china. $39.—$43.

Queen Elizabeth, The Queen Mother

G6-238 - Mug, 80th Birthday. Sepia portraits. Color decoration. Gold trim. 3½"h. Spode BC. $73.—$79.

G6-239 - Mug, 80th Birthday. Color and silver decoration. Silver trim. 3"h. 3"d. Boncay Pottery for the National Trust. $35.—$38.

G6-240 - Mug, 80th Birthday. Color decoration. Gold trim. Family tree and dates on reverse. 3¼"h. Aynsley BC. $59.—$65.

G6-241 - Mug, 80th Birthday. Puce decoration. Glamis Castle on front. Gold trim. 3"h. 3"d. LE 2500. Coalport BC. $72.—$79.

G6-242 - Mug, 80th Birthday. Color decoration. Gold trim. Arms, residences on reverse. LE 2500. 3½"h. Caverswall BC. $65.—$70.

G6-243 - Mug, 80th Birthday. Candles have gold flame. Gold trim. 3"h. 2½"d. Commemoration inside rim. J. & J. May. BC. $78.—$85.

G6-244 - Mug, 85th Birthday. Color decoration. Gold lettering and trim. 3½"h. 3"d. Sutherland bone china. $32.—$37.

G6-245 - Mug, 90th Birthday. Color portrait. Gold trim. Commemoration on reverse. 3¼"h. 3"d. Fenton BC. $26.—$29.

...

G6-246 - Mug, 90th Birthday. Color decoration. Gold trim. 3¼"h. 2¼"d. Parr Pottery bone china. $24.—$29.

G6-247 - Mug, 95th Birthday. Color portrait on pale blue surrounded by commemoration. 3¼"h. 3"d. Coronet BC. $26.—$29.

G6-248 - Plaque. White on pale blue jasperware. LE 1000 numbered. Made in 1977 for Silver Jubilee. 4¼"x3¼". Wedgwood. $89.—$99.

G6-249 - Plate, 80th Birthday. Color portrait. Gold rim. LE 5,000. 7½"d. Crown Staffordshire BC. $78.—$88.

G6-250 - Plate, 80th Birthday. Color portrait. Brown decorated border. Gold rim. LE 2500. 10"d. Crown Staffordshire. $125.—$137.

G6-251 - Plate, 80th Birthday. Color portrait and decoration. Gold rim. LE 1500. 10¾"d. Crown Staffordshire BC. $150.—$165.

G6-252 - Plate, 80th Birthday. Brown tone portrait. Gold commemoration and trim. Color decoration. 8¼"d. Royal Doulton. $67.—$73.

G6-253 - Plate, 80th Birthday. Maroon tone portrait. Gold rim. 8¼"d. Coronet BC. $63.—$68.

G6-254 - Plate, 80th Birthday. Sepia portrait. Color and gold decoration. LE 500. 9"d. Panorama bone china. $46.—$51.

G6-255 - Plate, 80th Birthday. Black and white portrait. Color decoration. Gold rim. 8½"d. $40.—$45.

G6-256 - Plate, 80th Birthday. Color flowers on border. Family tree beneath arms. Gold trim. 10½"d. Aynsley BC. $66.—$72.

G6-257 - Plate, 80th Birthday. Black silhouette. Pink roses. Gold decoration. LE 2000. 10½"d. Coalport bone china. $85.—$92.

G6-258 - Plate, 85th Birthday. Color portrait. Gold rim. Commemoration on reverse. 8"d. Bone china. $30.—$35.

G6-259 - Plate, 85th Birthday. Color portrait and flowers. LE 2000 numbered. 10½"d. Coalport bone china. $98.—$108.

G6-260 - Tin, 90th Birthday. Color portrait. Glamis Castle on sides. 3½"h.x9"x 6½". Walker's. $29.—$34.

G6-261 - Tray, 90th Birthday. Plastic. Color portrait and decoration. 11"d. Melamine by Montem Plastics. $22.—$26.

Princess Elizabeth

G6-262 - Bowl, Princess Elizabeth. Sepia portrait with name below. Gold rim. 8"d. 1¼"deep. Wedgwood & Co. Ltd. $220.—$245.

G6-263 - Cup and Saucer, Birth. "Two for Joy." Color decoration. Paragon bone china. $175.—$190.

G6-264 - Cup and Saucer, Birth. "Two for Joy". Color decoration. Cup 2¼"h. Saucer 4½"d. Paragon bone china. $200.—$225.

G6-265 - Cup and Saucer, Princess Elizabeth. Sepia Marcus Adams portrait. Gold trim. Paragon BC. $270.—$300.

G6-266 - Jigsaw Puzzle, Princess Elizabeth. 60 color plywood pieces. 6½"x8". George Newnes, Ltd. $65.—$75.

G6-267 - Mug, Princess Elizabeth. Sepia Marcus Adams portrait. Red and gold trim. 3½"h. Paragon bone china. $260.—$290.

Princess Elizabeth

G6-268 - Mug. Miniature. Sepia portraits. Pss. Margaret on reverse. Color decoration. 2"h. 2"d. Aynsley BC. $120.—$135.

G6-271 - Plate, Birth. "Two for Joy". Color decoration. Blue border. 6¼"d. Paragon bone china. $130.—$145.

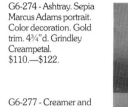

G6-269 - Plate, Birth. "Baby's Plate" on upper rim. Sepia portrait. Red and gold bands. 8¼"x5¾"x1¼" deep. Paragon. $250.—$275.

G6-272 - Plate, Birth. Sepia portrait. Gold rim. 5½"d. Paragon bone china. $260.—$290.

G6-270 - Plate, Birth. "Two for Joy". Color decoration. 9½"d. Paragon BC. $190.—$210.

G6-273 - Plate, Birth. Sepia portrait. Gold rim with fine red line. 6"d. Paragon BC. $260.—$290.

G6-274 - Ashtray. Sepia Marcus Adams portrait. Color decoration. Gold trim. 4¾"d. Grindley Creampetal. $110.—$122.

G6-277 - Creamer and Sugar. Play set. Color portrait. Orange trim. Creamer 1¼"h. Sugar 2"h. 2¾"across. Foreign. $60.—$70.

G6-280 - Cup and Saucer, Play. Color portraits. Orange border. Saucer 2¾"d. Foreign. $55.—$60.

G6-283 - Jelly Mold. "Elizabeth and Margaret Rose". Pressed glass. 6¾"x 4½"x3¼" deep. $85.—$95.

G6-286 - Plate. Sepia Marcus Adams portrait c. 1937. Color decoration. Gold trim. 10½"d. Grindley Creampetal. $115—$129.

G6-289 - Plate, Play. Color portraits. Blue border. 3¾"d. Foreign. $45.—$50.

G6-292 - Tin, Coronation. Black and white portrait on blue background. Hinged lid. 6¼"x3¼"x½"deep. City of Birmingham. $55.—$61.

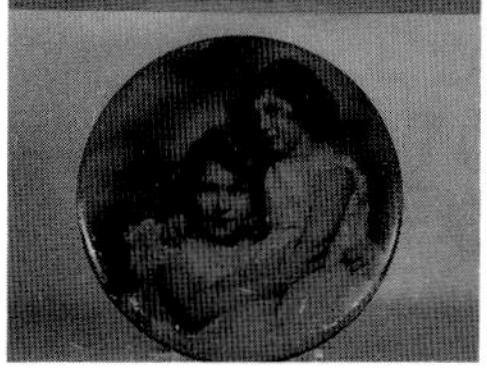

G6-275 - Bowl. Sepia Marcus Adams portrait. Color flowers. Gold trim. 6¾"d. 1"deep. C.W.S. Windsor bone china. $115.—$127.

G6-278 - Cup and Saucer, Play. Color portraits on both pieces. Cup 1½"h. 3"d. Saucer 4¼"d. Foreign. $60.—$70.

G6-281 - Dish. Sepia Marcus Adams portrait. Color flowers and crown. Gold rim. c. 1937. 4½"d. 1"deep. Melba BC. $100.—$110.

G6-284 - Mug. Sepia Marcus Adams portrait. Color flowers. Gold trim. c. 1937. 3¼"h. Grindley Creampetal. $265.—$290.

G6-287 - Plate. Sepia portrait. Color crown above. Color flowers below. Beige tone border. 9"d. Shelley. $165.—$185.

G6-290 - Saucer. Sepia Marcus Adams portrait. Their birth dates below. Blue rim band. Silver rim. 5¼"d. ¾"deep. Paragon BC. $300.—$330.

G6-293 - Tin. Sepia Marcus Adams portrait. Blue sides. 3¼"d. 1"deep. Wyllie, Barr and Ross. $56.—$62.

G6-276 - Calendar. Sepia picture of Princesses with "Lady Jane". 1938 calendar suspended below. 4¾"x7½". $38.—$42.

G6-279 - Cup and Saucer, Play. Color portraits. Cup 1"h. 2¼"d. Saucer 3¼"d. Foreign. $55.—$60.

G6-282 - Handkerchief. Black and white Marcus Adams portrait. Color flowers. 11¼"x11¼". $55.—$60.

G6-285 - Picture. Stand alone Marcus Adams black and white portrait. c. 1937. Printed on metal. 7"x6". $45.—$50.

G6-288 - Plate, Play. Color portrait. Orange border. 5"d. Foreign. $50.—$55.

G6-291 - Sugar, Play. Color portrait. Gold trim. 3¾"h. 4½"across. Foreign. $50.—$55.

G6-294 - Tin. Black and white Marcus Adams portrait. Blue border and sides. 7¾"d. 1½"deep. Gray, Dunn and & Co. Ltd. $59.—$66.

Princess Margaret

G6-295 - Creamer and Sugar, Birth. Color flowers. Gold trim. Deluxe edition. Creamer 2¾"h. Sugar 3½"d. Paragon BC. $185.—$205.

G6-296 - Creamer and Sugar, Birth. Color flowers. Blue trim. Creamer 3"h. 5¼" across. Sugar 2¼"h. x5¼". Paragon BC. $145.—$160.

G6-297 - Cup and Saucer, Birth. Color flowers. Gold trim. Deluxe edition. Paragon BC. $130.—$145.

Princess Margaret

G6-298 - Cup and Saucer, Birth. Color decoration. Blue border. Design also inside cup. Paragon bone china. $115.—$125.

G6-299 - Egg Cup. Sepia portrait. Color decoration. Gold rim. Pottery. 2½"h. $65.—$72.

G6-300 - Mug, Birth. Sepia portrait. Gold bands and trim. 3"h. 2¾"d. Crown Ducal. $250.—$275.

G6-301 - Plaque. "HRH Princess Margaret Rose". White composition. 5"x3¾". $55.—$60.

G6-302 - Plate, Birth. Color decoration. Roses, budgies, marguerites, heather. Blue trim. 7¾"d. Paragon bone china. $110.—$120.

G6-303 - Platter, Birth. Color decoration. Roses, budgies, marguerites, heather. Blue trim. 7"x6". Paragon BC. $105.—$115.

Miscellaneous and Mixed Monarchs

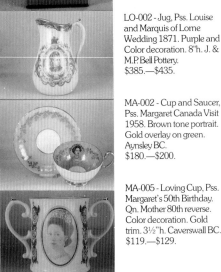

GE-001 - Tin, Pr. George, Duke of Kent, and Pss. Marina Wedding 1934. Sepia portrait on lavender. 5½"h.x4½"x3¾". $80.—$88.

HE-001 - Mug, B&W portrait of Prince Henry, Son of King George V and Qn. Mary. 5"h. "My Regards". Pottery. $130.—$145.

LO-001 - Autographed Note signed by Pss. Louise, 4th daughter of Qn. Victoria. 1884. B&W portrait. 6¾"x 4¼". Frame 10½"x13". $295.—$325.

LO-002 - Jug, Pss. Louise and Marquis of Lorne Wedding 1871. Purple and Color decoration. 8"h. J. & M.P. Bell Pottery. $385.—$435.

LS-001 - Tin, Pss. Louise (daughter of King Edward VII) Wedding to Duke of Fife 1889. 7"x4½"x 3"deep. Graham Bros. $185.—$205.

MA-001 - Bowl, Pss. Margaret Canada Visit 1958. Brown tone portrait framed in gold leaves. 7"x7"x 1½"deep. Aynsley BC. $255.—$280.

MA-002 - Cup and Saucer, Pss. Margaret Canada Visit 1958. Brown tone portrait. Gold overlay on green. Aynsley BC. $180.—$200.

MA-003 - Cup and Saucer, Pss. Margaret Canada Visit 1958. Color and gold decoration on blue. Paragon BC. $85.—$95.

MA-004 - Dish, Pss. Margaret Canada Visit 1958. Brown tone portrait framed in gold. 5½"x5". Gold rim. Aynsley BC. $85.—$95.

MA-005 - Loving Cup, Pss. Margaret's 50th Birthday. Qn. Mother 80th reverse. Color decoration. Gold trim. 3½"h. Caverswall BC. $119.—$129.

MA-006 - Plaque, Pss. Margaret 1973. White on pale blue jasperware. LE 1000. 4¼"x3¼". Wedgwood. $120.—$133.

MI-001 - Loving Cup, Year of Three Kings 1936. 3 panels. Sepia portraits. Color decoration. Gold trim. 4"h. 4"d. J. Kent Ltd. $215.—$240.

MI-002 - Plate, King Edward VII Proclamation, Queen Victoria In Memoriam. Sepia portraits. Gold rim. Beaded frames. 9¾"d. $290.—$320.

MI-003 - Plate, King Edward VII Accession, Queen Victoria In Memoriam. Color portraits. Gold embossed border. 9"d. $285.—$315.

MI-004 - Plate, Royal Ladies of August. Qn. Mother, Pss. Margaret and Pss. Anne. Gold trim. 10½"d. Coronet bone china. $75.—$82.

MI-005 - Plate, Year of Three Kings 1936. Color portraits. Gold rim. 9¾"d. Sovereign Potters Canada. $205.—$230.

MR-001 - Handkerchief, Pss. Mary (daughter of King George V) and Viscount Lascelles Wedding 1922. 10½"d. $43.—$48.

MR-002 - Mug, Pss. Mary Opening Cottage Hospital 1925. Sepia portrait. Gold rim. 2¾"h. Pottery. $100.—$110.

MR-003 - Tin, Pss. Mary and Viscount Lascelles Wedding 1922. Color portraits. 10"x5"x1¼"deep. Barringer, Wallis. $70.—$77.

MR-004 - Tin, Pss. Mary and Viscount Lascelles Wedding 1922. Color portraits and decoration. Gold trim. 6"h.x4¾"x3½". $64.—$69.

MR-005 - Tin, Pss. Mary and Viscount Lascelles Wedding 1922. Color portraits and decoration. 6"h.x3"x1¼" deep. Sharp's. $59.—$65.

MR-006 - Tin, Pss. Mary and Viscount Lascelles Wedding 1922. Color portraits. $75.—$82. - 9¼"h. $70.—$77. - 8"h.

MU-001 - Plate, Pss. Maud (daughter of King Edward VII) and Pr. Carl of Denmark Wedding 1896. Royal Copenhagen. LE 1200. $180.—$200.

PV-001 - Jug, Pss. Victoria and Pr. of Prussia Wedding 1858. B&W portraits. Copper luster trim. Blue background. 5"h. $245.—$270.

CA-001 - Bowl, "Long Live Queen Caroline." Black on white. Pink luster trim. 7¾"d. 1¼"deep. $275.—$305.

CA-002 - Cup and Saucer, "Long Live Queen Caroline." Black on white. Pink luster trim. $335.—$370.

CA-003 - Dish, "Her Majesty Queen Caroline, Queen of England." Blue decoration. Embossing. 5¾"d. 1½"deep. $485.—$535.

CA-004 - Jug, "God Save Queen Caroline." Black on white. Pink luster trim. "The Green Bag Crew" poem on reverse. 5"h. $925.—$1000.

CA-005 - Jug, "Success to Queen Caroline." Raised color portrait and flowers. Blue trim. Same reverse. 5½"h. 5¾"across. $900.—$990.

CA-006 - Jug, Queen Caroline. Applied medium blue decoration on white bisque. Oak leaf and acorn bands. 4½"h. $1375.—$1475.

CA-007 - Mug, Queen Caroline. Raised color portrait, flowers and wreath. Red trim. 3½"h. 3¾"d. $850.—$925.

CA-008 - Plate, Queen Caroline In Memoriam. Her likeness above tomb. Death date. Red and yellow flowers. 7½"d. $1100.—$1200.

CA-009 - Plate, Queen Caroline In Memoriam. Black center design. Color flowers. Birth and death dates. 7½"d. $1050.—$1150.

CA-010 - Plate, Queen Caroline. Raised color portrait, crown and flowers. Supported her in Bill of Pains and Penalties. 8¼"d. $925.—$1010.

CA-011 - Plate, Queen Caroline. Raised color portrait and decoration. Made to support her in Bill of Pains and Penalties. 6¼"d. $925.—$1010.

CH-001 - Bowl, Pss. Charlotte In Memoriam. B&W transfer. Her portrait on tomb. Pink luster trim. 5½"d. 1"deep. $160.—$190.

CH-002 - Bowl, Pss. Charlotte In Memoriam. B&W transfer. Pink luster trim. 8"d. 1½"deep. $260.—$285.

CH-003 - Bowl, Pss. Charlotte In Memoriam. Four B&W portraits. Pink luster trim. 6¼"d. 2½"deep. $335.—$375.

CH-004 Bowl, Pss. Charlotte In Memoriam. Three B&W transfers on sides. Her portrait on tomb. 6"d. 3"deep. $275.—$310.

CH-005 - Cup and Saucer, Pss. Charlotte In Memoriam. B&W transfer shows Britannia weeping at tomb. Pink luster trim. $215.—$240.

CH-006 - Cup and Saucer, Pss. Charlotte In Memoriam. B&W transfer shows her portrait on tomb. Pink luster trim. $250.—$280.

CH-007 - Jug, Pss. Charlotte and Pr. Leopold Wedding 1816. Bright colors and pink luster. 6"h. 7½"across. $850.—$925.

CH-008 - Teapot, Pss. Charlotte In Memoriam. B&W transfers. Pink luster trim. 6"h. 9½"across. $495.—$550.

G3-001 - Plate, King George III In Memoriam. Blue on white design. 10"d. 1½"deep. $1075.—$1175.

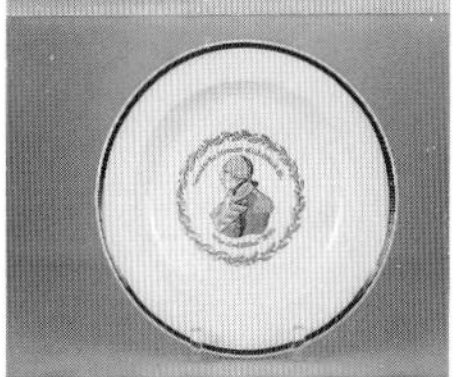

G3-002 - Plate, King George III In Memoriam. B&W portrait. Black oak leaves, acorns and rim band. 7½"d. $1000.—$1100.

G3-003 - Snuff Box, King George III In Memoriam. Gold tone raised portrait on black. 3¼"d. 3"deep. $675.—$750.

G4-001 - Jug, King George IV In Memoriam. Raised profile. Lion handle. Unglazed beige color. 8¾"h. 8"across. $1250.—$1355.

G4-002 - Jug, King George IV In Memoriam. B&W portrait and decoration. Dates listed. 6¾"h. 7½"across. $795.—$885.

G4-003 - Plate, King George IV Coronation. Black on cream. 9"d. Hartley Greens for Leeds Church School Dinner. 9"d. $1625.—$1775.

G4-004 - Plate, King George IV. Raised color portrait and decoration. Believed made at coronation time. 8½"d. $1425.—$1575.

W4-001 - Bust, King William IV. Bronze. 1831 publication information on reverse. Saml. Parker, London. 5½"h. $335.—$375.

W4-002 - Jug, King William IV Coronation. Qn. Adelaide on reverse. Black transfer. $725.—$800.—7½"h. $600.—$675.—5¼"h.

W4-003 - Jug, King William IV Coronation. Coronation scene front and reverse. Deep red decoration. 5"h. 5¼"across. $1450.—$1600.

W4-004 - Jug, King William IV Coronation. Blue on white embossed design. 9¼"h. 9"across. $1250.—$1375.

W4-005 - Mug, King William IV Coronation. Dark red portrait Queen Adelaide. Coronation scene on reverse. 2¾"h. $1350.—$1500.

W4-006 - Plate, King William IV Coronation. Dark red portrait. Embossed floral border. 5½"d. $825.—$925.

W4-007 - Tin. "Her Most Gracious Majesty Queen Adelaide" surrounds her raised profile. 2"d. 1"deep. $295.—$325.

VI-001 - Badge. Queen Victoria Fusiliers. "V R" below flame. Crown above. On 7"x5" glass mount. $205.—$230.

VI-002 - Beaker, In Memoriam. Color portrait. Purple decoration. Important dates. 3¾" h. Royal Doulton bone china. $400.—$450.

VI-003 - Beaker, 1887 Jubilee. Young and mature portraits. Brown tone decoration. 4"h. Doulton Burslem. $95.—$105.

VI-004 - Beaker, 1887 Jubilee. Color decoration partially hand painted. Gold rim. 3¼"h. Foley bone china. $70.—$77.

VI-005 - Beaker, 1887 Jubilee. Color decoration. Gold rim. 3½" h. W.H. Goss bone china. $75.—$85.

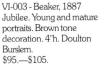

VI-006 - Beaker, 1897 Jubilee. Color decoration. Gold bands. Enamel on tin. 4¼"h. 3¾"d. at top. $110.—$120.

VI-007 - Beaker, 1897 Jubilee. B&W young and mature portraits. Color decoration. Enamel on tin. 4"h. $110.—$120.

VI-008 - Beaker, 1897 Jubilee. Color decoration partially hand painted. Gold rim. Mayor of Canterbury. 4"h. $100.—$110.

VI-009 - Beaker, 1897 Jubilee. Blue on white. Her name, titles, dates and "Diamond Jubilee". 4"h. $130.—$145.

VI-010 - Beaker, 1897 Jubilee. White on olive green. Light brown trim and inside. 4"h. 3"d. at top. Copeland Late Spode. $180.—$200.

VI-011 - Beaker, 1897 Jubilee. Color and gold decoration partially hand painted. Beading. 4¼". William Lowe design. BC. $110.—$120.

VI-012 - Beaker, 150th Anniversary of Coronation. Gold lion head handles and decoration. 4½"h. 3½"d. LE 150. Caverswall BC. $95.—$105.

VI-013 - Bottle Stopper, 1897 Jubilee. Blue glass. 2"h. 1½"d. $50.—$55.

VI-014 - Bowl, Crimean War. B&W portraits Queen Victoria and Napoleon. 8¼"d. 4¼"deep. $775.—$850.

VI-015 - Bowl, 1887 Jubilee. Black on white. Same portrait on reverse. Gold rim. 6"d. 3½"deep. $135.—$155.

VI-016 - Bowl, 1887 Jubilee. Brown tone portrait and decoration. Flowers on reverse. Gold rim. 4½"d. 2¼"deep. Plant. $95.—$105.

VI-017 - Bowl, 1887 Jubilee. Gold backed portrait. Pressed glass. 8¾"d. 1¾"deep. $80.—$90.

VI-018 - Bowl, 1887 Jubilee. Footed. Amber glass. Beaded commemoration. 5½"h. 6"d. at top. $95.—$105.

VI-019 - Bowl, 1887 Jubilee. Amber pressed glass. 9¼"d. $70.—$77.

VI-020 - Bowl, 1897 Jubilee. Color decoration. Gold rim. 4"d. 2¼"deep. W.H. Goss bone china. $77.—$85.

VI-021 - Bowl, 1897 Jubilee. Sepia portrait. Color decoration. Gold rim. 7¾"x6¼"x2"deep. Late Mayers bone china. $135.—$150.

VI-022 - Bowl. Applied white profiles and decoration on green. c. 1851. Profile Queen Victoria reverse. 4½"d. 4"deep. $255.—$280.

VI-023 - Bowl. Victoria and Albert in color. Pink luster trim. 4¾"d. 1½"deep. $75.—$85.

VI-024 - Bowl. Victoria and Albert in color. Pink luster trim. 6½"d. 3¾"deep. $165.—$180.

VI-025 - Bowl, Wedding. B&W portraits. Pink luster decoration and trim. 6½"d. 3¾"deep. $300.—$350.

VI-026 - Box. Gold raised portrait framed in gold. Black plastic. 2"x2"x2". $45.—$50.

VI-027 - Box, Covered. Staffordshire figure. Box separates above first skirt ruffle. Color decoration. 7½"h. $485.—$525.

VI-028 - Brooch, 1887 Jubilee. "1837 - Jubilee - 1887". 1¾"x½". Silver tone metal. $50.—$55.

VI-029 - Brooch, 1887 Jubilee. Color enamel arms. 2¼"x1¼". Sterling silver. $80.—$90.

VI-030 - Brooch, 1887 Jubilee. 1¼"x1". Silver tone metal. $50.—$55.

VI-031 - Brooch, 1887 Jubilee. Color enamel shield. 1¾"x¾". Sterling silver. $75.—$85.

VI-032 - Brooch, 1887 Jubilee. Profile portrait. 1½"d. Silver tone metal. $45.—$50.

VI-033 - Brooch, 1887 Jubilee. Red enamel in crown. 1¼"x1¼". Silver tone metal. $50.—$55.

VI-034 - Brooch, 1887 Jubilee. Profile portrait. 1½"x1". Silver tone metal. $45.—$50.

VI-035 - Brooch, 1897 Jubilee. 1¼"x1". Sterling silver. $75.—$85.

VI-036 - Bust. Prince Albert Profile. Gold tone color. Hanger on reverse. 7¾"h. 5"across at base. $60.—$66.

VI-037 - Bust. Queen Victoria. White bisque. Nice detail in lace. 7½"h. 4½"across at shoulders. $310.—$345.

VI-038 - Bust. Queen Victoria. White. 8¾"h. 4¼"across at shoulders. Bone china. $185.—$205.

VI-039 - Bust. Queen Victoria. Silver tone metal on black marble plinth. Bust 6"h. $210.—$235.

VI-040 - Card, In Memoriam. White embossed profile on purple. Black trim. Birth and death dates. 4½" x2¾". $43.—$48.

VI-041 - Cup and Saucer, 1959 Centenary of New Westminster Canada. Color portrait and decoration. BC. $75.—$85.

VI-042 - Cup and Saucer, 1887 Jubilee. Color decoration. Bone china. $65.—$72.

VI-043 - Cup, Saucer and 6" plate. 1887 Jubilee. Maroon tone portrait. Color decoration with gold highlights and trim. $165.—$180. Set.

VI-044 - Cup and Saucer, 1887 Jubilee. Color decoration. Gold trim. Bone china. RD No. 61464. $82.—$92.

VI-045 - Cup and Saucer, 1887 Jubilee. Color decoration partially hand painted. Gold trim. Foley BC. $86.—$96.

VI-046 - Cup and Saucer, 1887 Jubilee. Color decoration partially hand painted. Gold trim. Foley BC. $86.—$96.

VI-047 - Cup and Saucer, 1887 Jubilee. Color decoration. Beading in crown. Gold trim. William Whiteley bone china. $70.—$77.

VI-048 - Cup and Saucer, 1897 Jubilee. Color and gold decoration partially hand painted. Beading. W.L. Lowe BC. $135.—$150.

VI-049 - Cup and Saucer, 1897 Jubilee. Sepia portrait. Color decoration. Gold trim. By J. Aynsley for William Whiteley. BC. $125.—$143.

VI-050 - Cup and Saucer, 1897 Jubilee. Color portrait and decoration. Gold trim. Bone china. $125.—$143.

VI-051 - Cup and Saucer, 1897 Jubilee. Color decoration partially hand painted. Gold trim. Foley BC. $125.—$140.

VI-052 - Cup and Saucer, 1897 Jubilee. B&W portraits of four generations. Pink background. Gold trim. Germany. BC. $170.—$190.

VI-053 - Cup and Saucer with 6" plate. Color decoration. Gold trim. Hammersley BC. $140.—$155. Set.

VI-054 - Cup and Saucer. Royal Family. Bright colors and pink luster with cobalt blue background. BC. $165.—$180.

VI-055 - Cup and Saucer. Royal Family. Puce and luster colors. Bone china. $160.—$177.

VI-056 - Cup and Saucer. Victoria and Albert. Color decoration and pink luster. $140.—$155.

VI-057 - Dish. "The Last Coinage of The Nineteenth Century". 1900 one shilling coin in sterling silver dish. 2¼"d. ¼"deep. $97.—$107.

VI-058 - Dish, 1887 Jubilee. Clear pressed glass. 5"d. ¾" deep. $40.—$45.

VI-059 - Dish, 1897 Jubilee. Color decoration. Gold rim. 4"d. 1"deep. W.H. Goss bone china. $65.—$73.

VI-060 - Dish, 1897 Jubilee. Sepia portraits. Color decoration. 4½"x3"x ½" deep. Doulton Burlsem. $100.—$110.

VI-061 - Dish, 1897 Jubilee. Color decoration partially hand painted. Gold trim. 5¾"x4½". Foley China. $60.—$66.

VI-062 - Dish. The Royal Family. Pink luster and color decoration. 5½"d. 1"deep. $95.—$105.

VI-063 - Dish. Color portrait of Queen Victoria. 4¼"d. $55.—$60.

VI-064 - Dish. Queen Victoria. Edward, Prince of Wales with dog Carlo. Each 6¼"x 1¼"deep. Purple on white. $1225.—$1300. Pair.

VI-065 - Dish. Color Portrait of Queen Victoria. Gold rim. 6"x5½". Royal Doulton bone china. $110.—$123.

VI-066 - Dish. "Victoria & Albert". Profiles and crown in center. Clear pressed glass. 5"d. $95.—$105.

VI-067 - Dish. Queen Victoria and Prince Albert profile portraits. Each dish 5"d. Brass. $100.—$110. Pair.

VI-068 - Figurine. Queen Victoria with Pss. Victoria, the Princess Royal. Colorfully hand painted. 6"h. $525.—$575.

VI-069 - Figurine. Queen Victoria. Green press molded glass. By John Derbyshire. c. 1875. 8"h. 4½"d. at base. $350.—$385.

VI-070 - Flag, 1897 Jubilee. B&W portrait. Color flag. Red background. 25"x20". Cotton. $55.—$60.

VI-071 - Flask. Queen Victoria on front. Duchess of Kent on reverse. Treacle brown. c. 1837—38. 7½"h.x4"x2". $570.—$625.

VI-072 - Flask, Wedding. Raised portraits and incised names. Beige with flowing brown top. Salt glaze. 7"h. $560.—$615.

VI-073 - Handkerchief, 1887 Jubilee. B&W portrait. Blue border. 14"x14". $60.—$66.

VI-074 - Jar. Covered. "Victoria" molded beneath arms on base. White milk glass. 8½"h. $135.—$150.

VI-075 - Jug, Prince Albert In Memoriam. Molded design with pewter lid. His decorations and honors shown. 8"h. $420.—$460.

VI-076 - Jug, 1887 Jubilee. Color decoration partially hand painted. 3½"h. Foley bone china. $65.—$73.

VI-077 - Jug, 1897 Jubilee. Color portrait and decoration. Ships and servicemen. 5½"h. 5¼" across. Bone china. $150.—$165.

VI-078 - Jug, 1897 Jubilee. Color young and mature portraits. Color decoration. Gold trim. Embossing. 4"h. 3¼"across. BC. $125.—$140.

VI-079 - Jug, 1897 Jubilee. Color young and mature portraits. Color decoration. Gold trim. 5"h. Bavarian bone china. $145.—$160.

VI-080 - Jug, 1897 Jubilee. Sepia young and mature portraits. Nice embossing. Sepia decoration. 7½"h. 7" across. $240.—$265.

VI-081 - Jug, 1897 Jubilee. Young and mature profile portraits. Brown and beige. 6"h. 4½"d. Doulton Lambeth. $210.—$230.

VI-082 - Jug, 1897 Jubilee. Sepia portrait with gold highlights. Color decoration. 4"h. Pottery. $100.—$110.

VI-083 - Jug, 1897 Jubilee. White applied portrait and decoration on olive green. Beige trim and inside. 6"h. Copeland Spode. $295.—$325.

VI-084 - Jug, 1897 Jubilee. Color and gold decoration. Beading. William Lowe design. 3¾"h. 4¼"across. BC. $105.—$115.

VI-085 - Jug, 1897 Jubilee. Puzzle jug. Mainly blue and green decoration. 6¼"h. $525.—$575.

VI-086 - Jug, 1897 Jubilee. Color decoration partially hand painted. Gold trim. 3"h. Foley BC. $70.—$77.

VI-087 - Jug, 1897 Jubilee. Color and gold decoration. Beading. Wm. Lowe. $205.—$230. - 7¾"h. $160.—$175. - 6"h.

VI-088 - Jug. c. 1840. White raised figures on royal blue. Prince Albert in wedding attire on reverse. 5¼"h. 6½"across. $500.—$550.

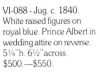

VI-089 - Jug, Wedding. Black on white. Queen Victoria in wedding dress. Pr. Albert in military uniform. 9"h. $1200.—$1300.

VI-090 - Jug, Wedding. Profile portraits. Medium brown. 6¾"h. $325.—$355.

VI-091 - Jug, Wedding. Black on white with pink luster trim. In Memoriam for John Wesley on reverse. 3"h. $540.—$590.

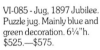

VI-092 - Jug, Wedding. Blue on white portrait and decoration. Prince Albert on reverse. 6½"h. 5½"across. $1375.—$1475.

VI-093 - Jug, Wedding. Black on white. Embossing. 4¾"h. 5"across. 4"d. at widest point. $525.—$575.

VI-094 - Jug, Wedding. Deep red portrait. Blue background. Pink luster trim. 6"h. 7"across. $410.—$460.

VI-095 - Loving Cup. Brown tone portrait. Color decoration. Pink background. Osborne House on reverse. 4"h. 6½"across. $190.—$215.

VI-096 - Loving Cup, 1897 Jubilee. Colorful decoration on cream. "V R I" and leaves on reverse. 5¾"h. 8½"across. $295.—$325.

VI-097 - Loving Cup, "1899 Transvaal War 1900". Three panels and handles. Color and gold. 5½"h.x7¾". Copeland for Goode. $1875.—$2000.

VI-098 - Medal, Coronation. "HM Alexandrina Victoria" around raised profile. 1¾"d. silver tone metal. $55.—$60.

VI-099 - Medal, 1897 Jubilee. Young portrait on reverse. Bronze. 2¼"d. $45.—$50.

VI-100 - Mug, Coronation. Hayter portrait. Duchess of Kent reverse. Deep red transfer. 3¼"h. 3¼"d. R&C. $1700.—$1875.

VI-101 - Mug, Coronation. Swansea design. Same purple portrait reverse. Birth, proclamation, coronation dates. 3¼"h. $1600.—$1750.

VI-102 - Mug, In Memoriam. B&W young and mature portraits. Death date. 4"h. 4"d. $280.—$310.

VI-103 - Mug, In Memoriam. Color portrait. Gold trim. Birth and death dates. 3¼"h. 2½"d. at top. Ceramic Art Co. $290.—$320.

VI-104 - Mug, 1887 Jubilee. Color and gold decoration partially hand painted. William Lowe design. 3¼"h. Bone china. $120.—$135.

VI-105 - Mug, 1887 Jubilee. Color decoration. Beaded crown. Gold trim. 3¼"h. William Whiteley bone china. $100.—$110.

VI-106 - Mug, 1887 Jubilee. Black on light blue. Gold trim. 4"h. 4"d. Foley Pottery. $155.—$170.

VI-107 - Mug, 1897 Jubilee. Sepia young and mature portraits. Color decoration. Gold trim. 3"h. 3"d. Empire Works. $105.—$115.

VI-108 - Mug, 1897 Jubilee. Pale sepia young and mature portraits. Tower Bridge. Man of War. 3¾"h. Pottery. $105.—$115.

VI-109 - Mug, 1897 Jubilee. Brown tone portrait and decoration. 3"h. 3"d. W.T. Copeland & Sons. $145.—$160.

VI-110 - Mug, 1897 Jubilee. Purple tone portrait and decoration. Gold trim. 3½"h. $120.—$135.

VI-111 - Mug, 1897 Jubilee. Sepia young and mature portraits. Color decoration. Gold trim. 4"h. $175.—$190.

VI-112 - Mug, 1897 Jubilee. Black on white portrait and design. 3¼"h. 3"d. $90.—$100.

VI-113 - Mug, 1897 Jubilee. Black on white portrait and decoration. 3"h. CTM. $95.—$105.

VI-114 - Mug, 1897 Jubilee. Sepia portrait. Sepia and gold decoration. 3"h. 3"d. By Aynsley for William Whiteley. $185.—$205.

VI-115 - Mug, 1897 Jubilee. Color decoration. Gold trim. 3¼"h. Foley China. $102.—$117.

VI-116 - Mug, 1897 Jubilee. Color decoration partially hand painted. Gold trim. 2½"h. BC. $95.—$105.

VI-117 - Mug, 1897 Jubilee. Cobalt blue glass. White commemoration with crown above. 3¾"h. $100.—$110.

VI-118 - Mug, 150th Anniversary of Coronation. Sepia portraits. Color decoration. LE 1500. 3½"h. Caverswall BC. $50.—$55.

VI-119 - Mug. "Q". Queen Victoria's portrait left of letter "Q". Green on white design. 2½"h. 2½"d. $345.—$375.

VI-120 - Mug, Victoria and Albert 1983-84 Exhibit London. White profiles, gold letters on black. LE 500. 4¼"h. Wedgwood. $235.—$255.

VI-121 - Mug, Wedding. Blue on white. Prince Albert on reverse. 4"h. 4"d. Union Pottery. $970.—$1050.

VI-122 - Mug. Osborne House. 3"h. 3"d. Hammersley and Asbury bone china. c. 1872—75. $255.—$280.

VI-123 - Paper Clamp. "His Royal Highness Prince Albert". Raised profile portrait and wreath. 2¼"d. 5¾"long. Brass. $50.—$55.

VI-124 - Pendant, 1887 Jubilee. Birth, coronation and wedding dates. 1½"x 1½"d. Brass. $45.—$50.

VI-125 - Pendant, 1897 Jubilee. "Sixty Years". Longest reign commemoration on reverse. 1½"x1¼". Silver tone. $50.—$55.

VI-126 - Picture. Color print of Prince Albert by Currier. 13"x12" in 16"x14" wooden frame. $145.—$160.

VI-127 - Picture. Color Print of Prince Albert from F. Winterhalter portrait painted in 1859. 10"x7½". Matted. $60.—$66.

VI-128 - Picture. Queen Victoria coronation scene on fabric. Brown tone decoration. Overall framed size 13"x17". $170.—$190.

VI-129 - Picture. In Memoriam color portrait on silk. "Presented with 'The Gentlewoman'". Black border. Frame 11"x9". $150.—$165.

VI-130 - Picture. In Memoriam photograph in sterling silver frame with crown above. "VR - 1819 - 1901". 2"x1½". $130.—$145.

VI-131 - Picture. 1887 Jubilee portrait of Queen Victoria in silver tone metal frame. Stand alone frame is 7¾"x4¼". $60.—$67.

VI-132 - Picture. Black and white print from a painting by G. Hayter. Engraved by J. Cochran. Overall 8½"x7". Fisher & Son. $40.—$45.

VI-133 - Picture. Color print Queen Victoria. 16"x12". $33.—$37.

VI-134 - Picture. Color portrait of Queen Victoria. Coat of arms brass frame with stand. 5½"x5". $230.—$255.

VI-135 - Picture. Color print of Queen Victoria in coronation robes. Hand colored. 4½"x3¾". Mat is 7"x5¾". $26.—$29.

VI-136 - Picture. Hand colored print of Queen Victoria in dress she wore for 1887 Jubilee service. 8½"x6½". Matted. $41.—$45.

VI-137 - Picture. Color portrait of young Queen Victoria. Wooden frame. Portrait is 1¾"x1½". Frame is 3¼"x3". $75.—$82.

VI-138 - Picture. Two tinted portraits by Thomas Sully (c. 1838) and F. Winterhalter (c. 1845). Matted size 8"x10". $35.—$40.

VI-139 - Plaque. Prince Albert c. 1855. Deep brown. 4½"d. Bois Durci. $230.—$255.

VI-140 - Plaque, In Memoriam. Color portrait. Birth, accession and death dates. Black border. 6½"d. Grimwade Bros. $270.—$300.

VI-141 - Plaque, 1887 Jubilee. Copper shield on wood. "Victoria Regina" and dates. Arms below. 12"x9". $210.—$230.

VI-142 - Plaque, 1897 Jubilee. Molded pottery. Beige, brown and red. 7"d. 1"deep. Austria. $75.—$82.

VI-143 - Plaque, 1897 Jubilee. Metal on wooden shield. Overall size 13"x10". $165.—$180.

VI-144 - Plaque, 1897 Jubilee. Blue tone portrait and decoration. Gold on green border. 8½"x7½"x1" deep. Pottery. $225.—$250.

VI-145 - Plate, Prince Albert In Memoriam. Black on white. Birth, marriage, death dates. Accomplishments listed. 11"d. $525.—$575.

VI-146 - Plate, Coronation. B&W portrait. Embossed floral border. Birth, proclamation and coronation dates. 6¾"d. $1050.—$1150.

VI-147 - Plate, Coronation. Blue tone portrait. Embossed floral border. Birth, proclamation and coronation dates. 7"d. $1050.—$1150.

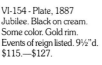

VI-148 - Plate, In Memoriam. Sepia portrait. Color decoration partially hand painted. Gold rim. 7"d. Foley BC. $130.—$145.

VI-149 - Plate, In Memoriam. Color portrait and decoration. Gold rim. Birth, accession and death dates. 10"d. Ridgway's. $300.—$335.

VI-150 - Plate, 1887 Jubilee. Color decoration partially hand painted. Gold rim. 7"d. Foley BC. $55.—$60.

VI-151 - Plate, 1887 Jubilee. Color decoration partially hand painted. Gold rim. 7"d. Foley BC. $55.—$60.

VI-152 - Plate, 1887 Jubilee. Color decoration. 6"d. Bone china. $55.—$60.

VI-153 - Plate, 1887 Jubilee. Blue on white decoration. Gold rim. 7"d. R.H. Plant BC. $88.—$98.

VI-154 - Plate, 1887 Jubilee. Black on cream. Some color. Gold rim. Events of reign listed. 9½"d. $115.—$127.

VI-155 - Plate, 1887 Jubilee. Brown tone portrait and decoration. Gold frame and gold trim. 8¾"d. $85.—$94.

VI-156 - Plate, 1887 Jubilee. "Jubilee Year Commencing June 20, 1886". Black on white. Gold rim. 9¼"d. $105.—$115.

VI-157 - Plate, 1887 Jubilee. B&W portrait. Blue, orange and gold decoration. 9½"d. $105.—$115.

VI-158 - Plate, 1887 Jubilee. Dark blue portrait and decoration. 8¼"d. $90.—$100.

VI-159 - Plate, 1887 Jubilee. Blue on white. "Compliments of A. Stowell & Co.". 10½"d. Royal Worcester. $115.—$127.

VI-160 - Plate, 1897 Jubilee. Sepia portraits. Color decoration. St. Paul's, Balmoral, Windsor. Gold rim. 10¾"d. $125.—$140.

VI-161 - Plate, 1897 Jubilee. Sepia young and mature portraits. Balmoral, St. Paul's and Tower Bridge. 7½"d. Pottery. $85.—$95.

VI-162 - Plate, 1897 Jubilee. Profile young and mature portraits. Color decoration. Gold rim. 7¼"d. Bone china. $73.—$80.

VI-163 - Plate, 1897 Jubilee. Color young and mature portraits. Gold rim. Swirl border. 6"d. BC. $60.—$66.

VI-164 - Plate, 1897 Jubilee. Young and mature portraits. Orange on white. Windsor and Balmoral. 9"d. $122.—$135.

VI-165 - Plate, 1897 Jubilee. Young and mature portraits. Blue on white. Gold trim. 9"d. Wedgwood & Co. Ltd. bone china. $130.—$145.

VI-166 - Plate, 1897 Jubilee. Pale sepia young and mature portraits. Color decoration. Gold rim. 7¼"d. Allertons. $90.—$100.

VI-169 - Plate, 1897 Jubilee. Brown tone portrait. Color decoration. Gold trim. Embossing. 8½"d. $115—$127.

VI-172 - Plate, 1897 Jubilee. Color portrait. Gold trim. 10"d. Royal Doulton. $90.—$100.

VI-175 - Plate, 1897 Jubilee. B&W portrait. Black decoration. Gold rim. Birth and accession dates. 7½"d. Hines Brothers. $95.—$105.

VI-178 - Plate, 1897 Jubilee. Sepia and color portrait. Royal residences in color. Gold rim. 9½"d. $150.—$165.

VI-181 - Plate, 1897 Jubilee. Windsor Castle in color with crown above. Gold rim. 9¼"d. $145.—$160.

VI-184 - Plate, 150th Anniversary of Coronation. Gold portrait. Gold on red and blue bands. LE 150. 10½"d. Caverswall BC. $160.—$175.

VI-187 - Plate. Color portrait of Queen Victoria. Green border. Gold rim. 9¾"d. Bone china. $85.—$93.

VI-190 - Plate. Queen Victoria at the Opera c. 1838. Infrequently seen transfer from painting by E.T. Parris. 7"d. $1030.—$1130.

VI-193 - Plate. Victoria and Albert. Color decoration. Copper luster trim. 8¾"x8¼"d. $150.—$165.

VI-196 - Plate, Wedding. Names, wedding date, crown and wreath in deep red. Color floral embossed border. 7"d. $300.—$330.

VI-167 - Plate, 1897 Jubilee. B&W young and mature portraits. Black decoration. Four events of reign. 9½"d. Wagstaff. $140.—$155.

VI-170 - Plate, 1897 Jubilee. Color portrait and decoration. Servicemen and ships. Angels above. 8"d. Bone china. $170.—$190.

VI-173 - Plate, 1897 Jubilee. B&W portrait by A. Bassano. Gold rim. Embossing. 8"d. Bone china. $90.—$100.

VI-176 - Plate, 1897 Jubilee. Brown tone portrait and decoration. Gold rim. 9¼"d. $155.—$170.

VI-179 - Plate, 1897 Jubilee. Color and gold decoration partially hand painted. Embossing. Gold rim. 9½"d. $95.—$105.

VI-182 - Plate, 1897 Jubilee. Color and gold decoration partially hand painted. Raised beading. Gold rim. 7"d. W.L. Lowe. $68.—$75.

VI-185 - Plate, Proclamation. B&W portrait and decoration. Birth and proclamation dates. Embossing. 8"d. $950.—$1050.

VI-188 - Plate. Queen Victoria color portrait. Dominion of Canada. Color decoration. Gold trim. $100.—$110. - 7½"d. $75.—$83. - 5¼"d.

VI-191 - Plate. "Victoria 1st". Black on white. Embossed animals around border. Late 1830's. 6"d. $975.—$1075.

VI-194 - Plate. Victoria and Albert. B&W portrait on horseback. Color embossed border. c. 1840. 7"d. $950.—$1050.

VI-197 - Pot Lid. "Tria Juncta in Uno". Crimean War. Color portraits and decoration. 4"d. $525.—$575.

VI-168 - Plate, 1897 Jubilee. 1837 portrait of Queen on horseback. 1887 Jubilee review scene. Black design. 7"d. $210.—$235.

VI-171 - Plate, 1897 Jubilee. Sepia portrait. Color decoration. Gold rim. 7"d. By Aynsley for William Whiteley. $100.—$110.

VI-174 - Plate, 1897 Jubilee. Brown on white. Events of reign listed around border. 10½"d. S.B. & S. $210.—$230.

VI-177 - Plate, 1897 Jubilee. Sepia portrait. Hand painted decoration. Gold rim. 9"d. Hines Brothers. $205.—$225.

VI-180 - Plate, 1897 Jubilee. Color decoration partially hand painted. Gold rim. 5¾"d. Foley BC. $58.—$63.

VI-183 - Plate, 150th Anniversary of Coronation. Sepia portrait. Color decoration. LE 1500. 8½"d. Caverswall BC. $61.—$67.

VI-186 - Plate. Color portrait of Queen Victoria. Color flowers. Gilded and embossed rim. 9"d. $80.—$88.

VI-189 - Plate. Deep red portrait of young Queen Victoria in palace garden. Raised alphabet border. c. 1837—38. 6½"d. $850.—$925.

VI-192 - Plate. Victoria and Albert. Color decoration. Pink luster trim. 9"d. 1"deep. $150.—$165.

VI-195 - Plate, Wedding. Black and white with some color. Embossed border. Pink luster band. 7¼"d. $350.—$385.

VI-198 - Pot Lid. "England's Pride" and "The Late Prince Consort". Color portraits and decoration. Gold frames. 5"d. $450.—$500. Pair.

VI-199 - Ribbon, Prince Albert In Memoriam. B&W portrait. 7½"x2". Dalton and Barton. $60.—$66.

VI-200 - Ribbon, Prince Albert In Memoriam. Black on white. Birth and death places and dates. 8¾"x2½". $65.—$72.

VI-201 - Ribbon, Queen Victoria In Memoriam. Birth, accession and death dates. Black frame is 7"x5". $90.—$100.

I-202 - Ribbon, 1887 Jubilee. B&W portrait. Color decoration. Stevengraph. 8¾"x2½". $80.—$88.

VI-203 - Seal. Victoria and Albert. National figures on other sides of cube. ½"x½"x½". Brass. $80.—$89.

VI-204 - Silk, Prince Albert In Memoriam. Black on white. Woven. Birth and death dates. 7¼"x4½". R. Sweitzer. $96.—$106.

VI-205 - Silk, 1897 Jubilee. Woven black and white. 15"x7¾". Made in France. $135.—$155.

VI-206 - Spoon, 1897 Jubilee. Queen's profile atop handle. Coronation scene in bowl. "VR" on box. 6¼"long. Sterling. $205.—$230.

VI-207 - Tape Measure, Prince Albert In Memoriam. White on black. Birth and death dates. 1¼"x½". $70.—$77.

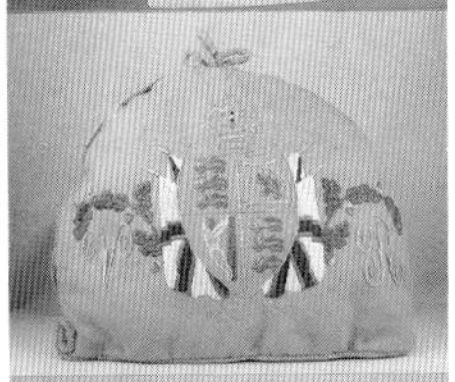

VI-208 - Tea Cozy, 1897 Jubilee. Color embroidery on tan. Same design reverse. 11"h. 13"wide. $170.—$185.

VI-209 - Teapot, 1887 Jubilee. Light gold on black. Color flowers. Birth, succession and coronation dates. 5½"h. 7¼"across. $175.—$190.

VI-210 - Teapot and Stand, 1897 Jubilee. Sepia portrait. Color decoration. Gold trim. 6¼"h. 9"across. $200.—$220.

VI-211 - Teapot, 1897 Jubilee. Blue on white. Gold trim. Raised decoration. 5½"h. 8¼"across. Wedgwood & Co. Ltd. BC. $410.—$450.

VI-212 - Teapot, 1897 Jubilee. B&W portraits of four generations. Color flowers. Gold trim. 3"h. 6¾"across. $240.—$265.

VI-213 - Teapot, 1897 Jubilee. Color young and mature portraits. Color decoration. Gold trim. 5"h. 7"across. Bone china. $175.—$200.

VI-214 - Teapot, 1897 Jubilee. Sepia young and mature portraits. Color decoration partially hand painted. 5½"h. 9"across. $325.—$355.

VI-215 - Teapot, 1897 Jubilee. Color young and mature portraits. Color decoration. Gold trim. 4"h. 7½"across. $175.—$190.

VI-216 - Teapot, 1897 Jubilee. White applied decoration on dark green. Beige handle, spout and trim. 7"h. Copeland Late Spode. $400.—$450.

VI-217 - Teapot, 1897 Jubilee. Color decoration partially hand painted. Gold trim. 6½"h. 7"across. Foley bone china. $185.—$205.

VI-218 - Teapot, Royal Family. Prince of Wales and Pss. Royal on lid. Color and pink luster. 7½"h. 9¾"across. $350.—$385.

VI-219 - Teapot Stand, 1897 Jubilee. B&W portraits of four generations. Color flowers. Gold trim. 6¼"d. Bone china. $185.—$205.

VI-220 - Teapot Stand, 1897 Jubilee. Color and gold decoration partially hand painted. 7"d. $85.—$95.

VI-221 - Teapot Stand, 1897 Jubilee. Color decoration. Gold trim. 4½"d. W.H. Goss BC. $90.—$100.

VI-222 - Teapot Stand, 1897 Jubilee. Color portrait and decoration. Gold trim. 6½"d. $80.—$90.

VI-223 - Teapot Stand. Black on white portrait and decoration. 6½"d. Pottery. $65.—$72.

VI-224 - Tile, 1887 Jubilee. Color portrait and decoration. 6"x6". $170.—$188.

VI-225 - Tile, 1887 Jubilee. Raised beige decoration on brown. 6"x6". $130.—$145.

VI-226 - Tin. Prince Albert brass cachou tin. Raised profile and decoration. 1½"d. ¼"deep. $70.—$77.

VI-227 - Tin, Boer War. Color portrait of Queen Victoria on lid. Military leaders on sides. 8½"x5½" x 4"deep. $70.—$77.

VI-228 - Tin, Boer War. Embossed gold profile portrait medallion. Red background. Blue border. 6"x3½"x¾"deep. $50.—$55.

VI-229 - Tin, In Memoriam. Queen and Pr. Albert on lid. Family members on sides. Color decoration. 5½"x4"x4½"deep. $240.—$265.

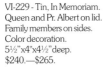

VI-230 - Tin, 1887 Jubilee. Color portrait and decoration. Royal residences on sides. 5¼"x5¼"x3¼"deep. Huntley & Palmers. $100.—$110.

VI-231 - Tin, 1887 Jubilee. Color portrait Queen in coronation robes on lid. Color decoration. 8½"x5¼" x 5¼"deep. $120.—$135.

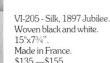

VI-232 - Tin, 1897 Jubilee. Color young and mature portraits. Ships and trains. Dates. Color decoration. 3¼"x3"x2"deep. $150.—$165.

VI-233 - Tin, 1897 Jubilee. Color young and mature portraits. Color decoration. 7¼"x7¼"x1¾"deep. Callard & Bowser. $120.—$135.

VI-234 - Tin, 1897 Jubilee. Color 1838 and 1897 portraits. Soldier and sailor on sides. Color decoration. 6"h.x4½"x3½". $155.—$170.

VI-235 - Tin, 1897 Jubilee. Accession portrait on lid. 1837 and 1897 ships on front and reverse. 5½"x3½"x3½". $110.—$120.

VI-236 - Tin, 1897 Jubilee. Color young and mature portraits. Royal residences on sides. 8"x3½"x 1½"deep. Parkinson's. $95.—$105.

VI-237 - Tin, 1897 Jubilee. Raised profiles of young and mature queen. Raised decoration on blue. 6"h.x5"x4". W.R. Jacob. $71.—$78.

VI-238 - Tin, 1897 Jubilee. Color young and mature portraits. 6"h.x8¼"x5½". $170.—$188.

VI-239 - Tin, 1897 Jubilee. Color young and mature portraits. Britannia, ships, Lord Nelson, soldiers. 4½"x3"x3½"deep. $75.—$82.

VI-240 - Tin, 1897 Jubilee. 1897 Jubilee procession around sides. Coronation scene on lid. 8"x5½"x 5¼"deep. Coleman's. $110.—$120.

VI-241 - Tin, 1897 Jubilee. Color portraits 1821, 1832, 1837 (with Prince Albert) and 1897. 6"x3¾"x4"deep. $140.—$155.

VI-242 - Tin. Queen Victoria color portrait. Color flowers and decoration. Gold trim. 6¾"h.x4½"x3¼". $81.—$89.

VI-243 - Tin. Queen Victoria color portrait. Royal residences on sides. Color decoration. 5½"h.x4"x4". $120.—$133.

VI-244 - Tin. Gold tone profile portrait. Brown base with gold band. "Victoria Regina". 10"d. 3"deep. $60.—$66.

VI-245 - Tin. Red profile portrait on color Union Jack. 2¼"x1¾"x¾"deep. $40.—$45.

VI-246 - Tin. Coronation scene on lid. Prime ministers on corners. Windsor and other scenes on sides. 8½"x6½"x5¼"deep. $195.—$215.

VI-247 - Tin. Victoria and Albert raised profile portraits. Names on lid. 2"d. $125.—$135.

VI-248 - Tin. Embossed profile portraits young and mature Queen and Pr. Consort on red medallions. 5½"h.x5"x3½". $95.—$105.

VI-249 - Tray, 1887 Jubilee. Profile portrait. Birth, coronation and marriage dates. Brass. 12"d. $220.—$245.

VI-250 - Tray, 1897 Jubilee. Raised profiles of Queen and family members. Silver plate. 11½"x10". $260.—$285.

VI-251 - Tumbler, 1897 Jubilee. Color portrait on white background. Glass. 5"h. 2½"d. at top. $55.—$60.

VI-252 - Vase, 1897 Jubilee. "Colchester". Color decoration. 3½"h. W.H. Goss BC. $70.—$77.

VI-253 - Vase, 1897 Jubilee. Color portraits and decoration. Opaline. Yellow at top and base. 10"h. 4½"d. $180.—$200.

VI-254 - Vase. Raised gold "penny" profile portrait. Raised gold wreath. White bisque background. 3½"h. $45.—$50.

VI-255 - Vase. B&W portraits of four generations framed in gold. Puce background. Gold trim. 4½"h. Germany. BC. $175.—$190.

Queen Victoria and Prince Albert — Family

VI-256 - Figurine. Angel watching over sleeping Pr. of Wales and Pss. Royal Staffordshire. 9¼"h. 7½"across. $460.—$510.

VI-257 - Jug. Royal Children c. 1848. Pr. Alfred as Autumn. Pss. Alice as Spring. Embossed design. 8"h. 7"across. $680.—$765.

VI-258 - Jug. Prince of Wales and Princess Royal in goat cart near Windsor Castle. Color decoration. 3½"h. 3¼"across. $170.—$185.

VI-259 - Plate. Prince of Wales. "England's Future King". B&W decoration. Color splashes. Red rim. 6½"d. $750.—$825.

VI-260 - Plate. Pss. Royal with her dog. c. 1840's. Deep green on white. "Royal Favourite". 7¼"d. $725.—$800.

VI-261 - Plate. Pss. Royal's Christening. "Bishop of Heliopolis". Color decoration. Embossed border. 7"d. $365.—$400.

Bibliography

Brisco, Virginia. *Torquay Commemoratives and Advertising Wares.* UK: The Torquay Pottery Collectors' Society, 1991.

Caunt, Pamela M. *Victorian Commemorative Jubilee Jewellery.* London: ARBRAS, 1997.

Davey, M. H. and Mannion, D. J. *Fifty Years of Royal Commemorative China 1837—1937.* UK: Dayman Publications, 1988.

_____. *Four Generations of Royal Commemorative China 1936— 1990.* UK: Dayman Publications, 1991.

Delderfield, Eric R. *Kings and Queens of England.* New York: Weathervane Books, 1978.

Edgar, Donald. *Britain's Royal Family in the Twentieth Century, King Edward VII to Queen Elizabeth II.* New York: Crescent Books, 1979.

Fraser, Antonia. *The Lives of The Kings and Queens of England.* New York: Alfred A. Knopf, 1975.

Gore, John. *King George V, A Personal Memoir.* London: Hazell, Watson & Viney Ltd., 1941.

Hallinan, Lincoln. *British Commemoratives - Royalty, Politics, War and Sport.* UK: Antique Collectors Club, 1995.

Johnson, Peter. *Royal Memorabilia.* London: Boxtree Ltd., 1988.

Knowles, Eric. *Miller's Royal Memorabilia.* London: Reed Consumer Books Ltd., 1994.

Lofts, Norah. *Queens of Britain.* London: Hodder and Stoughton, 1977.

Longford, Elizabeth. *The Queen, The Life of Elizabeth II.* New York: Alfred A. Knopf, 1983.

—. *Queen Victoria, Born To Succeed.* New York and Evanston: Harper & Row, 1964.

May, John. *Victoria Remembered.* London: William Heinemann Ltd., 1983.

May, John and Jennifer. *Commemorative Pottery 1780—1900.* New York: Charles Scribner's Sons, 1972.

Middlemas, Keith. *The Life and Times of Edward VII.* Garden City, New York: Doubleday & Company, 1972.

Murray, Jane. *The Kings and Queens of England, A Tourist Guide.* New York: Charles Scribner's Sons, 1974.

Palmer, Alan. *Kings and Queens of England.* London: Octopus Books Ltd., 1976.

Rose, Kenneth. *King George V.* New York: Alfred A. Knopf, 1984.

Warren, Geoffrey. *The First-Time Collectors' Guide to British Royal Commemoratives.* London: Quintet Publishing Ltd., 1994.

Weintraub, Stanley. *Victoria, An Intimate Biography.* New York: Truman Talley Books/E.P. Dutton, 1987.

Wheeler-Bennett, John W. *King George VI, His Life and Reign.* New York: St. Martin's Press, 1958.

Zeder, Audrey B. *British Royal Commemoratives With Prices.* Lombard, IL: Wallace-Homestead Book Company, 1986.

Ziegler, Philip. *King Edward VIII,* New York: Alfred A. Knopf, 1991.

More Titles from Schiffer Publishing

British Ceramic Art, 1870 to 1940 John A. Bartlett. This beautiful, color-illustrated reference of British art potteries includes detailed accounts of their histories, artists, designers, craftsmen and personalities, together with a comprehensive list of marks. The ceramics reflect the highly imaginative, diverse art styles of this period, evolving from Arts and Crafts naturalism through preatomic Modernism. Over 250 sharp color and 85 black and white photographs display the innovative, and often quite colorful, bowls, vases, plates and jugs of British manufacture. The book presents all the major art potteries, arranged alphabetically, with detailed text, photographs of typical wares, identifying marks, glossary, bibliography, and an index.

Size: 8 1/2" x 11"   336 photographs   240 pp.
Price Guide   Index
ISBN: 0-88740-456-1   hard cover $69.95

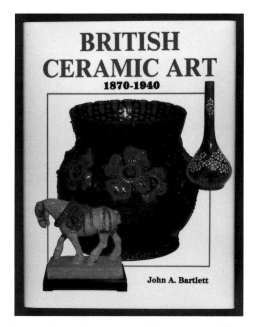

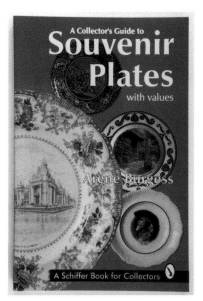

A Collector's Guide to Souvenir Plates Arene Burgess. Collecting and displaying souvenir plates first became a passion in 1893, a passion still very much alive today. Over 560 color photos illustrate this survey of souvenir plates dating back to the 1800s. The views of prominent potters such as Adams & Company, Wedgewood, and Wood and Sons are included. Short histories are provided for each manufacturers or importer to which specific views are attributed. A list of views is also provided, using the name given to the view by each manufacturer whenever possible, and including additional information on border designs, unusual features, color, and size when possible. Information on recent oriental imports similar to older souvenir plates are also discussed.

Size: 6" x 9"   564 color photos   224 pp.
Price Guide   Index
ISBN: 0-7643-0099-7   soft cover $19.95

Popular Souvenir Plates Monica Lynn Clements and Patricia Rosser Clements. Souvenir plates have long been representatives of America's history, whether commemorating special events or depicting places. Souvenir plates make attractive collectibles for several reasons, including their affordability and the fact that they come in a variety of designs and shapes. Popular Souvenir Plates has captured the versatility of the souvenir plate with examples that date from the 1880s through the present. More than 530 color photographs document plates depicting all fifty states and Canada, along with a sampling of European designs, each with its current market value. The work of American firms represented are Harker Pottery, Homer Laughlin, Kettlesprings Kilns, Edwin M. Knowles China Co., Sabin Industries, Salem China Co., Syracuse China Co., Vernon Kilns, and many others. The work of noted English potters such as Staffordshire, Adams, Jonroth, and Rowland and Marsellus are present. A chapter on foreign plates shows a variety of foreign-made souvenir ware including the beauty of "Made in Bavaria" and "Made in Germany" souvenir plates. This book and price guide is a valuable reference for anyone with an interest in souvenir plates.

Size: 8 1/2" x 11"   534 color photos   176 pp.
Price Guide
ISBN: 0-7643-0535-2   soft cover $29.95

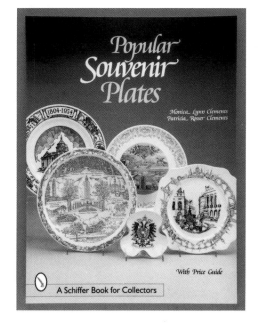

Chintz Ceramics, *2nd Edition\Revised* Jo Anne Welsh. The brilliant floral bouquets adorning chintz ceramics are displayed in over 400 full-color photographs. The major English chintz manufacturers, Royal Winton, James Kent, Lord Nelson, Shelley, Crown Ducal, and Empire, are discussed and many examples of their chintz wares are identified and shown. Over one hundred patterns are amply illustrated, including the popular DuBarry, Rosalynde, and Summertime patterns. Lesser known firms and American importers are also explored, along with the Japanese manufacturers of hand painted chintz. Manufacturer's marks are identified and dated. Chintz ceramics were introduced in the late 19th century, and rose to great heights of popularity in the first half of the 20th century as they were exported around the world. A value guide is included with newly updated prices.

Size: 11" x 8 1/2"	440 color photos	160 pp.
Price Guide		Index
ISBN: 0-7643-0451-8	hard cover	$39.95

Victorian Majolica Leslie Bockol. Beautiful color photographs of hundreds of Majolica ceramics from the Victorian age and more historical research contiue in this new study. The book traces majolica's roots and lists the manufacturers and their marks. Over 300 color photographs, taken in America and Britain, illustrate the high craftsmanship of majolica's nineteenth century potters. Artistic influences on majolica's designs are reviewed along with the evolving majolica markets England, America, Europe, and Canada. Specialty tablewares, decorative pieces, titles, and the controversial greenwares all are included. The price guide is a valuable tool.

Size: 8 1/2" x 11"	321 photos	192 pp.
Price Guide		
ISBN: 0-88740-953-9	hard cover	$39.95

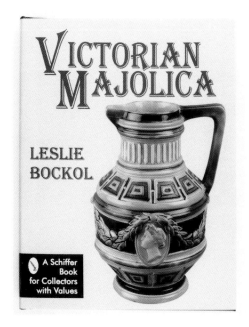

Majolica Mike Schneider. Majolica has been receiving growing recognition as a ceramic collectible and has experienced a consequent growth in value. In Majolica, Mike Schneider presents a comprehensive look at this soft-bodied, brightly colored pottery with its high-relief decoration and clear lead glaze. Amply illustrated with color photographs, the various forms Majolic took are covered in detail. They include pitchers, platters, plates, leaf plates, syrups, sardine boxes and other covered pieces, cigarette holders, ashtrays, and humidors. Also included are cups, saucers, mugs and teapots, cakeplates, planters vases, and other items. Schneider traces Majolica's history from its earliest roots in the 8th century to its emergence as a new form in London's Crystal Palace Exhibition in 1851 and the following decades of popularity. The leading manufacturers are documented using the latest research.

Size: 6" x 9"	170 color photos	144 pp.
Price Guide		
ISBN: 0-88740-769-2	soft cover	$14.95

Majolica: American and European Wares Jeffrey Snyder & Leslie J. Bockol. The colorful earthenwares known as Majolica are once again a popular part of the nostalgic revival of Victorian taste in interior decoration. This book presents a new analysis of Majolica set against its cultural-historical background. Hundreds of forms in dozens of patterns, especially American and British ware with a sampling of European pieces, are displayed in over 550 color photographs. The text presents new research and the examples are individually identified by style, pattern, maker, size and date. Short histories of the manufacturers are presented as they relate to Majolica wares. The price guide will be a valuable tool for collectors and dealers. Majolica's long history begins with Italian Renaissance tin-glazed wares; over the centuries its styles and techniques spread to France and England. With the advent of mechanization, the wares could be mass produced. Majolica became popular among the rising middle class in England, Europe, and the United States.

Size: 8 1/2" x 11"   554 color photos   160 pp.
Price Guide
ISBN: 0-88740-561-4   soft cover $29.95

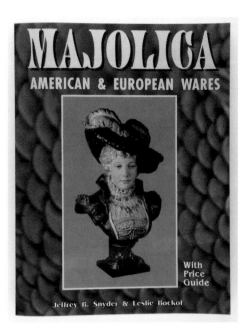

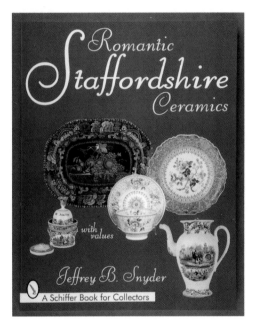

Romantic Staffordshire Ceramics Jeffrey B. Snyder. Linger over the images of finely detailed transfer prints produced by England's famous Staffordshire potters. Explore the wide range of early to mid-nineteenth century transfer prints which fall under the broad heading "Romantic Staffordshire." Over 500 color photographs capture the particulars of these beautifully decorated, sturdy, Victorian-era ceramics, including dinnerwares, tea sets, and other household ceramics. Included in the text is a discussion of the numerous series of prints produced by many of Staffordshire's potters. The potters and their manufacturer's marks are identified as well. Also included are a values guide, bibliography, and index.

Size: 8 1/2" x 11"   500 color photos   160 pp.
Price Guide
ISBN: 0-7643-0336-8   soft cover $29.95

Historical Staffordshire: American Patriots & Views Jeffrey B. Snyder. Patriotism was rarely more fervently displayed in America than in the early nineteenth century. Enthusiasm for the new country was especially felt in England where goods were produced specifically to commemorate America. This book presents in detail the transfer-printed ceramic dishes made in Staffordshire for the American market from 1820 - 1860. Here are the patriots, historical events and breathtaking new landscape views captured by fine artists and transferred to ceramics by the best companies in England. Today these dishes are actively collected. Written with a close view of the cultural changes that contributed to the enormous popularity of historical Staffordshire wares, Jeffrey Snyder has documented the scenes and the thinking of the people who so enjoyed displaying American history on their dishes. The makers, their marks, and information about the scenes is woven into this book to identify each of the examples in 485 color illustrations.

Size: 8 1/2" x 11"   485 color photos   160 pp.
Price Guide
ISBN: 0-88740-721-8   soft cover $29.95

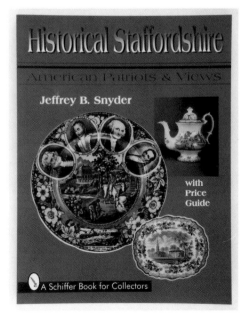

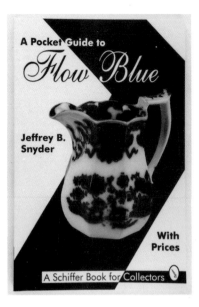

A Pocket Guide to Flow Blue Jeffrey B. Snyder. Here is the first concise handbook guide to the dining services and house wares with the distinctive Flow Blue transfer decoration. This handy reference work provides basic definitions of Flow Blue decoration and the wares on which it appeared throughout the Victorian era. Hundreds of color photos are grouped into three historic production periods recognizable by their artistic styles, and guidelines to identifying Flow Blue by these periods are presented. A brief synopsis of each English, American and European manufacturer whose ceramics appear in the text is presented with their marks. With this book in hand, the reader will be able to quickly identify and date Flow Blue wares with confidence. A Values Reference is included. This book will be a useful tool for all who collect these avidly-sought and highly-prized Victorian services.

Size: 6" x 9"	250 color photos	160 pp.
Price Guide		
ISBN: 0-88740-856-7	soft cover	$19.95

Fascinating Flow Blue Jeffrey B. Snyder. Enjoy a wide-ranging array of rare, unusual, and highly prized Flow Blue ceramic wares in 500 color photographs in this new study. The focus is on products of English potteries, although beautiful examples from America and elsewhere are included. Among the photos are lovely teapots in many shapes and sizes, children's tea and dinner services, potpourri jars, pitchers, platters, and plates. Also presented is a survey of the body shapes which Flow Blue adorns. Values for each of the items are included, along with an index and a bibliography. The index cross references patterns found in all four volumes of the author's Flow Blue books.

Size: 8 1/2" x 11"	500 color photos	160 pp.
Price Guide		
ISBN: 0-7643-0335-X	soft cover	$29.95

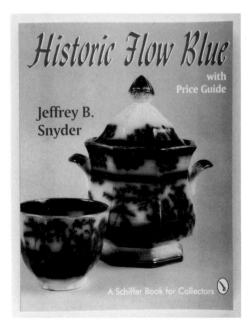

Historic Flow Blue Jeffrey B. Snyder. America in the nineteenth century Victorian age was changing as fast as the engines of the Industrial Revolution could carry it. At every turn, Flow Blue was there, first sparking the interest of the affluent and later the middle class with its rich colors and complete table services. This book puts Flow Blue in its historical context and covers the British, American and European manufacturers who produced it, the exhibitions that promoted it, the people who owned it and what moved them to buy it. Over 500 color photographs present the variety of forms and patterns in these popular wares from the 1840s to turn of the twentieth century.

Size: 8 1/2" x 11"	550 color photos	160 pp.
Price Guide		
ISBN: 0-88740-640-8	soft cover	$29.95